REBUILD AMERICA

SOLVING THE ECONOMIC CRISIS
THROUGH CIVIC WORKS

SCOTT MYERS-LIPTON

Paradigm Publishers
Boulder • London

Published in the United States by Paradigm Publishers, 3360 Mitchell Lane, Suite E, Boulder, CO 80301 USA.

Paradigm Publishers is the trade name of Birkenkamp & Company, LLC, Dean Birkenkamp, President and Publisher.

Library of Congress Cataloging-in-Publication Data

Myers-Lipton, Scott J.
 Rebuild America : solving the economic crisis through civic works / Scott Myers-Lipton.
   p. cm.
 Includes bibliographical references and index.
 ISBN 978-1-59451-721-1 (hbk. : alk. paper) — ISBN 978-1-59451-722-8 (pbk. : alk. paper)
  1. Public service employment—United States. 2. Manpower policy—United States. 3. Public works—Social aspects—United States. I. Title.
 HD5713.6.U54M94 2009
 363.0973—dc22

                                                                    2009016077

Printed and bound in the United States of America on acid-free paper that meets the standards of the American National Standard for Permanence of Paper for Printed Library Materials.

Designed and Typeset by Straight Creek Bookmakers.

13 12 11 10 09   1 2 3 4 5

To the people of the Gulf Coast, who have waited too long
for a working infrastructure, good jobs, restoration
of the social compact, the right to return, and dignity

REBUILD AMERICA

More praise for *Rebuild America: Solving the Economic Crisis Through Civic Works*

"*Rebuild America* provides a concise and persuasive argument for new civic works initiatives to address problems that existed in the U.S. Gulf Coast before Hurricane Katrina devastated New Orleans as well as strategies to address lingering poverty and unemployment problems among African Americans and other people of color."
—Robert D. Bullard, author of *Dumping in Dixie*

"Scott Myers-Lipton has created a must-read book for all those interested in our nation's economic recovery through job creation. It is a most engaging documentation of how a professor and his students became the 'can do' kids, forging ahead with a plan for the development and passage of a bill to put America and the Gulf Coast back to work. This is a great book."
—Beverly Wright, Founder and Director, Deep South Center for Environmental Justice

Contents

PREFACE

Today, our nation faces great difficulties. Our economy is teetering on collapse. Large banks fail daily. Stock markets are volatile, falling 300 to 500 points in a day. In a recent poll, 60 percent of Americans feel the nation is headed toward a depression. Importantly, the American worker faced hardship even before the current economic meltdown. More than 10 million middle-class jobs have been shipped overseas since 1980. The gap between rich and poor has widened to record levels, middle-class incomes remain stagnant, and recent housing gains for African American families have been all but wiped out by the foreclosure crisis.

At the same time, our public infrastructure is crumbling. It can be seen in our structurally deficient bridges, weak levees, poorly maintained dams, and dilapidated schools. The impact of this public infrastructure crisis further endangers the economy and the quality of our life. If ports are clogged, roads are congested, and air traffic systems are outdated, then the American economy suffers, our quality of life is diminished, and public safety is threatened.

Our nation desperately needs a plan to create jobs that will bring relief to Main Street. Seventy-five years ago, when our country faced the crisis of the Depression, public works were offered as a way to provide good jobs at a time when there were too few, to improve and expand our infrastructure, and to provide common purpose based on people working together to uplift our nation. In less than two months, the Civil Works Administration (CWA) hired 4 million people, and during its five-month history the CWA built or repaired 200 swimming pools, 3,700 playgrounds, 40,000 schools, 250,000 miles of road, and 12 million feet of sewer pipe. It was a great idea—and it can work again.

Today, 200 faith-based, human rights, student, and community-based organizations are once again calling for public works as a solution to our economic crisis. But this time, it is under the banner of civic works, because the "civic" no longer seems to work for the average American. This inability of government to work for the people was most clearly demonstrated by the botched recovery in the Gulf Coast after Hurricanes Katrina and Rita. Not only were thousands of people left on their rooftops to fend for themselves, but also since then there has not been a comprehensive solution offered to rebuild an entire region of the country that was so badly damaged from one of the worst natural disasters in the nation's history. The Gulf Coast still does not have adequate hospitals, housing, parks, or schools. The situation is so bad that in February 2008 two UN-appointed experts in housing and minority rights warned the United States that it was violating the human rights of African Americans and the poor in New Orleans by not providing affordable housing for its current and displaced residents.

The Gulf Coast Civic Works (GCCW) Act, which was introduced in Congress in 2007 after a campaign of persistent organizing, draws on a New Deal model for creating jobs and revitalizing infrastructure to rebuild the Gulf—and it is gaining support from Gulf Coast residents, community leaders, and members of Congress from both parties. The bill would create 100,000 good jobs and training opportunities for local and displaced workers to rebuild public infrastructure and restore the environment. It would empower residents to return with dignity, revitalize the local workforce, and help create more sustainable communities. And if it works in the Gulf Coast, it can serve as a pilot program for national initiatives to solve similar problems across the entire country. If the GCCW Act is enacted, it will teach a new generation one of the best lessons of American history: When we rebuild public infrastructure, provide living-wage jobs, strengthen the middle class, and reduce poverty, we can make real the promise of *e pluribus unum*— out of many, one.

This book is in many ways an extension of my first book, *Social Solutions to Poverty: America's Struggle to Build a Just Society*. In that book, I highlighted and examined most every major social solution to poverty that has been put forward by grassroots activists and elite policy leaders since the founding of the country. All in all, that book presented more than forty different public policy initiatives.

If you had asked me in July 2005, when I finished the first draft of the manuscript, what social solution to poverty was the most promising, public or civic works would have been at the bottom of the list. However, the political landscape was upended in August 2005 when Hurricane Katrina, and then three weeks later Hurricane Rita, struck the Gulf Coast. President George W. Bush, who held to a Reaganesque vision that government was the problem and not the solution, was seen by the American public to be unable to provide a competent response. Then, a series of highly public infrastructure problems occurred—a Minnesota bridge fell, a Hawaii dam broke, the northeastern part of the country's electrical grid was shut down—and now, most recently, the economy melted down. As a result, the idea of public or civic works entered into the mainstream dialogue in late 2008. Importantly, there is a group of students and faculty who have been calling for a civic works project in the Gulf Coast since the fall of 2006. This civic works message has caught the imagination of Gulf Coast communities, and after an almost three-year campaign there is movement in Congress and beyond to enact the GCCW Act.

This book provides an in-depth explanation of why the nation needs civic works at this time. Chapter 1 of this book examines the economic crisis in America, focusing both on the immediate crisis and its impact on the American workers and on the silent economic crisis that began in the early 1980s. This chapter also explores the dilapidated state of America's public infrastructure. Finally, it discusses the end of the conservative era and its implications for a new approach to the role of government.

Chapter 2 focuses on public or civic works as a solution to the economic and infrastructure crisis. Included in this chapter is a discussion of the history of American public works, as well as the lessons learned from that history, with a particular focus on what this means for a modern day civic works project.

Chapter 3 explores the story of a group of students and faculty and their attempts to create a modern-day civic works project in the Gulf Coast. This chapter looks at the role of service-learning in this campus movement, how students and faculty worked with coalition partners to build a regional and national campaign around the Gulf Coast Civic Works campaign and its tactics and strategy.

Chapter 4 explores the revisions of the GCCW Act as Gulf Coast residents continue to shape the bill to meet the reality on the ground and to take what they have learned and turn it into good policy. What has developed is a set of best practices on how to rebuild a community based on a project that (1) is led by residents and is participatory, (2) is a hybrid model (i.e., it has federal oversight and local control), (3) supports equitable economic development (e.g., first-source hiring and protection of vulnerable populations [low-income people, women, people of color, the disabled, immigrants, and the elderly] by including them in the hiring, planning, and implementation of civic works projects), (4) supports long-term development (i.e., job training and hiring of local contractors), and (5) is focused on the creation of green jobs. The project's development of these best practices may well be used as a pilot project to rebuild communities across this nation.

Chapter 5 allows experts in the field of public policy, community organizing, and economic development to weigh in on what a civic works project would mean for the nation as well as for the Gulf Coast. Authors in this chapter are Howard Zinn (Boston University), Jason Scott Smith (University of New Mexico), Robert Leighninger Jr. (Arizona State University), Jeannette Gabriel (JNESO, IUOE-AFL-CIO), Angela Glover Blackwell (PolicyLink), Emily Ryo (Stanford University), David Bowman (Louisiana Recovery Authority), Julie Kuklinski (Women in Construction), Stephen Bradberry (ACORN), and Jeffrey Buchanan (Robert F. Kennedy Center for Justice and Human Rights).

Lastly, Chapter 6 ties civic works to an economic bill of rights, which was an idea introduced by President Franklin Roosevelt and promoted by President Harry Truman and Dr. Martin Luther King. This chapter argues that with the current economic and infrastructure crisis, support for public works has grown tremendously, making it possible to create a permanent civic works agency and fulfilling this part of Roosevelt's, Truman's, and King's vision. The chapter concludes with twelve lessons on social action that have emerged from the GCCW campaign. The lessons are think big; act humbly; frame the "change idea" in a historical context; focus the demand on a specific target; get face-to-face with people in power; ensure that a campaign has movement; emphasize commonalities when working in coalition; develop media skills; be persistent; do not worry about money; recognize that democratic space is necessary for the long haul; and develop a bigger vision than the campaign.

I want to thank all of the students, staff, and faculty who have been involved in the Gulf Coast Civic Works Project. Without their drive and determination, the idea of 100,000 civic works jobs for the people of the Gulf Coast to rebuild their own communities simply would not have happened. I also want to thank Jeffrey Buchanan, from the Robert F. Kennedy Center for Justice and Human Rights, Stephen Bradberry and Darren Fenwick from ACORN, Jainey Bavishi and Ore Alao from the Equity and Inclusion Campaign, Sharon and David Gauthe from Bayou Interfaith

Shared Community Organizing, Mary Fontenot from All Congregations Together, Diane Yentel from Oxfam America, and so many more who have worked tirelessly to enact the GCCW Act. In addition, Representative Zoe Lofgren (D-CA) deserves special recognition for having the courage to introduce the bill into Congress, even though her district is 2,100 miles away. She did so because she understood that a grave wrong had taken place, and she wanted to right it. Lastly, I want to thank the public policy and community organizing folks who contributed articles to this book. I greatly appreciate their expertise and analysis of civic works.

Finally, every effort has been made to ensure the accuracy of information in this book. Possible errors should be brought to the attention of the publisher and author. They will be researched, and if verified, they will be corrected in future editions.

Scott Myers-Lipton

CREDITS

Chapter 1

I-35 Bridge: Courtesy of Heather Munro.

New Orleans levee break: Courtesy of Vincent Laforet, REDUX Pictures.

Ko Loko Dam: Courtesy of Casey and Cyndi Riemer, Jack Harter Helicopters, Lihue, Kauai.

New York City blackout: Courtesy of Vincent Laforet, REDUX Pictures.

Mark Keppel High School gym: Courtesy of ACLU of Southern California.

Chapter 3

Campus Sleep-Out: Courtesy of Eric Austin.

Louisiana Winter logo: Courtesy of Mark Macala.

Louisiana Winter students: Courtesy of Bill Snyder, Mississippi Gulf Coast Community College.

Tusculum College students: Courtesy of Tusculum College.

CSU Fullerton students: Courtesy of Lezlee Hinesmon-Matthews.

National Campus Sleep-Out: Courtesy of Scott Myers-Lipton.

Dillard Student Conference: Courtesy of Scott Myers-Lipton.

Mardi Gras Celebration for HR 4048: Courtesy of Scott Myers-Lipton.

Stephen Bradberry and students: Courtesy of Scott Myers-Lipton.

Chapter 5

Raised fists: Courtesy of Mark Macala.

CHAPTER I
THE CRISIS IN AMERICA

Main Street America is suffering. With the housing slump and the financial meltdown of Wall Street, the U.S. economy plunged into a deep recession. The federal government's early response to the economic crisis was to bail out large and wealthy financial institutions. In March 2008, the federal government provided a $29 billion bailout to Bear Stearns. In September, the federal government took over Freddie Mac and Fannie Mae, the two largest mortgage lenders, at a projected cost to taxpayers of up to $200 billion. Then, ten days later the federal government provided an $85 billion bailout to American International Group (AIG). All of these bailouts were surpassed when in early October the Bush administration pushed through Congress a $700 billion bailout for the wealthiest banks and financial institutions, plus $110 billion in tax breaks offered as "sweeteners" to ensure the bill's passage. By the time President Barack Obama took office, the federal government had spent more than $2 trillion and allocated $10 trillion to rescue the economy. It appeared to some that loss and risk had been socialized while profit had been privatized.[1]

Even though the vast majority of the initial federal assistance went toward Wall Street, the citizens on Main Street were suffering greatly from the economic crisis. From December 2007 to May 2009, 6 million jobs have been lost, with 4 million of those jobs being lost since September 2008, when the financial meltdown accelerated the economic downturn. The first to be affected were the construction and housing sectors, but job losses are now widespread and span the leisure, hospitality, and retail sectors. The hardest hit have been men and blacks, with their unemployment jumping from 4 percent to 8.1 percent and from 9.8 percent to 14.9

percent, respectively. By May 2009, the overall unemployment rate was 9.4 percent (14.5 million), up from 4.9 percent (7.5 million) the previous year. Economists warn that the unemployment rate will continue to rise, possibly reaching 10 percent by the end of 2009. Incredibly, unemployment jumps to more than 14 percent when we count the total number of people out of work, including those who have not worked for the past six months, which the official unemployment rates do not reflect. By May 2009, about 6.7 million people were drawing state unemployment insurance, up from 2.7 million the previous year.[2]

Globalization, Technology, and Conservative Public Policy

The crisis for American workers is now quite apparent. However, American workers faced hardship even before the current meltdown. This hardship has been caused by globalization, technology, and conservative public policy. Globalization has led to millions of living-wage jobs being shipped overseas. The offshoring of U.S. jobs has fueled a decline in the manufacturing sector from 26 percent of the economy in 1969, to 19 percent in 1984, and to 12 percent by 2007. Since 2001, 35,000 manufacturing firms have been closed, which has cut 3 million jobs, with more than one-half being union jobs. This loss of manufacturing jobs has decreased the strength of unions. Today, only 13 percent of manufacturing jobs are unionized, down from 28 percent in 1983. Many of these living-wage jobs have been replaced with low-skilled, poverty-wage jobs. In the 1980s, one-half of all new jobs paid wages below the poverty line. In the 1990s, 30 percent of American workers earned poverty-level wages, up 7 percent from the early 1970s.[3]

Advances in technology have also increased job loss. Some economists argue that job loss caused by increases in productivity due to automation, computerization, and mechanization has been even more destabilizing than globalization because jobs are not just shifted, but eliminated. *Business Week* argues that for every 1 percent of annual productivity growth, U.S. corporations eliminate approximately 1.3 million jobs. With productivity rising 2 percent since 2001, this increase would account for all of the 2.5 million jobs that were lost between 2004 and 2007.[4]

At the same time, workers faced hardship because of the conservative policies put in place during the last three decades, which decreased minimum wage, opposed unionization, and passed tax laws benefiting the rich at the expense of the middle class and poor. First, conservatives have opposed increasing the minimum wage. The federal minimum wage was not increased during the eight years of the Reagan administration or the nine years between the end of the Clinton administration and the last part of the Bush administration. In 2007, the Bush administration finally relented and signed off on a minimum wage increase from $5.15 an hour to $5.85, and then to $6.55 in 2008 and $7.25 in July 2009. Until this latest increase, the minimum wage had been at historically low levels. If we look back in ten-year increments since 1958 and use 2007 as a baseline, the minimum wage was $6.50 in 1998, $5.92 in 1988, $8.49 in 1978, $9.61 in 1968, and $7.23 in 1958. Even at the end of this latest increase, when the minimum wage is at $7.25 an hour, these jobs will pay below the poverty line because it takes $8.25 an hour for a worker with a family of three to get above it. Currently, 3.1 percent of American workers, or 1.2 million people, earn the prevailing minimum wage or below.[5]

Conservatives have opposed an increase in the minimum wage because they feel that a higher minimum wage hurts business. But this argument overlooks the fact that the economy was booming in the late 1960s, exactly at the same time that the minimum wage was at an all-time high. Moreover, many social scientists point to the low minimum wage as a key factor in explaining why the American poverty rate has climbed to almost 13 percent of the population, with children's poverty at 18 percent. This level of want makes the United States the leader in poverty in the industrialized world.[6]

Second, American workers have faced hardship because of conservative opposition to unions. Ever since industrial capitalism developed in the mid to late nineteenth century, conservatives—particularly business leaders–have mostly opposed the unionization of workers. After an almost century-long struggle, unions were finally legalized in 1935 with the passage of the Wagner Act, which guaranteed the right of workers to choose their own unions, picket, boycott, and strike. The Wagner Act also made it illegal for employers to blacklist union leaders, to hire spies to infiltrate a union, and to operate company unions. These changes in labor policy led to an increase of union membership from 3.7 million in 1935, to 7.3 million in 1940, and to 15 million by 1950. They also led to many important labor victories, such as increased pay and job benefits.

However, this is not the end of the story, as conservatives and business leaders fought back. In 1947, congressional conservatives passed the Taft-Hartley Act, which fundamentally altered the balance of power in favor of business by outlawing sympathy strikes in support of other unions and secondary boycotts (e.g., the grape boycott by the United Farm Workers was a secondary boycott, but it was not illegal because farmworkers were not covered by the National Labor Relations Board). Taft-Hartley also allowed management to work against a union organizing drive and allowed the president to force strikers "back to work" for up to eighty days when the nation's "safety and health" were at stake.[7]

In the 1960s, businesses fought unionization by relocating to the Sun Belt or overseas to countries that were hostile to unions. More recently, businesses have hired specialized consultants to actively work against union organizing drives, sometimes using illegal tactics such as firing workers sympathetic to unionization. This attack on the unionization of workers has been successful, reducing unionized workers from 35 percent of the workforce in 1950 to 12.6 percent in 2008, with only 7 percent of those in the private sector. Clearly, workers have suffered because union workers earn 27 percent more than nonunion workers ($781 a week versus $612), receive better health care (81 percent covered versus 50 percent covered), and have pensions (72 percent versus 15 percent).[8]

Third, American workers have faced hardship due to a conservative tax policy that favored the wealthy over the middle and working classes. For example, the top 1 percent (incomes of $1 million or more annually) received 33 percent of all the benefit from President George W. Bush's tax cuts. In dollar terms, the top 1 percent received an average tax cut of $78,460, while households in the middle received a tax cut of $1,090 and the bottom 20 percent received $250.[9]

Combined, these policy changes have led to the greatest income and wealth gap that the United States has experienced since the Great Depression. When we examine real family income from 1979 to 2003, we see that more than one-half of the U.S. population either lost ground or held steady by working more hours, while the top 20 percent took home one-half of all the income. More specifically, real family income changed as follows:

- the bottom 20 percent (up to $24,000) dropped by 2 percent
- the second 20 percent ($24,100–$42,100) increased by 8 percent
- the middle 20 percent ($42,100–$65,000) increased by 15 percent
- the fourth 20 percent ($65,000–$98,200) increased by 26 percent
- the top 20 percent ($98,200 and more) increased by 51 percent
- the top 5 percent ($170,000 and more) increased by 75 percent
- the top 1 percent ($337,000 or more) increased by 106 percent

Incredibly, the top 1 percent of the population garnered 82 percent of all the income between 1980 and 2005. What makes this more surprising is that worker productivity increased 71 percent during this time period. Clearly, American workers have not been receiving their fair share of company profits.[10]

This income inequality is not the way it has always been. From 1947 to 1979, when unions and the minimum wage were relatively strong and tax policies were more progressive, real family income increased about the same for all groups, with the poorest actually growing the most and the richest growing the least. To use a colloquial expression, all boats rose together. More specifically, from 1947–1979 real family income changed in these ways:

- the bottom 20 percent increased by 116 percent
- the second 20 percent increased by 100 percent
- the middle 20 percent increased by 111 percent
- the fourth 20 percent increased by 114 percent
- the top 20 percent increased by 99 percent
- the top 5 percent increased by 86 percent

This growing inequality between the highest and average wage earners can also be seen in a comparison of executive pay with the pay of an average worker in a company. This gap between CEO and average worker shot up from 41:1 in 1975 to 525:1 in 2000. By 2007, the gap dropped a bit to 364:1, with the average CEO of a large U.S. company making $10.8 million in comparison to the average worker's $29,544.[11]

As a result of offshoring, technological advances, and conservative social policy, wealth inequality has also risen, with almost all of the new growth in wealth (assets such as real estate, stocks, and bonds) going to the top 1 percent of the population. In 1976, the top 1 percent owned 20 percent of the wealth and the top 10 percent owned 50 percent. By 2001, the top 1 percent, which included those households whose net worth was $5.8 million or more, controlled 33 percent of the wealth. In fact, the top 10 percent controlled 84 percent of all stocks and mutual funds, with the top 1 percent controlling 43 percent and the next 9 percent controlling 41 percent.[12]

The bottom line is this: When conservative social policy was the dominant political force throughout the 1980s and 1990s, culminating in conservative control of all branches of the federal government from 2001 to 2006, America saw record levels of wealth accumulation for the top 1 percent, stagnation of middle-class incomes, and an increase in poverty. This change in American society to more economic wealth and income inequality has undermined the security of our families. For the average American worker, it has meant less free time with family because people have had to work more hours to maintain their standard of living, fewer households with health insurance, rising debt, a decline in savings, less money for retirement, and an increase in temporary jobs that provide no benefits. This inequality may have also led to the conditions that caused this current economic downturn because the rich have had more than enough wealth to make extremely risky investments. This rise in inequality also threatens our democracy because the elite has used its increased wealth to shape public policies through political contributions and philanthropic endeavors. As Bill Gates Sr. claimed, once a person makes $15 million dollars, the purpose of making more money becomes gaining power to influence the rules of society.[13]

In light of the current economic crisis and the conservative assault on workers, Main Street was in need of a stimulus package as we entered 2009. America was desperate to get people back to work at living-wage jobs. As highlighted previously, the initial bailout under the Bush administration was directed at wealthy institutions. Yet working Americans were still waiting for a bailout. Many felt that if the government bailed out Wall Street, why could it not bail out Main Street? In late 2008, President-elect Obama began to articulate a plan for Main Street, a major focus of which would be to rebuild America's infrastructure.

America's Crumbling Infrastructure

Our nation's infrastructure is crumbling. This can be seen in our structurally deficient bridges, weak levees, poorly maintained dams, and dilapidated schools. The impact of this public infrastructure crisis endangers the economy and the quality of our lives. When the highways resemble parking lots, the water system has difficulty delivering clean water, and the bridges are outdated and in need of repair, then the American economy cannot function optimally and our standard of life decreases. Clearly, a plan to rebuild the infrastructure will help the economy, the American worker, and our quality of life.

At the beginning of the twenty-first century, a series of dramatic events have made more Americans aware of the importance of our public infrastructure. Whether it is a bridge collapsing in Minnesota, the levee system failing in New Orleans, a dam breaking in Hawaii, the electrical power grid shutting down throughout the Midwest and Northeast, or schools in California falling into disrepair, we have all become aware of this "silent crisis."

Bridges

Even though the word *infrastructure* may sound abstract, it describes a situation in which lives are in the balance. Here are just a few examples. On August 1, 2007, rush hour traffic filled the Interstate 35W bridge in Minneapolis. The I-35W was one of the busiest bridges in the state, carrying 140,000 people daily. Suddenly, the 1,907-foot bridge collapsed into the Mississippi River with approximately 120 vehicles and 160 people on it. As a result, 13 people died and 144 were injured.[14]

What many did not know the day the I-35 bridge collapsed was that it was one of the 77,000 American bridges deemed *structurally deficient*—a term used to describe a bridge that may be safe but can no longer tolerate the speed it was designed for or carry the current vehicle load because of deteriorated structural components. These 77,000 structurally deficient

I-35 Bridge in Minnesota.
(Courtesy of Heather Munro)

bridges need to be continually monitored and possibly repaired or replaced. Another 80,000 American bridges are *functionally obsolete*—a term used for a bridge that no longer provides the necessary width or vertical clearance to serve the current traffic demand. Incredibly, 47 percent of the nation's 468,095 rural bridges have been determined to be either structurally deficient or functionally obsolete. Moreover, the average age for American bridges is forty-three years; most bridges are designed for a maximum age of fifty years. Today, 20 percent of American bridges are more than fifty years old.[15]

The American Society of Civil Engineers (ASCE) produces a report card on American infrastructure every couple of years. In its most recent report card of 2009, the ASCE gave U.S. bridges the letter grade of "C" and estimated that it will cost $17 billion a year for fifty years to eliminate all bridge deficiencies.[16]

Levees and Dams

On August 28, 2005, Hurricane Katrina approached the Gulf Coast as a Category 5 storm. By the time Katrina passed the east side of New Orleans

New Orleans levee break. (Courtesy of FEMA/Jocelyn Augustino)

on August 29, its winds were at a Category 2 or less. Unfortunately, the levees were improperly designed and maintained to protect the city from even this level of storm. Even though President Bush was surprised that the levees broke, many engineers had warned for years that the weak levees surrounding New Orleans might fail. When the levees broke in fifty-three places, 80 percent of New Orleans flooded and almost 1,000 people died in the city as a consequence.[17]

Weak levees are not just a New Orleans issue. The U.S. Army Corps of Engineers reports that today almost 150 levees pose a serious risk of failing. This was evident in Cedar Rapids, Iowa, on June 11, 2008, when an ill-maintained levee broke and caused 100 city blocks to flood. Yet again, engineers had warned that the levee "would likely fail in a future major flood event." And as was the case in New Orleans, Cedar Rapids knew of the threat but did not have the money to fix the problem. The Cedar Rapids levee had been on a waiting list for federal money since 1993.[18]

Levees are not the only water-containing structure in need of repair; the other structure is dams. On March 14, 2006, the Ko Loko Dam in Kauai burst, spilling more than 400 million gallons of water onto the communities below. An eighteen-foot wall of water came crashing down, killing seven people and destroying several houses. Inconceivably, Ko Loko Dam had never been inspected, even though state law required an inspection every five years. Today, 4,095 dams have been deemed deficient, with 1,819 dams considered high hazard. The ASCE report card gave American dams the letter grade of "D" and estimated a repair cost of $50 billion.[19]

Ko Loko Dam, Kauai. (Courtesy of Casey and Cyndi Riemer, Jack Harter Helicopters, Lihue, Kauai)

New York City darkened by blackout. (Courtesy of Vincent Laforet/The New York Times/Redux)

Electrical Grid

Another wakeup call occurred on August 14, 2003, when the largest blackout in North American history turned off the lights to 50 million customers in the Northwest, Midwest, and parts of Canada. An area covering 3,700 square miles lost power; regional airports were shut down; New York subways came to a standstill, stranding 400,000 commuters in tunnels; the Cleveland water system was closed, leaving 1.5 million people thirsty; and Michigan schools were closed. After $10 billion in economic loss and an untold number of lives put at risk, weak infrastructure was once again identified as a cause.[20]

As with the other emergencies, experts had warned that the infrastructure was outdated and that a major blackout was probable. Experts had urged the United States to modernize the transmission grid system because it was not designed for the needs of the twenty-first century. They had noted that whereas production of energy had generally increased 2.4 percent annually from 1992 to 2003, there was no significant corresponding investment in transmission facilities. This increase in demand without the necessary upgrading of transmission facilities has led to more "bottlenecks" and blackouts. The United States needs to increase annual spending from $283 million to $3–4 billion for the next ten years to upgrade transmission lines. In its latest report card, the ASCE gave a "D" grade to the overall energy system.[21]

Schools

Schools are also part of the public infrastructure crisis. Although the school infrastructure crisis is not as viscerally shocking as when a bridge falls, a levee or dam breaks, or the electricity shuts off, a similar tremor was created in the summer of 2005 when California parents won a $1 billion settlement because of the state's dilapidated facilities.[22]

The lawsuit, which was brought by parents of the state's students, charged that thousands of California's schoolchildren were "forced to study in 'overcrowded, unsafe, poorly ventilated buildings with terrible slum conditions.' These conditions include infestation of cockroaches, rats, and mice, toilets that back up or leak, faucets that do not work, and lack of air conditioning and/or heat, leaving children in a constant sweat in temperatures of 90 degrees and above or with a persistent chill so severe that they have to wear coats, hats, and gloves in the classroom." The settlement forced the state to provide $800 million for emergency repairs to broken air conditioners and heaters, ceilings, roofs, toilets, walls, and windows.[23]

California is not the only state that needs to reinvest in education infrastructure. The American Schools and Universities' Thirtieth Annual Official Education Construction Report estimated that $118 billion were needed for new construction, additions, and renovations to K–12 schools. The ASCE estimated that $127 billion to $268 billion were needed to put school facilities in good condition. This high level of need earned schools a "D" letter grade on the ASCE report card.[24]

These are some of the more dramatic events that have highlighted our run-down infrastructure. Less dramatic but still important are the poor state of our roads ("D–" rating), drinking water ("D–" rating), and public parks ("C–" rating). Taken as a whole, it is clear that our public infrastructure is in crisis. That is why the American infrastructure received

Mark Keppel High School gym, Alhambra, CA.
(Courtesy of ACLU, Southern California)

an overall rating of a "D" on the ASCE report card. To fix this crisis, the ASCE estimated that the United States would have to spend $2.2 trillion on public infrastructure during a five-year period.[25]

The United States is an anomaly when it comes to investing in infrastructure. Today, the United States spends about 2 percent of its gross domestic product (GDP)—which includes federal, state, local, and private-sector spending—on building and maintaining its public infrastructure. In comparison, Europe and sub-Saharan Africa spend about 5 percent of their annual GDP on infrastructure, whereas India and China spend 8 and 9 percent, respectively.[26]

Surely, most Americans can agree that the United States, the richest country in the world, should have a public infrastructure that is worthy of a great power. Our nation's economy depends on having good roads, efficient airports, an effective power grid, and well-maintained schools; our health and well-being depend on clean water and good public parks. The benefit of investing in infrastructure—in addition to having new bridges, dams, and schools—is that it spurs the economy, creates living-wage jobs, and provides the foundation for future economic development. Terrence Sullivan, president of the construction workers Laborers' International Union of North America, estimates that for every $1 billion invested in infrastructure, 47,500 jobs are created. In addition to the creation of jobs, public infrastructure investment brings a high rate of return. Ryan Macdonald with Canada's National Statistics Agency recently released a report showing that infrastructure investment brought an annual rate of return of 17 percent, which was a greater yield than long-term government bonds from 1961 to 2005. There is also historical evidence to demonstrate that infrastructure investment spurs the economy, as many economists claim that major infrastructure investment played a significant role in strengthening the American economy from the 1930s to the 1960s.[27]

So why has the United States not invested in public infrastructure? The answer is found in the reigning conservative ideology, according to which government is the problem and not the solution, with a corollary belief in limiting the scope of government and lowering taxes. Some on the right have called this strategy "starve the beast"; some on the left characterize it as the "dismantling of the New Deal and War on Poverty." Whatever we name it, this dominant ideology has led to a sharp reduction in infrastructure investment, from more than 3.5 percent of GDP in the years 1950 to 1970, to less than 2 percent in the 1980s and 1990s. This level of investment in public infrastructure is the lowest since before the Great Depression. Fortunately, the governing philosophy that led to this low investment in infrastructure, as well as to the social policies that exacerbated the problems facing the American worker, is over.[28]

The End of an Era

The end of an era has arrived. This is certain. Conservatism, with its goals of deregulation and privatization, has been discredited with the economic meltdown. With large financial companies going bankrupt or being bought out at bargain basement prices, credit has become difficult to obtain and the stock market has reacted with wild swings. Average Americans, who will be saddled with a possible $10 trillion bailout tab, still wait for a massive bailout like the megafirms received.[29]

The cause of this financial crisis is found in the deregulation and privatization polices that are at the heart of conservative philosophy. Conservatism has been the dominant ideology of the country since the election of President Ronald Reagan and is based on a laissez-faire, hands-off approach to the economy. Modern conservative philosophy is summed up in President Reagan's famous remark that "government is not the solution to our problem, government is the problem." To get government out of the way and to "free" the market, conservatives relentlessly pushed for deregulation, which minimized oversight of business. By 2001, conservatives were in control of all three branches of government, and by 2008 they had achieved many of their deregulation objectives.

However, the results of their "achievements" have been troubling. In the financial arena, we can see the troubling effects of deregulation in three areas: (a) the overall structure of the financial sector, (b) subprime mortgages, and (c) the credit derivative markets.

Financial Sector Structure

First, the overall structure of the financial sector was fundamentally altered with the repeal of the Glass-Steagall Act. Glass-Steagall, which was passed in 1933 during the height of the Great Depression, made it illegal for banks to own insurance companies and brokerage firms. This New Deal legislation was designed to stop a key cause of the Depression. Before Glass-Steagall, banks were incentivized to promote stocks rather than protect investors. Glass-Steagall was based on the assumption that without regulation, banks had a fundamental conflict of interest because they were both lending money to investors and underwriting stocks. In this structure, banks were seen as unable to provide impartial advice to a client on a possible investment because the banks also made money on selling stock. Glass-Steagall also insulated people's deposits from a stock market collapse because banks and investment firms were separated.

In 1999, conservatives achieved their goal of overturning Glass-Steagall when they enacted the Financial Services Modernization Act. At the signing ceremony for the bill, Representative Phil Gramm, one of its key advocates, commented that "in the 1930s, at the trough of the Depression, when Glass-Steagall became law, it was believed that government was the answer. It was believed that stability and growth came from government overriding the functioning of free markets. We are here today to repeal Glass-Steagall because we have learned that government is not the answer. We have learned that freedom and competition are the answers. We have learned that we promote economic growth, and we promote stability, by having competition and freedom. I am proud to be here because this is an important bill. It is a deregulatory bill. I believe that that is the wave of the future."[30]

As a result of this change to Glass-Steagall, many large and powerful banks and investment firms merged, creating even more powerful corporations, such as JPMorgan Chase and Citigroup. These new megafirms offered a plethora of services that included personal and commercial banking, credit cards, investment services, and wealth management. When the current financial crisis struck, there was little diversity in the market (i.e., separation between banks and investment firms) to cushion the blow, and the federal government felt compelled to bail out these megafirms because they were so large and important to the economy, even though deregulation had created them in the first place.

Subprime Mortgages

Second, a lack of regulation of the financial markets allowed financial institutions to offer subprime mortgages, which is a fancy word for a high-interest loan. Subprime mortgages are a relatively new method of lending money and were created in the early 1980s; before that subprime mortgages had been illegal. Moreover, the Alternative Mortgage Transaction Parity Act of 1982 made it possible for financial institutions to make more risky loans by allowing balloon payments and variable interest rates, which had also been illegal before the passing of this act. Then, Congress passed the Tax Reform Act of 1986, which no longer allowed the deduction of

interest on consumer loans but continued to allow deduction for mortgages on primary residences and second homes. This change encouraged
homeowners to refinance their homes and roll their consumer debt (car
loans and credit cards) into their mortgages, where it was tax deductible.
It is not surprising that more than one-half of all subprime loans involved
cashouts in order to pay debt.

This need for cash reflects the stagnation of incomes for working
Americans. Today, the median household income is lower than it was in
1999. This stagnation and decline of incomes forced Americans to look
for other ways to maintain their standard of living, and many turned to
subprime loans. In addition, stagnating wages presented an obstacle to
buying a home when housing prices soared from 1998 to 2005. Subprime
loans were inviting because they offered low introductory "teaser" rates to
people with low credit scores. In addition, some subprime loans offered
no downpayment and no credit check or income verification. In 2006,
banks offered 60 percent of the subprime loans to people with no credit
check or income verification.[31]

To make matters worse, mortgage companies then sold these subprime
loans to middlemen who bundled and sold them as mortgage-backed
securities. The investor in these bonds now held the risk, while the mortgage companies and middlemen walked off with a large profit. In 1995,
there were only 21,000 subprime loans; by 2003 that number had risen
to 866,000; by 2006 subprime lending was a $600 billion business, with
20 percent of all mortgages being subprime.[32]

It is important to note that subprime mortgages have a racial and ethnic dimension. In 2005, blacks received subprime loans 53 percent and
Latinos 38 percent of the time when refinancing a home; white borrowers
received subprime loans 26 percent of the time. Disturbingly, the majority of people of color qualified for a conventional prime-rate loan. This
targeting of people of color for subprime loans has huge consequences,
as foreclosures on these loans will affect 10 percent of black borrowers
and 8 percent of Latino borrowers, in comparison to about 4 percent of
white borrowers. Black and Latino homeownership, which had reached
record levels, growing at twice the rate of white homeownership in the late
1990s, is now on the decline. For example, black homeownership, which
was at 49 percent in 2004, was at 46 percent in 2007 and may drop to
44 percent in the near future.[33]

Interestingly, Congress saw the problem coming. In 1994, it passed
the Homeownership Opportunity and Equity Protection Act (HOEPA),
which called on the Federal Reserve to put restrictions on subprime loans

to reduce the risk of foreclosure and predatory lending. For example, HOEPA made illegal balloon payments in the first five years of a loan and prepayment penalties after five years. However, Alan Greenspan, chairman of the Federal Reserve from 1987 to 2006, decided not to apply HOEPA because it contradicted his free-market philosophy, and the Republicans controlling Congress did not press Greenspan on the matter. Other governmental officials were equally disdainful of regulating subprime loans. To show their contempt, representatives of the five government agencies charged with overseeing financial institutions held a press conference in June 2003—at a time when subprime loans were growing exponentially—and attacked with tree shears and a chainsaw a stack of paper representing bank regulations. On top of this disdain for regulation, the federal regulators basically waived the law that required mortgage lenders to have adequate capital in reserve.[34]

As the new interest rates kicked in on subprime loans, people were unable to pay their mortgages, causing them to foreclose. In 2007, 1.3 million homes were in some stage of foreclosure, up 79 percent from the previous year; 405,000 people actually lost their homes. Foreclosures accelerated even more in 2008: In August more than 300,000 homes received foreclosure filings. By February 2009, the United States experienced its tenth straight month in which more than 250,000 households filed for foreclosure. Currently, about 24 percent of all subprime mortgages are delinquent or in foreclosure. This foreclosure crisis burst the housing bubble and sent home prices downward. This downturn was not just bad news for homeowners; it was also catastrophic for the megafirms. To understand why the megafirms went bankrupt, or were pushed to the brink of bankruptcy, it is necessary to understand the other major change in regulation, which was to the credit derivatives market.[35]

The Credit Derivative Markets

Credit derivatives, or "credit default swaps," were created as a "hedge," or insurance, against investment losses, and in this current crisis they were used by institutional investors to hedge against the risk of default in mortgage-backed securities. At the same time, credit derivatives became an investment tool themselves because they allowed people to speculate on future prices of stocks or commodities without owning the underlying investment. What began as a way to protect investors became a vast game of speculation. In a way, credit default swaps may be best understood as a "side bet," with megafirms and other institutional players using them to make bets on the direction of markets. This type of unregulated side bet on stocks and commodities was illegal for most of the twentieth century until the Republican Congress legalized it at the end of the Clinton presidency in 2000.[36]

Before long, people began to raise concerns about credit default swaps as a threat to the overall financial system, with Warren Buffet in 2003 going so far as to call derivatives "financial weapons of mass destruction." However, Greenspan, who had previously refused to regulate subprime mortgages, also declined to regulate credit default swaps. Thus, these derivatives were traded without federal oversight, which meant that there was no central exchange to monitor and oversee these bets.[37]

Even though credit default swaps were high-risk investments, they also were extremely lucrative for the megafirms. In the 1980s, the derivative market played an insignificant role in the financial world. By 2002, unregulated credit default swaps were a $2.2 trillion business; by 2008 it had increased to $62 trillion, with about 80 percent in speculation. Investment banks, as well as Wall Street traders, made millions as they collected premiums for the "insurance" protection they offered for taking on the risk of default. Yet as long as the bonds did not default, the gambling continued. But when the housing bubble burst, lots of the bonds—particularly mortgage-backed securities—defaulted, exposing these megafirms to huge losses. It was this combination of losses in mortgage-backed securities and in credit default swaps that was so devastating to Bear Stearns, Citigroup, Morgan Stanley, Lehman Brothers, and AIG. When housing prices began to fall, these firms lost billions of dollars as their mortgage-backed securities became "toxic," and they were forced to pay out on their side bets as well. A further problem was that these mortgage-backed securities were leveraged, and so the losses became magnified. Ultimately, they came up short. When financial firms were not able to cover their losses, they were forced into bankruptcy or near bankruptcy. Warren Buffet's prediction had come true. Thirty-seven banks failed in the first half of 2009, following on the heels of the twenty-five banks that had failed in 2008. In comparison three banks had failed in 2007, and none had in 2006 and 2005.[38]

* * *

Today, there is growing consensus across the political spectrum that the deregulated market is at the center of the financial meltdown. Even the architects of this philosophy, such as Alan Greenspan, have admitted that the free-market ideology was flawed. At a congressional hearing in October 2008, Greenspan stated, "I made a mistake in presuming that the self-interests of organizations, specifically banks and others, were such as that they were best capable of protecting their own shareholders and their equity in the firms." This "flaw" in Greenspan's thinking about markets, regulation, and the limited role of the government has led to the end of the conservative era in America. Perhaps the demise of this era will bring about major change in the structure of the global free-market system, which has been dominated by the American-British model of capitalism since its development at Bretton Woods, a New Hampshire resort, in 1944. It is time for something different.[39]

A "New" Approach

After almost thirty years of conservatism being the dominant ideology in America, a new approach is needed in this country. Barack Obama rode this desire for change to victory in the presidential election on November 4, 2008, by soundly defeating Senator John McCain by a margin of 52.9 to 45.6 percent and winning 365 electoral votes to McCain's 173. What ideology will replace conservatism as the new dominant paradigm has yet to fully emerge. What we do know is that the government will be seen as part of the solution, not part of the problem. This will mean that the federal government will play a powerful role in the economy, both in creating jobs and in providing oversight and regulation.[40]

In January 2009, President-elect Obama provided his clearest articulation until then of his governing philosophy when he stated that "only government can break the cycle that is crippling our economy, where a lack of spending leads to lost jobs, which leads to even less spending, where an inability to lend and borrow stops growth and leads to even less credit. That's why we need to act boldly and act now to reverse these cycles." Reflecting on Obama's words, Allan Lichtman, a scholar on the American presidency, commented that "Reagan famously said government is not the solution, it's the problem.... Obama is saying government is the solution and, in fact, the only real solution to the crisis we're experiencing today." Ironically, we saw this change in philosophy evident even before Obama took office. In October, President Bush led the effort to pass a $700 billion bailout of the megafirms. This partial nationalization of these megafirms—taxpayers are now the largest shareholders in Citgroup, with 36 percent of the stock; in Bank of America, with 6 percent; and in AIG, with 80 percent—was followed by Bush's authorization to use $13 billion from the bank bailout to provide a loan to help General Motors and Chrysler avoid bankruptcy. To justify these governmental intrusions into the economy, Bush argued that "government has a responsibility to safeguard the broader health and stability of our economy." In a strange twist, Bush put an end to Reagan's antigovernment philosophy.[41]

Upon talking office, President Obama and the Democratically controlled Congress went to work on bringing relief to Main Street. On February 17, 2009, Obama signed into law a $787 billion package focused on creating or saving 3.5 million jobs as well as rebuilding infrastructure. Clearly, Obama's plan has given new life to the ideas of John Maynard Keynes, an economist who advocated government spending as a way to stimulate the economy during the Great Depression of the 1930s. However, there are still questions and concerns surrounding the structure of the job-creation projects and what type of oversight they will have. These questions are the focus of Chapter 2.

CHAPTER 2

PUBLIC WORKS

AN AMERICAN SOLUTION

As the economic crisis deepened in late November 2008, President-elect Barack Obama called on Congress to pass immediately a large-scale infrastructure bill with the goal of saving or creating 2.5 million jobs. With this announcement, the media and pundits declared the end of the conservative era and the dawning of a new epoch of government involvement in the economy. In recognition of this change, *Time* magazine placed on its front cover a picture of President Obama's face superimposed on an iconoclastic image of President Franklin Roosevelt, with the title "The *New* New Deal." David Demerjian of *Wired* argued that a modern-day Works Progress Administration (WPA) was the best way to save the economy and provide good jobs to Main Street.[1]

Four weeks after taking office, President Obama signed a $787 billion stimulus package with the goal of saving or creating 3.5 million new jobs. The infrastructure component of the bill will build bridges, schools, and electric grids, with a focus on "green-collar" jobs. However, the question remains: Is Obama's public works initiative truly a *New* New Deal, and does it bear any resemblance to the Public Works Administration (PWA), Civil Works Administration (CWA), Works Progress Administration (WPA), or the Civilian Conservation Corps (CCC), all signature New Deal public works projects?

Yes, it is true that Obama's bill will build public structures using federal dollars. It is also true that this initiative will create jobs. However, for the most part the Obama plan is not a New Deal–like public works project, and it may lead to waste, corruption, and inequality. To understand why this may occur, it is necessary to understand the history of public works in America, the lessons learned from such projects, and the ideology that guided them.

Public Works: Getting People Back to Work

Using public works to get people back to work and reduce poverty has a long tradition in America. During the second half of the nineteenth century, American cities conducted public works projects to deal with wild fluctuations in the economy and the resulting unemployment. For example, during the depression of 1882–1885, during which 2 million people lost their jobs, cities hired unemployed workers to do such public works as clean the streets. However, it was during the depression of 1893 that Jacob Coxey, a wealthy businessman from Ohio, first proposed the idea of national public works to solve the unemployment crisis. With millions of Americans unemployed, Coxey demanded that the federal government employ people to build modern roads and civic buildings such as courthouses and fire stations. Under his plan, each state would receive $20 million. In addition to advocating for the creation of jobs and the building of public structures, Coxey argued that the pay, which was to be no less than $1.50 for an eight-hour workday, would provide upward pressure on wages, as well as make the eight-hour day the standard during a time when the average person worked ten to twelve hours a day.[2]

More than 1,000 men participated in Coxey's "army of the unemployed," as they marched from several American cities toward Washington, DC. Throughout this first "march on Washington," Coxey argued that public works would provide good jobs, build necessary infrastructure, and drive up wages. However, when Coxey arrived in DC, he was arrested for trespassing: Walking on the Capitol grass and having a banner (he had a small lapel pin) were illegal. Congress largely overlooked the pleas of Coxey's army of the unemployed, and the idea for a national public works project would have to wait another two generations.[3]

Forty years later, President Franklin D. Roosevelt put Coxey's vision into action. In 1933, Roosevelt created a series of national public works programs to deal with the unemployment crisis; these programs included the PWA, CWA, WPA, and CCC. As a part of the first 100 days of his presidency, Roosevelt created and signed into law the National Industry Recovery Act of 1933, which created the Public Works Administration.

The PWA utilized private contractors to employ mostly skilled workers to build large infrastructure projects such as aircraft carriers, airports, tunnels, bridges, and dams that produced electricity. The PWA defined public work as "the construction and report of public highways and parkways, and public buildings; the conservation and development of natural resources including the control, utilization, and purification of waters; prevention of soil and coastal erosion, development of water power; transmission of electrical energy, and reconstruction of river and harbor improvements and flood control, and also the construction of any river or drainage improvement; construction, reconstruction, alteration, or repair under public regulation or control of low-cost housing, and slum-clearance projects."[4]

The PWA was based on President Herbert Hoover's public works model, which had been started as part of the 1932 Emergency Relief and Construction Act (ERCA). This limited public works model was expanded under Roosevelt, and by 1940 the PWA had awarded 54,637 construction contracts to more than 20,000 contractors. Between 1934 and 1939, PWA projects allowed private contractors to employ on average 221,000 workers a year, which was one-eighth of the total of all workers directly employed in public works. The PWA's peak year was in 1934, when it hired 463,100 workers. PWA workers were primarily from the skilled trades, and union workers were hired from the trade union locals rather than from the local employment and welfare agencies. In its eight-year history, the PWA spent more than $6 billion (about $92 billion in 2009 dollars) and completed more than 34,400 construction projects, building 7,488 schools, 11,428 road projects, 25,000 affordable housing units, and some of our nation's landmark structures, such as the Bay Bridge in California, the Hoover Dam in Nevada, the Lincoln Tunnel in New York, and the Ronald Reagan Washington National Airport.[5]

Secretary of the Interior Harold Ickes led the PWA, and his official title was administrator of public works. A special board was created to manage the PWA, and it was composed of Ickes and several cabinet members (the secretaries of agriculture, commerce, labor, and war; the attorney general; and the director of the budget). Projects were funded according to two principles: They provided immediate employment to workers, and they had a high level of social usefulness. Each week, Ickes met with FDR to discuss which PWA projects should move forward.[6]

The positive aspects of this model were that the contractors had the skills to complete the work and they handled the direct supervision of workers. The contract method also fit well into capitalism, as it kept

*PWA workers build a wall
for the Lincoln Tunnel in
New York. (Courtesy of
the National Archives and
Records Administration)*

jobs within private industry. However, by the mid-1930s Roosevelt was
frustrated with the contractor model because he felt that it was not creating enough jobs and that not enough money was getting into workers'
hands. First, contractors wanted to minimize expenses on a project, which
included labor costs, in order to maximize profits. Second, more money
was spent on materials than on salaries. According to PWA records, sixty-
four cents of every dollar went to materials, whereas only thirty-six cents
went for labor costs, which were paid at a prevailing wage. However, PWA
supporters argued that the contractors did the work efficiently and that
it was necessary to take into account the "indirect employment" created
through the purchase of materials in any evaluation of the effectiveness of
the PWA to employ people. When we take into account both direct and
indirect employment, the PWA employed on average 1,177,000 workers
each year. However, Roosevelt was interested in direct, rather than indirect,
employment. He argued that "there is no use mentioning indirect labor
in these discussions. Indirect labor does not count in our figures.... It
does not enter into the consideration of our projects."[7]

In response to the PWA's inability to hire directly large numbers of
adult workers, Roosevelt created by executive order the CWA and then the
WPA. They differed from the PWA in that they utilized a government-run
model. In other words, the federal government was directly involved in the
hiring and supervising of workers, which allowed the government to hire
large numbers of unemployed workers quickly. For example, Roosevelt
signed the executive order in November 1933, and within two weeks the
CWA hired 814,511 people from the relief rolls to do construction work,

and within four weeks the total number of CWA workers was almost 2 million. During the next month, more than 9 million workers applied for the remaining 2 million CWA jobs. By mid-January 1935, the CWA employed 4,263,644 workers. The WPA continued this model of using local public welfare agencies to sign up large numbers of workers quickly and efficiently. Conservatives criticized this government-run model as "socialism," but Roosevelt believed that he was acting to save American capitalism.[8]

Some have argued that, even though a government-run public works project may be able to efficiently hire mass numbers of unemployed and unskilled workers, it surely is not as productive as the private contractor model because the latter workers have a higher level of skills. However, as Jason Scott Smith points out in his book *Building New Deal Liberalism: The Political Economy of Public Works, 1933–1956*, the record does not fully support this perspective. For example, in its five-month history the CWA built or repaired 200 swimming pools, 1,000 small airports, 3,700 playgrounds, 40,000 schools, 250,000 miles of road, and 12 million feet of sewer pipe. Clearly, the CWA was successful at building infrastructure projects utilizing unemployed and unskilled workers. In addition, it pumped more than $1 billion into the economy. This extra money in the pocketbooks of consumers would, it was hoped, lead to more consumer spending, which in turn would lead to businesses hiring more people, thereby leading to even more consumer spending. This is known as the multiplier effect, which was made popular by economist John Maynard Keynes and is based on the idea that output goes up by a multiple of the original spending change.[9]

Despite the success of the CWA, President Roosevelt feared that Americans were becoming too dependent on the federal government, and he abruptly shut down the project in March 1934. However, a year later the economy had yet to recover, so he once again turned to a large-scale, government-run public works project. In March 1935, President Roosevelt signed another executive order, this one creating the WPA. In its eight-year history, the WPA spent $10.8 billion (about $165 billion in 2009 dollars), employed 8.5 million people, and worked on 1.4 million projects. The WPA built or improved 103 golf courses, 853 airport landing fields, 2,500 hospitals, 2,500 sports stadiums, 3,000 schools, 8,192 parks, 12,800 playgrounds, 124,031 bridges, 125,110 public buildings, and 651,087 miles of highways and roads. In addition, the WPA hired artists for the Federal Art, Theater, Writing, and Music Projects. For many working Americans, the concerts by the WPA's 238 orchestras and bands were the first time they had ever heard live music.[10]

WPA crew working on a tunnel for Charity Hospital in New Orleans, Louisiana. (Courtesy of WPA Photograph Collection/ Louisiana Division, New Orleans Public Library)

The CWA and WPA, both of which were directed by Harry Hopkins, differed sharply from the PWA because they used a government-hiring model to employ unemployed workers who were receiving welfare. The WPA continued the CWA model of using local public welfare agencies to sign up large numbers of workers quickly and efficiently. Hopkins, whose official title for the WPA was commissioner of work projects, believed that the solution to the employment crisis was to provide jobs to unemployed, and often unskilled, workers. Hopkins stated: "Give a man a dole and you save his body and destroy his spirit. Give him a job and pay him an assured wage, and you save both the body and the spirit."[11]

The CWA and WPA were incredibly successful in hiring several million workers a year throughout the mid- to late 1930s. Importantly, the average WPA construction project had 75 percent unskilled laborers working

A Civilian Conservation Corps (CCC) member uses an engineer's level for a construction project in Yanceyville, North Carolina. (Photo courtesy of USDA Natural Resources Conservation Service)

on road construction projects and 50 percent unskilled laborers on public buildings. To overcome this lack of skilled labor, local communities used their own monies to hire skilled workers to help oversee and carry out the projects. The CWA paid its workers a prevailing wage, which was generally the rate paid to union workers for that region. The main reason for this pay rate was that the CWA was funded out of PWA money and therefore was obliged to follow its wage policies. However, the WPA moved away from this CWA commitment to pay a prevailing wage and substituted for it a "sustainable wage." This amount was similar to what the government paid for "welfare." The WPA workers were outraged by this lower pay and through organizations such as the Workers Alliance of America struggled for higher wages. After a succession of strikes at WPA offices and job sites, the federal government acquiesced and provided regular wage increases that moved workers closer toward a prevailing wage. To maximize the number of workers hired, 80 percent of the WPA allocation went toward worker salaries, with only 20 percent going toward material.[12]

In spite of what some historians have suggested, the CWA and WPA were successful at putting people to work *and* building infrastructure. Seventy percent of the 1.4 million WPA projects were in the field of construction. The success of the WPA in building infrastructure gives pause to anyone who claims that the PWA was more successful or doubts that a similar program using unemployed and unskilled workers would not work today. At the same time, contractors and other businessmen disapproved of this model because they felt that private plumbers, electricians, and road builders were being cut out of the construction business, even though the historical record does not indicate this to have been the case.[13]

President Roosevelt also developed a public works project focused on young unemployed workers. The CCC, created in 1933 through executive order, was overseen by the U.S. Army and provided government-created jobs to 500,000 young men a year (aged eighteen to twenty-five) to work on environmental conservation projects. In its nine-year history, the CCC employed a total of 3.5 million young people and built 800 state parks, saved 40 million acres from soil erosion, stocked 1 billion fish in lakes and rivers, and planted 3 billion trees. The total cost for the CCC was $3 billion (about $46 billion in 2009 dollars).[14]

With the entrance of the United States into World War II, the New Deal public works projects came to a close as the unemployment rate plummeted. However, before the WPA closed in 1943, it participated in the internment of 120,000 Japanese Americans by organizing and staffing assembly centers and relocation, or concentration, camps. Sadly, a program that was created to help remove societal inequalities provided the workforce to forcibly and unconstitutionally relocate Americans in the largest forced removal program since Native Americans were forced to move west of the Mississippi River. After the end of World War II, public works contin ued in the form of building dams, bridges, and highways, but the social democratic ideal of reducing inequality had been eliminated.[15]

Public works as a method of reducing inequality was resurrected by Dr. Martin Luther King Jr. As part of his 1968 Poor People's Campaign, King advocated for a return to public works investment as one of his three main strategies to end poverty in America. In combination with a guaranteed income pegged at middle-class-income levels for those who could not work and the creation of 5 million low-income homes in ten years, King argued that a public works program would provide the poor with the money they needed to pay for adequate housing, food, clothing, and health care. King felt that there was no reason that the richest nation in the world could not end poverty through public works, a guaranteed income, and the creation of 5 million low-income homes.[16]

Lessons for the Obama Administration

As President Obama and his administration move forward with their public works agenda, there are five key lessons to be learned from New Deal public works. These are (1) public works programs need strong oversight and management to safeguard against waste and corruption; (2) the federal government must work together with local and state part- ners at all stages of public works projects, (3) the contract model and the government-hiring model are both effective ways to build infrastructure, but the most effective way to create millions of jobs is the government-run model; (4) funding must be large enough to create the number of jobs needed to solve the problem and not be based on loans; and (5) public works projects must take into consideration issues of equity.

Oversight and Management

First, President Obama and his administration need to know that the New Deal public works projects had strong oversight and management to safeguard against waste and corruption. New Deal public works projects did not just give money to the states, with the hope that it would reach the local level; rather, the public works agencies were involved throughout the various stages of the projects. For example, the PWA rooted out waste and corruption by having PWA officials present, in conjunction with local officials, when a contract was offered for a project. The presence of the PWA ensured that the lowest bid received the contract. After the lowest bid was accepted, the PWA official would immediately research the chosen contractor's qualifications to ensure that the contractor was qualified to do the work. The PWA then assigned a resident engineer to each project to make sure that the work was conducted at high standards. A PWA report noted: "As the projects were built by local authorities, local inspectors were, of course, required. But the tradition of lax local inspection was intrenched in American practice. Too often local inspectors winked at substandard material or wage 'kick practices.' The practice had grown to be accepted in a number of communities."[17]

In addition, the PWA and WPA created investigative divisions that were active and aggressive in combating waste and corruption. The Investigative Division was included in Roosevelt's executive order creating the WPA, and its goal was to investigate fraud, corruption, and abuse. In such a large government-run construction program, there were many opportunities for criminal activities. That was why the WPA Investigative Division functions included

> the handling of complaints alleging that funds were being diverted to other than public benefit; that false statements had been made in obtaining allocations or benefits from Federal funds; that pay rolls for personal services were being padded; that false compensation claims had been filed by WPA employees; that fraud existed in competitive bidding on Government contracts; that vendors to the Government were not delivering goods or materials in accordance with their contracts; that forgery had been committed in work assignments, time reports, or other official documents, and complaints of extortion, kickbacks, theft, embezzlement, bribery, and collection of illegal fees.

During its eight-year existence, the Investigative Division of the WPA examined 17,352 cases. Of these, 8,811 cases were substantiated. Out of those, 2,215 cases were forwarded on to the attorney general for criminal prosecution, and in 4,496 cases people received debarments, demotions, dismissals, and reprimands.[18]

This PWA and WPA oversight allowed projects to be selected based on social usefulness and maximization of employment. The Division of Application and Information would screen the public works project applications. After the initial screening, the project applications were sent on to the Advisory Committee on Allotments, which would review the screened list and make recommendations to President Roosevelt, who would make the final decision. This process screened out such inappropriate or boondoggle projects as a plan to hire 10,000 men to kill snakes and a project to build a people-mover sidewalk from coast to coast. These oversight policies allowed the administrators to claim that public work projects, "on the whole, have been well built and honestly built, and that the schools, hospitals, courthouses, bridges, roads, waterworks and other public works of a permanent nature have met definite community needs." Even President Ronald Reagan, the father of the modern-day conservative movement, talked glowingly about how public works provided socially useful projects and jobs, including one for his father, Jack, from Dixon, Illinois. Reagan commented: "Now a lot of people remember [the WPA] as boondoggles and raking leaves. . . . Maybe in some places it was. Maybe in the big city machines or something. But I can take you to our town and show you things, like a riverfront that I used to hike through once that was a swamp and is now a beautiful parklike place built by the WPA."[19]

In order to have the most effective public works programs, the PWA and WPA also created divisions of administration, finance, engineering, legal issues, and statistics. Both models divided the country into seven regions, with each having a regional office for the two public works programs. For example, each state had its own WPA administrator who was responsible for all WPA activities within the state. This state administrator, who reported to the commissioner of work projects, was responsible for supporting local and state authorities in initiating projects; the administrator then passed these requests on to the commissioner and the president. If a decision was made to go forward, the state administrators and their staff made the funds available to the project sponsors and worked with them to assign local supervisors and workers to the project. Most states also had WPA district offices, which brought together the WPA work supervisors, the local sponsors, various government agencies that might be affected by the project, and the larger general public.

This lesson of providing oversight for public works is one of the most important lessons for the Obama administration. Without strong oversight, such as was developed in the New Deal, much of the money for the public works projects will go toward pork-barrel projects or quarterly profits or both. Look at what happened just two months after the I-35 bridge collapsed in Minnesota: The Senate approved a transportation and housing bill that contained $2 billion for pet projects, including a Montana baseball stadium and a Las Vegas history museum. Or take a look at what happened to the 2005 Gulf Opportunity Zone Act (GO Zone), which was signed into law by President Bush four months after Hurricane Katrina and gave businesses $3.5 billion in tax breaks to jump-start the recovery process. Two years later, only one GO Zone project was located in New Orleans, the city that had suffered the most damage from Hurricane Katrina. Incredibly, many GO Zone tax breaks were given to regions outside the most affected areas, such as the $1 million deal to develop ten luxury condos across from the football stadium at the University of Alabama, even though it is a four-hour drive from there to the Gulf Coast.[20]

Research shows that "bridges to nowhere" are part of a wasteful system in which only about twenty states actually do cost-benefit analysis when evaluating projects such as transport. Moreover, this waste is part of a larger problem of not having a national strategy or a federal office to oversee infrastructure spending. *The Economist* notes that "congressmen appropriate money for individual projects, a few of which are ludicrous (Alaska's 'bridge to nowhere') and most of which bear no relation to each other. Cash for roads is given to states with few strings attached." Robert Puentes of the Brookings Institution adds that with at least one type of infrastructure spending, that of highway funds, "it is as close to sending states a blank check as you can get. Unfortunately, when it comes to transportation most states have not proven themselves to be good stewards of the public dollar." This wasteful system was also evident in the large infrastructure projects undertaken after Hurricanes Katrina and Rita, where congressional staffers discovered that nineteen federal contracts totaling $8.75 billion had significant overcharges, wasteful spending, and mismanagement. Similar abuses may occur with Obama's stimulus package without New Deal–type oversight.[21]

Federal Partnerships

The second lesson for the Obama administration is that the federal government must work together with local and state partners at all stages of public works. A key lesson of the New Deal public works projects is that there was a partnership among the local, state, and federal governments, with each level of government playing a particular role: The local communities initiated and planned the vast majority of projects, the state determined whether the projects fit under public works regulations, and the federal government selected the projects and provided support and oversight to ensure project completion and protect against corruption. When describing this federal, state, and local partnership, Commissioner

Hopkins said: "We would have been awful damned fools if we thought for a minute that we have either the power or the ability to go out and set up 100,000 work projects as we are going to have to do, probably 200,000 before the year is over, without the complete cooperation of local and state officials. We couldn't do it if we wanted to." To help with this coordination, a plethora of WPA and PWA officials were made available to work through all the legal and logistical questions that arise in the conduct of large-scale public works projects.[22]

Compare this with what has taken place with the Gulf Coast rebuilding efforts, where there has been a lack of coordination among federal, state, and local officials. Examining the Gulf Coast is instructive because there was a massive infusion of capital appropriated to create jobs and rebuild the infrastructure. For example, more than $116 billion have been allocated for post-Katrina recovery, but the money has had a difficult time making its way down to the local level because of the inability of the federal government to help solve the problems faced by state and local officials. For example, the federal government provided $16.7 billion for Community Development Block Grants, but by March 2007 only $1 billion had been spent by local communities, most of it in Mississippi. By the second anniversary of Katrina, less than 70 percent had been used. Jeffrey Buchanan from the RFK Center for Justice and Human Rights states: "The White House has not done enough to make sure the funds get to the places that need it quickly and efficiently, instead choosing to take a hands off attitude, leaving itself in a position to point fingers at overwhelmed state and local officials who have had to deal with significant federal red tape while rebuilding their communities from the ground up without the logistical and operations help of their federal government." To make a modern-day public works project successful, federal, state, and local governments must coordinate their activities so that potential roadblocks are dealt with quickly.[23]

Models for Building Infrastructure

A third lesson for the Obama administration is to understand the different potentials of the contract and government-run models. Even though both models were successful at building infrastructure, the government run model was more successful at hiring massive numbers of the unemployed. Recall that the two government-run programs hired the largest number of workers, with the CWA hiring 4.2 million people in 1935 and the WPA hiring on average 2.1 million each year, with a peak of 3.3 million in 1938.

Overall, the WPA employed 8.5 million people, which was three-fourths of all public workers. Thus, history demonstrates that a government-run model creates more jobs, and does so faster, than a contract model.

Large-Scale Funding

Fourth, funding for public works projects must be large enough to create the number of jobs needed to solve the problem, and this funding must not be based on loans. The amount of funding has been an issue in the large-scale recovery efforts in the Gulf Coast, where the Federal Emergency Management Agency provided only $3.4 billion to rebuild public infrastructure, which covered about one-eighth of the damage that had taken place in Louisiana alone.

Funding was also an issue during the New Deal public works projects. During the Great Depression, unemployment was 23.6 percent, or 12.8 million people, in 1932, but the combined public works projects (PWA, CWA, WPA, and CCC) were funded to hire on average about 3 to 4 million people a year. And although public works, along with other New Deal measures, had the positive effect of decreasing unemployment to 9.5 million in 1935 and 7.6 million in 1936, these measures were not enough to end the unemployment crisis; another 5 million-plus jobs were needed. The WPA, which was by far the largest employer of unemployed workers, only helped between 30 and 39 percent of all unemployed workers. Thus, there were not enough public works jobs in relation to the need for them, so high levels of unemployment remained. At one point, Ickes, the head of the PWA, sadly reported that "there are many hundreds of worthy projects still pending with no money to be allotted to them unless Congress should make a further appropriation."[24]

Clearly, it is incorrect to think that this decrease in unemployment, which would have been even greater if more money had been provided, did not lead to an economic recovery; it did. In Roosevelt's first two terms (1933–1941), the economy grew at a rate of 9–10 percent a year, which is now considered "spectacular" by some modern economists. It is true that there was a short recession in 1937–1938, when Roosevelt prematurely cut public spending; however, this short recession did not undermine the overall upward direction of the economic recovery. Ultimately, the New Deal public works of the PWA, WPA, and CCC injected more than $21.7 billion (about $336 billion in 2009 dollars) into the economy and in combination with other New Deal initiatives cut unemployment from 23.6 percent in 1933 to 14.6 percent by 1940. This 9 percent decrease was the single greatest drop in the unemployment rate in U.S. history. Thus, when Senate minority leader Mitch McConnell (R-KY) argued against President Obama's stimulus package, stating that "the big spending programs of the New Deal did not work; in 1940 unemployment was still 15 percent," he was just flat wrong. Incredibly, these unemployment numbers do not even include the approximately 3 million people a year who were hired as employees of the public works programs themselves. If people with public works jobs are included, the unemployment rate drops to 10 percent in 1940.[25]

In addition to the amount of money appropriated, another key part of funding public works projects has to do with whether the money is given as loans or grants. For example, Roosevelt argued that the original funding method of the PWA, which was through loans, slowed down public works projects. In many respects, the PWA inherited the funding strategy that had been adopted by President Hoover in his initial attempts at public works as part of the Emergency Relief and Construction Act (ERCA). In 1932, the Hoover administration and Congress made $1.5 billion ($23 billion in 2008 dollars) available to the states as loans for "self-liquidating" public works projects, which meant that the federal loan would be paid back through the self-generating income of the projects (e.g., electricity-producing dams and bridge tolls). Even though Harold Ickes, director of the WPA, attempted to ease the ERCA loan requirements, the reality was that the PWA continued Hoover's model because a main factor in determining whether a PWA project was selected depended heavily on whether the loan was self-liquidating. If the project was accepted, the PWA provided states and municipalities with a grant of 30 percent for the project's cost and then offered a loan at 4 percent.

This model was criticized by some New Dealers and led to the WPA financing model, which was based primarily on grants-in-aid to states and municipalities. Out of the $4.88 billion ($76 billion in 2009 dollars) appropriated in 1935 for the WPA, more than $4 billion were in grants to states and municipalities, with only $450 million for self-liquidating loans. This funding method was designed to encourage the employment of workers on public works projects as quickly as possible without putting a burden on the states and municipalities. This funding strategy, which the Obama administration should learn from, was successful at getting people to work throughout the country, as the WPA had projects in all but three counties in the country. Note that even though local communities did not provide labor costs for the WPA, they did contribute materials and equipment, providing two-thirds of those for WPA projects; the WPA contributed the remaining one-third. As mentioned, local communities also hired some skilled workers to assist WPA workers, who were often unskilled for the jobs they were on.[26]

Equity Issues

A fifth lesson for the Obama administration is that equity issues must be considered when contractors and workers are chosen. These issues cover a broad range of topics but include at least four questions: Who will receive the jobs (e.g., will women, people of color, the poor, and immigrants be included)? Who will receive the contracts (e.g., small businesses, people of color, women)? Which communities will get infrastructure projects (uptown or the inner city)? Will the workers be paid a living wage?

As was discussed earlier, the New Deal public works projects were careful to avoid favoritism in assigning contracts. PWA officials were involved in every stage of the process to make sure that businesses were given contracts based on their low bids and their ability to complete jobs. Nevertheless, New Deal public works projects did not meet their democratic ideal when they favored white over black workers. However, the PWA did have a nondiscrimination policy and even designed it to ensure that contractors paid skilled black workers a percentage of the total project salaries equivalent to a least one-half of their percentage in the regional workforce. And even though PWA officials tried to enforce this nondiscrimination policy, particularly in the South, they were not always successful. One of the problems the PWA ran up against was that in cases of discrimination it was difficult to get African American workers to testify against contractors for whom they were working or had worked because such testimony damaged the workers' future employment opportunities.

Black workers did benefit from WPA jobs because decent-paying jobs were offered to unemployed workers. As a result of discrimination, blacks had disproportionately high unemployment rates and therefore could obtain WPA jobs. Furthermore, blacks also benefited from the fact that pay rates for these government jobs were based on skill level, not race or ethnicity.[27]

In addition to racial discrimination, there was gender discrimination in the New Deal projects. A New Deal official noted that "for unskilled men, we have the shovel. For unskilled women, we have only the needle." Thus, even though the WPA did hire women, they often worked in community sewing rooms making clothes for poor children, as well as in school lunch rooms, libraries, or canneries. Because women were classified as unskilled labor, they were paid the lowest wage rate, which was twenty to thirty cents (about $3.05 to $4.49 in 2009 dollars) an hour.[28]

A related issue is how much workers were, and are, paid. The CWA and PWA paid living wages; the WPA did not. On average, a WPA wage was $55 a month, or $660 a year (about $10,000 in 2008 dollars), which was about one-half the salary of an average factory worker. In *America's Struggle Against Poverty in the Twentieth Century,* James Patterson calls this wage "a pittance" and argues that from the late 1930s until the late 1960s, "few used the WPA as an example of a 'successful' agency that would justify public employment as a major weapon against poverty." Clearly, a modern public works project must pay a living wage.[29]

A vivid example of how these equity issues have played out more recently has been in the post-Katrina aftermath. In the Gulf Coast, large corporations received the contracts over small and medium-sized businesses to do the cleanup and begin the rebuilding process. Within a month of Katrina, more than fifteen large corporations—including Ashbritt Inc., Bechtel Corporation, CH2M Hill Inc., Fluor Corporation, Kellogg, Brown & Root (a Halliburton subsidiary), and the Shaw Group Inc.—received $100 million plus, no-bid or "limited competition" contracts, including five contracts of $500 million or more. Of course, these no-bid contracts went to the companies that had the best political connections.[30]

The problem with favoring large corporations over medium and small corporations—besides the fairness issue—is that it is inefficient. After receiving a major federal contract, large corporations often subcontract out the work to medium-sized contractors, which then subcontract the work out to smaller contractors. At each level of subcontracting, taxpayer money is skimmed off the top, and the money ends up as quarterly profits rather than as funds for hiring workers and building infrastructure. This scheme was clearly evident in the aftermath of Katrina. For example, the federal government gave Ashbritt a $500 million contract to remove debris at the rate of $23 a cubic yard in Mississippi. At that time, according to reports, Ashbritt did not even own a single dump truck, but it had given $50,000 to the Republican Party and another $40,000 to Barbour, Griffith & Rogers, a GOP lobbying firm that had been led by Haley Barbour, the Republican governor of Mississippi and former chair of the Republican National Committee.[31]

After receiving the contract, Ashbritt subcontracted the work to C&B Enterprises at the rate of $9 per cubic yard, which turned around and hired Amlee Transportation Inc. at $8 per cubic yard. Amlee Transportation then subcontracted the work to Chris Hessler Inc. at $7 per cubic yard, which ultimately hired Les Nirdlinger, a New Jersey hauler, at $3 per cubic yard. When informed about what had taken place, Nirdlinger was unhappy, stating that "it's a pyramid ... and everybody is taking a piece of the pie as you work your way up, and we're at the bottom. We're doing the work!" The three other companies (Ceres Environmental Services Inc., Phillips & Jordan Inc., and Environmental Chemical Inc.) that had each received $500 million contracts for debris removal also used this subcontracting scheme. Clearly, this method of contracting is inefficient because a sizable portion of taxpayer money does not end up in the hands of the people actually doing the work.[32]

This aversion to hiring local contractors was endemic in the Gulf Coast rebuilding. One year after Katrina, only 16.6 percent of the federal funding for rebuilding had been awarded to businesses in Louisiana, Mississippi, and Alabama, the states most damaged by Katrina. As the nation reflected on the second anniversary of Katrina in August 2007, the House of Representatives Small Business Committee held hearings to draw attention to the problem of local businesses not receiving federal grants. The committee pointed out that federal procurement law requires that a minimum of 23 percent of government contracts be granted to small businesses, with the goal of supporting community development and the creation of local jobs. However, according to the committee only 7.4 percent of Katrina contracts had gone to small businesses from May to August 2007.[33]

Even worse, the large corporations that received federal contracts generally did not hire local workers; rather, they hired the cheapest possible labor force, which meant workers from outside the Gulf Coast and even outside the country. With the local workforce overlooked, the long-term development of the region was undermined. This policy of not hiring locally was supported by the federal government, which suspended employer sanctions for forty-five days for companies hiring workers who did not possess documents to prove they could work legally in the United States. After Katrina, an estimated 50,000 workers, many of them from Bolivia, the Dominican Republic, and Peru, were brought to the United States under H2-B visas to clean up and rebuild.

These foreign workers are in an extremely vulnerable position, and there have been widespread reports that workers have been treated poorly. Human rights organizations report that the Katrina foreign workers have been underpaid or not paid, that they live in poor housing conditions, and that some companies claim they "own" these workers, selling them off to the highest bidder, much like slaves. In a recent case, more than

100 workers from India who were recruited to work in the Mississippi shipyards for Signal International walked off the job to protest their working conditions. They claimed they had paid a Signal recruiter $20,000 a person in exchange for green cards and permanent residency. When they arrived, they were given ten-month H-2B visas and then forced to live in unsuitable housing, with 24 workers in a small room. That did not stop Signal from charging the workers more than $1,000 per month for company housing.[34]

This top-down approach does not lead to equitable communities, nor does it develop the local economy because much of the money awarded to large corporations leaves the affected community. This model also leaves unskilled and underdeveloped communities that are vulnerable to stagnation at best and exploitation at worst. In any new public works project, the questions of who gets the contracts and the jobs need to be at the forefront. There is already some concern that women, people of color, and the poor will not have equal access to the jobs created by the Obama stimulus plan.

Where Do We Go from Here?

Currently, a group of students, community, faith, labor, and human rights organizations have taken the lessons learned from the New Deal public works projects and used them to create a civic works project for a twenty-first-century New Deal. This movement is entitled the Gulf Coast Civic Works Campaign, and its promoters see it as a national model for President Obama and Congress to solve the human rights crisis in the Gulf Coast, as well as a solution to the economic and infrastructure crises in the United States.

CHAPTER 3

THE IMPROBABLE HISTORY OF THE
GULF COAST CIVIC WORKS PROJECT

Civic works can rebuild public infrastructure and provide good jobs for the American worker. Today, 200 student, community, faith, labor, and human rights organizations are promoting this age-old American idea in the form of the Gulf Coast Civic Works (GCCW) Act. This federal bill has been put forward as a major solution to the continuing crisis in the Gulf Coast.

On August 29, 2005, Hurricane Katrina took the lives of more than 1,836 people, displaced more than 1 million residents, and destroyed or damaged more than 250,000 Gulf Coast homes in a 90,000-square-mile area. The damage caused by the flooding, storm surge, and high winds destroyed schools, hospitals, roads, community centers, bridges, parks, and forestlands. In the end, the Gulf Coast suffered more than $100 billion in damage, making Katrina the costliest and most deadly hurricane in the history of the United States. Then, three weeks later, the Gulf Coast was struck again, this time by Hurricane Rita, which caused $11 billion in damage. Unfortunately, the government's response to these hurricanes, which affected Alabama, Louisiana, Mississippi, and Texas, has been ineffective and weak. The stark reality is that in 2009 the Gulf Coast's public infrastructure is still badly damaged from Hurricanes Katrina and Rita.

In Louisiana, the housing situation is dire. In total, approximately 107,000 homes were completely destroyed and another 98,000 suffered major damage. And even though more than 121,000 home owners have received Road Home checks, how many have actually been able to successfully rebuild is still unclear. The situation for renters is even worse.

Although 40 percent of the damaged homes were rental properties, only 15 percent of the Community Development Block Grants (CDBGs) money went toward programs that develop rental properties. The most critical needs are in affordable housing for low- and moderate-income families where shortages combined with increased insurance and utility costs have created a 69 percent increase in rental rates. As of November 2008, the Federal Emergency Management Agency (FEMA) estimates that 9,300 families are living in toxic trailers, with 1,600 families living in hotel rooms in the Gulf Coast. The situation is so bad that some first responders live and work in FEMA trailers. In 2008, New Orleans led all other U.S. cities in the percentage of vacant or ruined houses, with 69,727 unoccupied residential addresses.[1]

In Orleans Parish, where 80 percent of the city was underwater, 44 percent of the hospitals, 57 percent of child care centers, and 71 percent of the schools are still closed compared to pre-Katrina levels. At the same time, the New Orleans population is at 74 percent of pre-Katrina levels, whereas the larger metro area is now at 88 percent of pre-Katrina levels.[2]

In Mississippi, 60 percent of the housing stock in three counties (77,000 units) was damaged in Hurricane Katrina. The homes that experienced the most severe damage, as well as multifamily units, still lag far behind in the rebuilding efforts. In Alabama, where more than 1,000 homes were destroyed or damaged, $96 million were made available by the federal government through CDBGs to assist with the rebuilding, with $31 million set aside for housing. Of the $96 million allocated for recovery, $19 million have been spent. Of the $31 million specifically set aside for recovery, only $6 million have been spent, and that has resulted in 40 modular homes and 22 surplus mobile homes.[3]

Why is the recovery taking so long? First, the Gulf Coast has received relatively little support for its long-term recovery. Yes, Congress appropriated more than $116 billion to the region in the aftermath of Hurricanes Katrina and Rita, but less than $40 billion have been dedicated for long-term recovery. Worse yet, much of the money for long-term recovery has yet to be spent. For example, three and one-half years after the 2005 hurricanes, FEMA reported that it had spent only one-third of the $5.8 billion appropriated for roads, libraries, schools, and sewer systems. As Senator Mary Landrieu (D-LA) put it, these delays have led to "dilapidated buildings, roads and sewer systems in our communities." Moreover, local and state officials from the Gulf Coast complain that FEMA often underestimates how much a project costs, imposes too many restrictions on how the money can be spent, and does not pay its bills. For example,

New Orleans has yet to be repaid almost $7 million for a police head-quarters it rebuilt and has had opened for more than a year. This lack of long-term spending in a region that suffered more than $100 billion in infrastructure damage has led to a public infrastructure crisis.[4]

Second, the recovery has been slow because multinational corporations received large, no-bid contracts and then subcontracted out the work. As stated earlier, this subcontracting process was incredibly wasteful because it allowed money to be directed toward profit rather than toward the rebuilding effort. To make matters worse, the corporations hired workers from outside the region at very low pay rather than paying a living wage to local or displaced workers. These large, no-bid contracts have produced uneven economic development.[5]

Third, the recovery is slow because the Gulf Coast was in poor condition before the hurricanes. Mississippi and Louisiana are the poorest two states in the nation. Before the storm, the New Orleans poverty rate was 23 percent, and for women with children it was 41 percent. Nine percent of households in New Orleans did not own or have access to a car, which meant that 25 percent of the population was carless. The public schools were underfunded: Louisiana spent $7,605 per student, which was $1,096 less than the national average, ranking it thirty-fourth in the nation in school spending. As a result, New Orleans adults had a 44 percent illiteracy rate and a high dropout rate (more than 50 percent of black ninth graders did not graduate from high school). Public housing provided homes for 5,000 families, most of which were African American. This segregation caused these families to be isolated from the other parts of the city.[6]

On September 15, 2005, just two weeks after Katrina, President George W. Bush spoke from Jackson Square and firmly committed the nation to the rebuilding of New Orleans and the Gulf Coast. He promised that the nation would take bold action to confront the poverty in the Gulf Coast, which "has roots in racial discrimination." He committed to the creation of minority-owned business, houses that are owned instead of rented, and job-training programs for the regional economy. Unfortunately, these things did not happen.[7]

To realize this commitment to rebuild the Gulf Coast equitably, students and community organizations have led a relentless effort to introduce and pass a federal civic works bill. The students' dream of getting a bill into Congress was realized when Representative Zoe Lofgren (D-CA), along with Representatives Charlie Melancon (D-LA) and Gene Taylor (D-MS) as original cosponsors, introduced the Gulf Coast Civic Works

Act of 2007 into Congress on November 1, 2007. Within a year, the bill had twenty-seven cosponsors. The GCCW Act is based on a simple idea: Create 100,000 living-wage jobs for Gulf Coast residents and displaced survivors to rebuild the public infrastructure that was damaged in Hurricanes Katrina and Rita.

The GCCW Act is a resident-led effort that creates good jobs and training opportunities for local and displaced workers to rebuild public infrastructure and restore the environment. More specifically, the act (a) creates a minimum of 100,000 good jobs and training opportunities for local and displaced workers to rebuild hospitals, roads, schools, parks, police and fire stations, water and sewer systems, and workforce housing; (b) creates a civic conservation corps for youth aged seventeen to twenty-four to focus on wetland restoration, forestation, and urban greenery; (c) provides summer and after-school employment or training opportunities for youth aged twelve to nineteen; (d) provides oversight and transparency through Local Advisory Councils; and (e) provides grants for artistic projects to highlight Gulf Coast culture and history and to chronicle the stories from the hurricanes. The program has been conceptualized from the very beginning as a pilot project. The hope has been that if it works in the Gulf Coast, the GCCW Act could be used as a model for the rest of the nation.

The goal of the GCCW Act is to spur equitable and sustainable community development by engaging community leaders and local officials in determining projects based on community needs through Local Advisory Boards. The Local Advisory Councils would include city and county officials, business leaders who have an expertise in infrastructure and workforce development, and leaders of community organizations. The bill cuts through bureaucracy, which has in the past stalled and sometimes skimmed from economic development projects. The GCCW Act overcomes this problem by providing communities with the opportunity to apply for federal funds directly through a grant-making process. This model will be effective because it allows the money to reach the communities in need directly and builds on the good work that local community organizations and faith-based groups have been able to accomplish, many times with little support from the government. Community efforts, such as the Beacon of Hope Resource Center in Lakeview or the Lower Ninth Ward Village, demonstrate that local groups that are in control of the decisionmaking process can have successful results and with greater funding can do even more to encourage the long-term development of their communities.

The GCCW Act focuses on developing local workers through first-source hiring provisions, which give priority to Gulf Coast residents and displaced survivors in the hiring for any civic works projects. The bill also strengthens the workforce by providing funds to create jobs and provide much-needed skills training. As part of the job training, the Local Advisory Councils will work with local Workforce Investment Boards and community colleges to identify and fund job-training companies and apprentice programs. If there are no providers of job training in a community, the Local Advisory Councils can create them. With this focus on funding the development of the local workforce, the bill provides the community with the necessary resources, skills, and organization to survive future economic downturns or natural disasters. Thus, the GCCW Act is not a band-aid solution; rather, it works to restore the health of a community by investing in its people. This will avoid the existing top-down, outsiders-in approach in which money flows to multinational corporations, which hire workers from outside the region, and when the projects or funds come to a close, the companies leave with the knowledge and profits.

The GCCW Act utilizes a hybrid model (i.e., a mixture of federal and local control) in which the federal government partners directly with communities in planning, overseeing, and administering recovery projects to assist the survivors of these disasters, protect the region from future disasters, and revitalize the region economically. At the time of the writing of the bill, asking for a government-run, Works Progress Administration (WPA)–type public works project seemed impossible. The dominant political paradigm was still that of rugged individualism. In light of that reality, the idea emerged of a civic works project that would be a partnership between the federal government and local communities. The GCCW Act could authorize the federal government to hire workers, but generally the bill is a contract, Public Works Administration (PWA) model, but with a twist: Community-based organizations, in conjunction with the municipalities, decide on which projects to pursue. Thus, the GCCW Act is an integration of local control (a conservative idea) with federal involvement in the economy (a liberal idea).

Representative Lofgren's idea was to have a Tennessee Valley Authority–like agency oversee the civic works projects to ensure transparency; in that way the American public knows exactly where the money is going. In the GCCW Act, this turned into a federal Gulf Coast Recovery Authority, which would oversee and coordinate the projects, as well as serve as a grant-making body to the Local Advisory Councils. And even though in the

2009 version of the act, the Recovery Authority Office has been replaced by the Office of the Federal Coordinator for Gulf Coast Rebuilding—which was created by President Bush after Hurricane Katrina to coordinate the federal government's response—the emphasis on oversight and a close partnership between the federal government and local communities has been maintained (see Appendix 1 for the full text of the bill).

The GCCW campaign estimated the cost of the bill, which was based on a ratio of labor to materials of eighty to twenty (the split used during the New Deal), at between $5 and $10 billion. Initially, Lofgren thought that even the lower of the two numbers was "a lot of money" to ask for. However, as time for the introduction of the bill got closer, Lofgren changed her mind and was thinking about asking for $12 billion, which was what the United States was spending in the Iraq and Afghanistan wars each month. However, after discussions with Representatives Charlie Melancon and Gene Taylor, both Blue Dog Democrats (i.e., a coalition of fiscally conservative Democrats), the bill's sponsors took a specific amount out of the 2007 bill. The funding language in the bill was innocuous and vague: "There is authorized to be appropriated to the Corporation such sums as may be necessary for fiscal years 2008 through 2012 to carry out this title."

Jonathan Rhodes, a law student at Chicago-Kent College of Law, wrote most of the 2007 bill. Rhodes is an active member of the Student Hurricane much, which is a coalition of law students from around the country working on legal issues facing Gulf Coast residents. In the summer of 2007, he was working as a fellow at the Democratic Caucus, an organization of House Democrats that formulates party policy, when he reached out to the GCCW Project, which was the campus advocacy wing for the campaign. During the next several months, he worked closely with students and faculty, taking the ideas and principles that guided the project and turning them into legal language appropriate for a federal bill. Of course, members of Congress made changes to the bill, but Rhoades's wording runs throughout the GCCW Act of 2007.

The GCCW campaign has now gained support from more than 200 organizations, including All Congregations Together (ACT), the Association of Community Organizations for Reform Now (ACORN), Bayou Interfaith Shared Community Organizing (BISCO), ColorofChange.org, the Equity and Inclusion (E&I) Campaign, the RFK Center for Justice and Human Rights, Oxfam America, the Student Hurricane Network, and Women in Construction. It also has the support of the Louisiana Republican Party, the New Orleans City Council, the Bayou Parishes of

Lafourche and Terrebonne, and the California and Missouri Democratic parties.

Service-Learning and the GCCW Project

Importantly, the Gulf Coast Civic Works (GCCW) Project developed out of service-learning, which integrates theory and action in the classroom. For the past twenty years, I have been deeply involved in the service-learning movement. I have personally taken twenty student groups on domestic and international summer service-learning trips, taught more than thirty service-learning courses, developed three service-learning leadership programs, and written my dissertation and six scholarly articles on service-learning. Basically, I have dedicated almost my entire professional career to service-learning. However, several years ago I began to have doubts about the effectiveness of what I was doing.

Yes, I and hundreds of others in the service-learning movement had transformed individual lives. Research shows that service-learning makes students more civically and intellectually engaged, more racially tolerant, and more globally concerned. Based on this research, we know that service-learning can transform individual lives. Yet at the same time, service-learning has not fulfilled its promise of changing society. Sadly, the service-learning movement has not even changed our college campuses. Academe is basically running as it did before the service-learning movement. Yes, our university uses service-learning to demonstrate its engagement in the community, but the movement has had very little effect on the culture of the campus or on the social structures in the larger society. In fact, we have gone backward on many of the issues (e.g., poverty rate and inequality) that service-learning is supposed to be addressing.[8]

So in 2003, I set out to see if it was possible to bring about social transformation at my campus (San Jose State) and community. The focus was not to be on individual change, even though this would still occur, but rather on social policy change. I decided to develop an action-oriented, service-learning course in which students would choose a project to work on that would entail changing some type of social policy. The only requirements were that students would work in teams and that projects would be designed to continue after the end of the semester. Course topics included the history of community organizing, strategy and tactics, small-group skills (active listening skills, facilitation, consensus, group dynamics and process), coalition building, and media skills. The pedagogy was highly interactive and included group activities, small- and large-group discussions, videos, guest speakers, and community service-learning projects.

What was unique about this course, Sociology 164: Social Action, was that it was designed to *do social action*. Students did not just read about social change in a book; they were actually involved in it. Of course, "book knowledge" was still used, but throughout the course students were encouraged to integrate course content with what they were learning in the community, with the hope that they would develop a more critical and deeper understanding. Practically, about one-half of each class was spent discussing the text and the other one-half was used to discuss the community action projects. Of course, wherever possible, text and action were integrated.

During a two-year period, six viable student organizations were created from this social action course: the Student Homeless Alliance, Students Against Intimate Violence, Students Advocating Global Education, a student chapter of the Worker Rights Consortium, a student group pushing for the reinstatement of the Education Opportunity Program, and, ultimately, the GCCW Project.

At the same time as I was creating this new course focusing on policy and institutional change, I became involved in a student-led effort to build statues for Tommie Smith and John Carlos, two San José State University (SJSU) student-athletes. In the 1968 Summer Olympics in Mexico City, Smith and Carlos won gold and bronze medals, respectively, in the 200-meter track and field event. However, this athletic accomplishment was not the reason the Associated Students (the SJSU student body organization) decided to spend more than $300,000 of its own money on twenty-three-foot statues of the two young men. Rather, it was what they did when they were on the Olympic podium during the award's ceremony that SJSU students decided to honor: During the playing of the national anthem, they raised their fists and bowed their heads to protest racism and poverty in the United States. As part of the Olympic Project for Human Rights, Smith and Carlos had tried to mount a boycott of the Olympics, but when that did not transpire, they decided, along with their fellow male black athletes, to take individual stands in Mexico City. Smith and Carlos were punished for their courageous action: They were banned from the Olympics for life, and when they returned home, they had difficult times finding employment.

I began to see this work to build these statues as part of the larger project to change social structure, for if change was to happen, students and faculty needed to have democratic space, in the manner of a commons, for them to meet and gather to *do* democracy. From the beginning, it was clear that the statues had the potential to be a focal point for student activism because they were a daily reminder to the campus community about the importance of taking a stand for justice. After several years of hard work by the students, as well as by faculty and staff supporters, the statues were dedicated in the spring of 2006. Four thousand people gathered, including Smith and Carlos, for the unveiling of these historic statues. And as if on cue, a semester after the statue unveiling forty student leaders gathered at the Smith and Carlos statues on election night and initiated the GCCW Project.

How the GCCW Project Came to Be

On a crisp November evening in 2006, a group of forty SJSU students and faculty gathered on campus to highlight the fact that Silicon Valley—home to Cisco, Adobe, and many other wealthy high-tech corporations—had recently become the "homeless capital" of Northern California. On any given night, 7,600 people in Silicon Valley were without housing. In response, students called for a "campus sleep-out" entitled "Poverty Under the Stars" to show their solidarity with the poor. The sleep-out was to be held in front of the newly unveiled statues of Tommie Smith and John Carlos.

During the evening event, the students talked to the gathered crowd about how 13 percent of Americans, or 37 million people, lived in poverty. The students highlighted the fact that the United States was ranked number one in the industrialized world in child poverty (18 percent) and that on any given night 727,000 people were without homes in America. The evening's highlight was the showing of Spike Lee's film *When the Levees Broke: A Requiem in Four Acts*. The students had set up a large movie screen in front of the Smith and Carlos statues. Each one-hour "act" was shown and was followed by a twenty-minute discussion.

The students exhibited the racial and ethnic diversity of America: black, Latino/a, white, and Asian. They also represented a variety of groups. But even though they were of different ethnicities and student groups, they had two things in common—they were all Americans, and they had come together to discuss poverty in America and what was happening in Silicon Valley and the Gulf Coast in particular. In a powerful demonstration of democracy, students had come together of their own volition to dialogue and debate these important social issues. During the dialogue, the students expressed shock and outrage at what had taken place in the

Students sleep out at the Tommie Smith and John Carlos Statues at San José State University. (Courtesy of Eric Austin)

aftermath of Katrina. They could not fathom how the richest country in the world had responded to this crisis in such an ineffectual manner, both in the first days after Hurricane Katrina struck and during the following year.

The film began at 7 p.m., but with the intense discussions that occurred between the four acts the film ended around 1:30 a.m. The students and faculty then slept out on campus to be in solidarity with the homeless. The students had asked me to sleep out with them, which I was glad to do. When we awoke, the students decided to march across the street to the newly completed San José City Hall, which had cost $500 million to build. Ironically, the new City Hall towered over the First Christian Church, which opened its doors nightly to more than thirty homeless adults and kids. At City Hall, the students held a spontaneous protest, in which they marched, drummed, and sang about the need to end homelessness.

After returning from City Hall, I ate breakfast at a local eatery and then stumbled into my morning class, bleary-eyed from a lack of sleep. That morning's class discussion was coincidentally on the public works projects of the New Deal. In this class, we discussed how the Civil Works Administration (CWA) employed 814,511 in two weeks and 4.2 million in two months. We also explored how the CWA, along with the WPA, the PWA, and the CCC, totally rebuilt the public infrastructure of the country.

Upon returning home from class, I sat down at the kitchen table to read the paper, which focused on the election results from the previous night. (Interestingly, many of the students had brought their laptops to the sleep-out, so that they could follow the election results from their tents.) As I read about the Democrats winning control of both the House and the Senate, I noticed a short article about Gayle McLaughlin, a white woman from the Green Party who had been elected mayor of Richmond, California, a predominantly African American city, on the platform of creating a public works project for 1,000 youth to combat crime and poverty.

It was then that the idea came. Why not do in the Gulf Coast what had been done some seventy years ago in the New Deal public works projects or what was being proposed in Richmond, California? This new public works project could rebuild the schools, hospitals, and playgrounds that had been so badly damaged in Hurricane Katrina. Surely, if the United States had once put more than 800,000 people to work in two weeks, the nation could now put 100,000 people to work to rebuild New Orleans and the Gulf Coast.

That was the birth of GCCW Project. Based on the knowledge I had gained in writing *Social Solutions to Poverty: America's Struggle to Build a Just Society,* I scratched out the general outline of the project: Hire 100,000 Gulf Coast residents and displaced residents to rebuild the hospitals, houses, schools, parks, and forests. As I wrote this short outline, I noted that federal legislation would need to be introduced into Congress, and that a social movement would have to be created, if the nation was to enact this project. I also spelled out how there were three imperatives at stake in the Gulf Coast:

1. The economic imperative: To rebuild the Gulf Coast, residents needed living-wage jobs and a functioning public infrastructure.
2. The psychological imperative: For Gulf Coast residents to regain their empowerment and hope, which had been stolen from them, they needed to be directly involved in rebuilding their communities.
3. The social imperative: The social compact between citizen and government was badly torn due to a loss of faith in the latter, and it needed to be repaired.

I also began to articulate how the GCCW Project would be part of a larger goal of ending poverty in America. As stated earlier, Dr. Martin Luther King Jr. spent the last several years of his life dedicated to this goal of ending poverty through a public works program. Dr. King's vision was of the "Beloved Community," in which all citizens had decent housing, a living-wage job for all who were able to work, and a social insurance program that guaranteed a middle-class income for those who were not able to work. The GCCW Project was a step toward creating King's Beloved Community.

After I wrote down these initial thoughts about the project, I e-mailed the basic concept to friends and colleagues in the Gulf Coast and around the country. Within a few days, I received several positive responses. Importantly, several Gulf Coast residents stepped up and said they would be willing to help make the GCCW Project a reality. Tracie Washington, director of the National Association for the Advancement of Colored People Gulf Coast Advocacy Center; LeeAnn Gunn-Rasmussen, an instructor at Mississippi Gulf Coast Community College; and Marty Rowland, a community activist, all offered their services. In fact, Washington commented that she had thought of this type of idea, but because people were just trying to survive in the Gulf Coast, they had not put the idea down on paper.

The students were also positive. In my "Poverty, Wealth, and Privilege" course, which was the same course that had been discussing the New Deal public works projects, several students stepped forward to help, and we began meeting outside of class. At our first meeting, the students and I decided to travel to New Orleans to discuss the GCCW Project with local residents. I was going to speak at a conference in New Orleans that January, so I offered the floor of my hotel room to the students, and they readily accepted. Then, a photography student, who ended up coming to New Orleans, asked if we could take some photos and uplink them to my Web site so that SJSU students and students at other campuses could follow our actions. Inspired by the student's creativity, I suggested to her that we should invite students from around the nation to come to the Gulf Coast. I half-jokingly suggested we call the experience "Louisiana Winter" because it had parallels to "Mississippi Freedom Summer." In 1964, 800 college students from around the country had gone to Mississippi to register African American voters, who were being denied this constitutional right.

After the run-in with the photography student, I went to my service-learning internship course. That night the class was discussing social solutions to the issues at their internships, and I had encouraged them to "think big." After a group of students had presented their grandiose plans to solve the social issues at their sites, I decided to present my "big idea." I must admit, I was a bit sheepish, because the idea of Louisiana Winter was so big and, at some level, totally audacious, given that SJSU was 2,100 miles away from the Gulf Coast. After a brief discussion of the project and the plan to travel to the Gulf Coast, I invited students to stay after class if they were interested in participating in Louisiana Winter. I expected one or two students to take up this offer, but to my surprise, ten students remained. This group formed the beginning of the GCCW Project student movement.

People often ask why students from California care about the Gulf Coast. Some have even suggested that the students' efforts should be directed to problems closer to home. However, this perspective misses several key points. First, most of the students who have been involved in the project are also involved in local social justice projects. Second, Katrina represented the unmasking of the racial and class inequalities in American society. The whole world saw the images of the poor and African Americans being left to fend for themselves for five days without adequate food and water. In fact, the media were so unaccustomed to covering poverty that they had difficulty explaining what they were seeing and incorrectly labeled the people fleeing the floods as "refugees," as if the winds of Katrina somehow blew away their citizenship. No, these were not refugees; they were American citizens who usually lived in the shadows of society but were now exposed to a worldwide television audience. Third, many students had relatives or friends from the Gulf Coast who had been directly affected. They had heard about their struggle for survival and were incensed. For all of these reasons, students from California were committed to the idea of struggling for justice in the Gulf Coast.

Louisiana Winter

Not surprisingly, students across the country were interested in the Gulf Coast. Almost 100 college students from fifteen universities responded to

Louisiana Winter logo that was on students' t-shirts. (Courtesy of Mark Macala)

our "Internet call" to come to the Gulf Coast in January 2007 to begin the process of developing federal legislation.

Louisiana Winter students went to the Gulf Coast to educate people about the GCCW Project, to hear firsthand what people thought of it, and to learn what specific items the community wanted in the federal legislation. To get this information, students knocked on trailers in New Orleans in such neighborhoods as Gentilly, Pontchartrain Park, Uptown, St. Bernard Parish, and the Lower Ninth Ward. Students also traveled to Mississippi, where they went trailer to trailer in Bay St. Louis, Pass Christian, Long Beach, Gulfport, and Biloxi. As part of their outreach, they passed out 10,000 fliers, held two town hall meetings, sponsored two rallies, and gave a series of interviews to local, state, and international media. Throughout the Gulf Coast, the students were greeted warmly, and most all of the feedback about the project was positive, as residents saw it as a potential solution to the slow recovery process. In fact, support for the GCCW Project cut across political parties: Conservatives saw it as an opportunity for the locals to control the recovery process, whereas liberals saw it as a way for the government to become actively and efficiently involved in rebuilding. This perspective would influence the supporters of the project to talk about it not as a Democratic or a Republican idea but as an American solution.

One of the reasons that both conservatives and liberals supported the GCCW Project as a way to rebuild their communities was that both groups felt that the federal government had broken its social contract by not properly taking care of the people. For example, in Mississippi students learned how the state's residents had a strong independent streak but nevertheless felt let down by the government's inadequate response to Hurricane Katrina. Kay Bethea, who lived on the beach in Gulfport, described how a twenty six-foot surge of water from the Gulf Coast hit her house. She stated: "Gulf Coast people are very tough-minded and independent. I have taken care of myself—for what feels like 100 years. I do not expect much from my government, and I have got even less. My neighborhood would still be stinking and rotten if I depended on the government. From the top on down to the city level, I would pretty much say ... " and then she blew a raspberry. An instructor at the local community college, Leeann Gunn-Rasmussen, remarked: "In light of our independence, self-help, and strong will, I decided to support the Gulf Coast Civic Works Project because it makes sense and it is practical. If we can rebuild our own communities, we can rebuild not only the houses that we lost, but our spirit as well. We can get our voice back."

One of the participants in Louisiana Winter was Rachel Recore, a first-year student at Mississippi Gulf Coast Community College. Standing in the midst of destroyed houses, she noted: "It is obvious that we need to re-build our community. Just look at the destruction all around us." She went on to describe how in the first several days after Katrina, people of Gulfport desperately needed help. The U.S. government did communicate to the res-idents that help was on the way, but agents of the government did not show up until five days after the hurricane. In fact, Rachel told the other students how the Royal Canadian Mounted Police arrived in Gulfport before the U.S. government. She was a strong supporter of the project, saying: "The reality is that we are still suffering, and you cannot imagine until you come down and actually see it. That is the reason that I love the Gulf Coast Civic Works Project because it has the possibility to jump-start the rebuilding, and it is taking into consideration the needs of my community."

The students heard similar stories in New Orleans about the possibil-ity of the project rebuilding communities. When the students drove into Gentilly, Nikki Najiola, a community resident, met their bus and gave the students a tour of her neighborhood. When asked about how civic works might help in the recovery, Nikki replied: "I think a civic works project is an excellent idea. In fact, that is exactly how our city park was built here in Gentilly in the 1930s. The Works Progress Administration brought in thousands of people and built our park. It just makes sense to do the same thing now."

In Pontchartrain Park, Norma Hedrick, who had lived there for three years, led students through her almost abandoned community. Picking up on the need to develop parks, Hedrick stated: "I see a civic works project rebuilding our parks, which were completely destroyed. They could also

Louisiana Winter students passing out fliers in Mississippi. (Courtesy of Bill Snyder, Mississippi Gulf Coast Community College)

rebuild Mary Coghill and Parkview Schools, as well as the Joe Bartholomew Golf Course—which was named after the first black golf course designer." She wanted New Orleans to "green it up," because she believed that green space is connected to lower crime rates. Norma concluded: "I think a civic works project is a great idea. We really need this right now. And what happens here has national implications because the issues in New Orleans are the same ones as Baltimore, Oakland, and Detroit."

In addition to educating people about the idea for a civic works project, the students asked the local residents for their ideas about what should be included in a federal bill. From these conversations, five key principles emerged, which were then used to guide the development of the federal bill. These principles were as follows:

1. Civic works jobs should be in the areas of construction and the arts. If workers do not have construction skills, paid apprenticeships should be provided.
2. Civic works jobs should be simple to obtain. A streamlined process should be developed with the county employment service offices or the faith-based and community initiatives already connected to the White House.
3. Civic works jobs need to pay a living wage so that people can support themselves. This wage should not be lower than $15 an hour.
4. Civic workers should have the right to join unions.
5. The local communities should play a key role in deciding which projects and buildings get rebuilt and in what order.

In retrospect, the students discovered that the economic, psychological, and social imperatives outlined at the very beginning of the project were valid. The economic imperative was real and could be solved by providing residents with living-wage jobs to rebuild infrastructure. The psychological imperative surfaced in firsthand stories of seniors who had lost the will to live in the face of such a limited government response, and the students heard how young people had become alienated because few had places to play now that the community centers and parks had been destroyed. Finally, the students learned that the social imperative was real, as they heard both liberals and conservatives talk about how the government had let them down. The students came to understand that, even though citizens had various responsibilities (e.g., pay taxes, sit on juries, and serve our country), government also had responsibilities, one of which was to respond effectively when its citizens were in need. Passing federal legislation would be a major step in repairing the social compact that had been so badly damaged.

The Louisiana Winter trip and subsequent trips to the Gulf Coast have been critical to the development of the GCCW Project. In January and October 2008, the project sponsored two other large-scale trips to the Gulf Coast in order to connect the students to the issues. We have also tried to breach the distance by connecting the issues that people are facing in the Gulf Coast (homelessness, poverty, racism) to the issues surrounding college campuses. For example, San José State students held an event in November 2008 called "Tent City America" to dramatize homelessness both in the Gulf Coast and in the Bay Area.

Next Steps After Louisiana Winter

Since its inception in 2006, a major goal of the GCCW Project has been to develop a college movement to support this federal legislation. To do so, the project has focused on providing students with a firsthand experience of civic engagement. For example, when the project started, a group of fifteen students met almost every night for a month, blasting out e-mails to college students and organizations around the country about Louisiana Winter. When the project was introduced to the media in November 2006, students played a major role in planning and presenting at two of the three simultaneous press conferences held at San José State and Mississippi Gulf Coast Community College.

The project has continually tried to design ways to get students to become directly involved in the democratic process and social change. As part of doing democracy and building a campus movement, students have (a) sponsored two post-Katrina summits, which were held simultaneously on college campuses; (b) held two national campus strategy meetings in the Gulf Coast; (c) sponsored national phone-in and call-in campaigns to various members of Congress; and (d) met directly with lawmakers. The key point is that everything the GCCW Project does attempts to engage students in democracy.

Simultaneous Events on College Campuses

After Louisiana Winter, the project's first major event was a national summit held simultaneously on college campuses. In April 2007, the project initiated the "National Post-Katrina Summit," which was a nationwide,

Students at Tusculum College gather signatures in front of a Katrina banner that listed the names of the 1,836 victims. (Courtesy of Tusculum College)

weeklong effort to raise awareness about the Gulf Coast through documentary films, speakers, spoken word, blood drives, rallies, petition drives, solidarity dinners, reading of the names of Katrina victims, and other events. In the first annual event, students and faculty from more than forty colleges, including California State University at Fullerton, the State University of New York at Stony Brook, San José State, the University of South Florida, Stanford, Tulane, the University of California, the University of Michigan, Tusculum College, and Woodrow Wilson College, signed up to host a summit on their campuses.

At the University of Michigan, students held events throughout the week. The highlight was when Lieutenant General Russel Honore, the person whom Mayor Ray Nagin credited with finally getting supplies to New Orleans, spoke to a large group of students, faculty, and community members. At the University of North Carolina, students held a campus vigil for the Katrina survivors and victims. Mary Small, cochair of the campus group Extended Disaster Relief, was quoted in the local paper as saying that this vigil was different: "The ones in the past have been in memory of those who have died, but this one is to stand in solidarity for those still alive and struggling to survive." The newspaper article concluded that the goal of the vigil was to obtain "signatures to petition the U.S. Congress to enact legislation that would create 100,000 jobs for Gulf Coast residents." At Tulane University, students stood in front of a coffin with a sign in front that read "death to apathy" and encouraged other students to sign petitions. At California State University at Fullerton, the students and faculty held a New Orleans–inspired second line march across campus. At the conclusion of the processional, they read the names publicly of the more than 1,836 Katrina victims. As part of the summits, students gathered more than 7,000 signatures to support this federal legislation.

The following semester, five campuses signed up to hold simultaneous second anniversary commemorations of Hurricane Katrina on August

Students signing project petitions at CSU Fullerton as part of the Post-Katrina Summit. (Courtesy of Lezlee Hinesmon-Matthews)

29. By far, the largest commemoration was held at San José State, where 300 students, Katrina survivors, and community members participated in a march and rally. The group gathered in front of San José's Municipal Stadium, which had been built by the WPA. By beginning the march in front of a public works project, the GCCW Project was attempting to highlight the fact that there is an effective solution to the crisis in the Gulf Coast. After the two-mile march, students, scholars, survivors, clergy, and nonprofit leaders gave a series of speeches. It was the largest second anniversary event in California, and it was a main story on all of the major San Francisco Bay Area television stations.

Another simultaneous event held on college campuses was the "National Campus Sleep-Out," which was based on the original "Poverty Under the Stars" event. With the tag line "A New Deal for the Gulf Coast," students, faculty, and Katrina survivors gathered on November 14, 2007, at Loyola University, Northeastern, Sarah Lawrence College, San José State, the University of North Carolina, and Wartburg College to participate in the event.

As with all project events, the goal was to highlight the crisis as well as a solution. At SJSU, students held a large march across campus. They ended the march at a FEMA trailer, which had been brought to campus by Derrick Evans from Turkey Creek, Mississippi. The trailer dramatized the fact that 150,000 Katrina survivors were still living in FEMA trailers. Coincidentally, two days before the event, the media broke the story that FEMA employees had been banned from entering the FEMA trailers due to the high levels of formaldehyde, a known respiratory irritant and carcinogen. To highlight this fact, students wore masks to dramatize the insanity of a policy that bans government employees from entering these

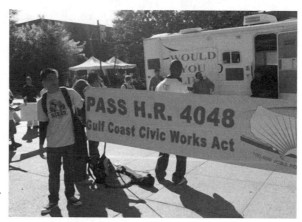

Victor Ngo, SJSU '09, in front of a FEMA trailer as part of the National Campus Sleep-Out. (Courtesy of Scott Myers-Lipton)

toxic FEMA trailers, but allows for 150,000 Gulf Coast residents to live in them. That night, 150 students gathered to hear speakers, watch Gulf Coast documentaries, and listen to spoken word. The media loved the toxic trailers, and once again the majority of TV stations in the Bay Area covered the event, with several of them doing live shots from the campus.

National Campus Strategy Meetings in the Gulf Coast

In January 2007, the project sponsored a national gathering in New Orleans to discuss the campus campaign strategy to pass the GCCW Act. Fifty-nine students, staff, and faculty from ten college campuses met at Loyola University, and they took some major steps forward. This student led gathering included a discussion of the project's history and an in-depth discussion of the federal bill. Students then broke into five groups and discussed the following questions:

- What part of the bill are you most excited about? Do you have any concerns about the bill?
- What has worked on your campus to promote social justice causes? In light of that learning, how can we promote the GCCW Act at your campus?
- How do we build a national student coalition around the GCCW Act?
- Do you have a powerful experience from New Orleans that you want to share? Does it connect to the GCCW Act?

• Have you experienced Katrina fatigue on your campus? And if so, what have you done to overcome it?

At the meeting, various campaign strategies were discussed, including the setting up of a GCCW Project MySpace and Facebook account and how to get students involved in the upcoming campus Mardi Gras Celebration for the GCCW Act and the Post-Katrina Summit.

This gathering of students at Loyola University was a part of Louisiana Winter 2. In addition to the meeting, students worked with ACORN in the Lower Ninth Ward on cutting "Katrina grass," which was more than six feet tall. They also met with such organizations as the Louisiana Recovery Authority and the Workforce Investment Board in the mayor's office, where they advocated for the GCCW Act.

Nine months later, on November 13–16, 2008, the GCCW Project and the Dillard University Deep South Center for Environmental Justice joined forces to bring together eighty students and faculty from twenty-seven campuses and sixteen states to New Orleans for a three-day conference entitled "Rebuild the Gulf Coast: Rebuild America—Do It Green!" The two organizations came together to cosponsor this event with the hope of bringing the green jobs and the civic works movements together. On Friday, the students took a trip to the bayou country to see firsthand how the Louisiana wetlands are losing one football field every thirty-six minutes and to discuss how GCCW projects could be utilized to address this issue. Students also heard from local activists about how

Students in the bayou get a firsthand view of the loss of Gulf Coast wetlands. (Courtesy of Scott Myers-Lipton)

Louisiana communities along "cancer alley" have been damaged by the pollution from the oil industry. On Saturday and Sunday, students set up a framework for the national campaign to pass the GCCW Act in the first hundred days of the Obama administration. Four regional coordinators were set up. The students also discussed meeting again in the spring of 2009 in Washington, DC, possibly when the House Education and Labor Committee, or subcommittee, holds a hearing on the GCCW Act.

National Phone and Call-In Campaigns

Coming out of the Dillard conference, the project began sponsoring national call-in days. Our first action was chosen for November 19–20, 2008, and the targets for the "call-in" were Louisiana senators Mary Landrieu (Democrat) and David Vitter (Republican). The "ask" was for them to introduce a complementary bill into the next session of the Senate. This call-in was so successful that students decided to do monthly call-ins in which they would target a different official every month (see Appendix 2 for call-in material).

Nevertheless, call-ins had been used by the project even before the Dillard conference. For example, students in the Sociology 164: Social Action course decided to target Speaker of the House Nancy Pelosi (D-CA). Pelosi had stated on her Web site that she would do everything possible for the Gulf Coast, so the students took her at her word and called in asking her to cosponsor the GCCW Act. Beginning on October 1, 2007, the students made more than 100 calls to her office during a four-day period. The students had organized their compatriots, and each had lined up five others to help make the phone calls. As the week wore on, the flood of calls coming into the Speaker's Office increasingly exasperated Pelosi's staff. At the same time, the students felt empowered, as they demonstrated they had the skill and the human power to pull off a large-scale call-in to the Speaker of the House. And the students' action was registered, as representatives of the campaign were in a meeting the next month with Cheryl Parker Rose, director of intergovernmental affairs for Speaker Pelosi, and when it got to the GCCW Project, she remarked, "Oh, you were the ones who kept calling our office."

Students also used phone calls to congressional staff to get House members to sign on. During the summer of 2008, fifteen students each took one or two states and made phone calls and sent e-mails to the legislative directors. The students learned that the legislative directors were easily found. The students just did an Internet search for "contact Congress" and chose one of the Web sites that provided the Web sites of members of Congress, such as http://www.visi.com/juan/congress. Then they clicked on the name of the member of Congress they wished to contact and scrolled down and looked at the bottom left side of the page for the name of the legislative director. They copied her or his name, put a period in between first and last name, and added the ending @mail.house.gov. If the legislative director's name was John Smith, his e-mail was John .Smith@mail.house.gov. This e-mail address went straight to the legislative director. This process of contacting legislative directors was successful at getting several House members to cosponsor the GCCW Act.

Direct Contact with Lawmakers

As stated earlier, this movement has tried to generate as many ways as possible for students and the larger campus community to engage in democracy. One of these ways was to have students talk directly to lawmakers. The first time the GCCW Project used this strategy was in March 2007, when Sally Lieber (D-22nd Assembly District), speaker pro tempore of the California General Assembly, invited the students to give testimony to lawmakers and their staff at a public hearing focusing on the students' recent trip to the Gulf Coast as part of Louisiana Winter. At this public hearing, more than ten students provided testimony. Importantly, the students requested that Lieber introduce a nonbinding resolution into the California legislature calling on the state's congressional delegation in Washington and the president to support the project. A month later, Lieber introduced Assembly Joint Resolution (AJR) 22. As part of the process to pass AJR 22, students traveled to Sacramento, where several of them provided testimony to an assembly subcommittee.

The idea to introduce a state resolution had originated with Jeanette Oxford (D-St. Louis), a representative in the Missouri General Assembly. In January 2007, Representative Oxford contacted the project and said she would like to support the idea for federal legislation because both her parents had been in the New Deal public works projects and she knew from their stories the power of public works. One way she said she could support the project was to introduce into the legislature a resolution calling on Missouri's members in Congress and the president to enact a public works project for the Gulf Coast. Even though the state legislature's resolution would be only symbolic, it would provide momentum for the project. In late February, Oxford, along with twenty-one cosponsors, introduced such a resolution. And although it never got out of committee, other state and local resolutions would follow.

When the California resolution, AJR 22, passed the California State Assembly in September 2007, Lieber noted that "regardless of where we live, we have an obligation to call for action in the Gulf Coast region. As Californians, we are also vulnerable to a variety of natural disasters, and we would not want to endure the kind of dismal federal response that the Gulf Coast residents received." Then on March 10, 2008, the California State Senate passed AJR 22 on a 24–11 vote. The vote represented the first legislative victory for the students and faculty.

The students have also participated in numerous direct meetings with lawmakers. Some of these meetings occurred in their home offices, such as the meetings with Representatives Zoe Lofgren (D-CA), Anna Eshoo (D-CA), and Lynn Woolsey (D-CA). Some of these meetings happened after speeches by members of Congress; for instance, students met with Representative John Lewis (D-GA) after a speech at a Georgia community service conference. And other meetings happened at national conventions; for example, students and faculty traveled to the Democratic National Convention (DNC) in Denver in August 2008. For example, GCCW Project members talked one-on-one with Senator Landrieu (LA) and Representatives John Conyers (MI), Bennie Thompson (MS), Carolyn Kilpatrick (MI), Alcee Hastings (FL), Maxine Waters (CA), Charles Rangel (NY), Hilda Solis (CA), and Niki Tsongas (MA). Asking Congress members directly for their support at the DNC was very empowering, and it led directly to four House members signing on to cosponsor the GCCW Act.

A Service-Learning Course and the Campaign

The student campaign continued to develop leadership and provide energy for the movement through my course titled Sociology 164: Social Action. Each semester, twenty to thirty students enrolled in the course, and a sizable number of them ended up choosing the GCCW Project as part of their service-learning component. This course has played a key role in providing the leadership and energy for the overall student movement.

The social action course is unique because students are asked to read and reflect upon social action, as well as participate in it. As stated earlier, students in the course gain civic knowledge and skills by writing press releases,

Roberto Ceballos-Garcia, Marcus Kilgore, Rochelle Jackson-Smarr, and Tenah Flores "Celebrate for HR 4048" as part of Mardi Gras. (Courtesy of Scott Myers-Lipton)

speaking to the press, facilitating meetings, developing strategy, raising funds, and building coalitions with students from around the country. For example, students in the course took the lead in planning a Mardi Gras celebration to promote the GCCW Act on February 5, 2008. Students and faculty held a "Celebrate for HR 4048" (HR 4048 was the House resolution number for the GCCW Act of 2007) procession around campus with the jazz band Bug Horn Rex. The celebration included the throwing of beads, New Orleans cuisine, films, speakers, and a student report on a recent trip to the Gulf Coast.

In 2008, Mardi Gras fell on Super Tuesday, when twenty-two states held caucuses or primary elections to choose their presidential candidates. The students tried to integrate Mardi Gras and Super Tuesday, hoping to send a message to the nation and to the presidential candidates that the GCCW Act was a key part of the solution to the crisis in New Orleans and the Gulf Coast.

The Larger GCCW Campaign

Even though the campuses took the lead in creating the bill and pushing the project forward, the goal from early on was to find regional and national coalition partners to help push Congress and the president to enact this legislation. As stated earlier, some of the key coalition partners that stepped forwarded were ACORN, ACT, BISCO, ColorofChange .org, Equity and Inclusion Campaign, and the RFK Memorial Center

Stephen Bradberry, ACORN national campaigns coordinator, Scott Myers-Lipton, and Louisiana Winter students at the ACORN national office in New Orleans. (Courtesy of Scott Myers-Lipton)

for Justice and Human Rights. Some of the key players of the campaign have been Jeffrey Buchanan, RFK Memorial Center; Stephen Bradberry, national campaigns coordinator for ACORN; Sharon Gauthe, director, BISCO, and her husband, David; Mary Fontenot, director, ACT; James Rucker, director, ColorofChange.org; Jainey Bavishi, manager, the E&I Campaign; Jeremy Hughes, Bay Area Women's Coalition in Alabama; and Karissa McClane and Julie Kuklinski, Women in Construction in Biloxi, Mississippi.

These coalition partners have been central to the larger GCCW campaign. The coalition members have met several times in New Orleans, and they have stayed connected through weekly, sometimes daily, e-mail messages and phone calls. The main focus of the coalition has been to obtain congressional support for the legislation, while at the same time working to obtain a presidential executive order to create the structure for Gulf Coast Civic Works. During the transition, the campaign sent President-elect Barack Obama a letter signed by more than 130 organizations asking him to sign an executive order in the first 100 hours of his administration (see Appendix 3 for draft of executive order). There is historical precedent for an executive order to create public works projects, as this was how President Franklin Roosevelt created the CWA, WPA, and CCC. The executive order strategy has always been appealing because the bill would be less altered if created in this manner rather than by going through Congress.

Early in the campaign, the coalition tried to influence the presidential debates by sponsoring a "Bring the Gulf to the Debates" campaign, which focused on getting a question about the Gulf Coast Civic Works Act into the national presidential debates. The campaign decided to submit a question to Politico.com, the host for the California debates in January

2008. The question read: "Two years after Katrina and Rita, Gulf Coast schools, hospitals, police stations, roads and flood protection still lie in ruins, keeping displaced residents from returning and communities from recovering. Will you support H.R. 4048, the Gulf Coast Civic Works Act, as President to rebuild community infrastructure and create job and training opportunities for residents?"

An e-mail blast to campaign supporters noted that the candidates had not fully answered the question of how he or she would rebuild the Gulf Coast if elected president. In fact, in the previous twenty-five presidential debates, hardly any questions had addressed the Gulf Coast crisis, and New Orleans had been rejected as a host city for a presidential debate. After coalition members and supporters started voting online, the Gulf Coast Civic Works question soon rose to the number one rated question on the Democratic side and the number three rated question on the Republican side. Incredibly, on the day of the debate Politco.com released a list of the questions it had chosen from, and the Gulf Coast Civic Works question was not on the list. Unfortunately, Politico.com decided to ignore the will of the people and did not ask the Gulf Coast question in either debate. To make matters worse, the rules were changed at the last moment. Several of the coalition partners e-mailed Politico.com and conveyed their disappointment that the process seemed unfair.

The second project the GCCW campaign took on was to get the Democratic and Republican National Committees to include in their party platforms a statement about the GCCW Act. After many phone calls and discussions with politicians from both parties, the campaign did succeed in passing resolutions with the Louisiana Republican Party, as well as the California and Missouri Democratic Parties. The campaign has worked hard to be nonpartisan, and there was great excitement when the Louisiana Republican Party Central Committee passed a resolution supporting the act. The resolution stated, "Resolved by the Louisiana Republican Party Central Committee that the Louisiana Republican Party supports the passage of policy based on the Gulf Coast Civic Works Act for a resident led partnership rebuilding public infrastructure for stronger, safer and more equitable communities, train a new generation of skilled trade workers, create job and training opportunities for returning and displaced workers and contracting opportunities for local businesses." More recently, the New Orleans City Council passed a resolution supporting the GCCW Act (see Appendix 4).[9]

The campaign has also tried to influence lawmakers by reaching out to the faith community. On September 15, 2008, on the third anniversary of President Bush's Jackson Square speech, in which he committed to rebuilding New Orleans, the campaign released an interfaith statement signed by 108 prominent Jewish, Christian, and Muslim leaders calling for a moral response to the hurricanes, for a charitable response, and for justice through long-term human rights–based recovery policy to help Gulf Coast families (see Appendix 5). The statement urged national leaders to create bipartisan resident-led federal solutions, such as the GCCW Act, to help families return and participate in rebuilding their communities, to create living-wage jobs, to restore the coastal wetland, and to make human rights along the Gulf Coast a national moral priority. On June 1, 2009, to mark the beginning of hurricane season, several of these faith groups sent out national appeals to the congregations urging them to contact their Congressmembers about cosponsoring the GCCW Act. Representatives from these faith traditions are currently exploring what else they might do together to move the campaign forward.

Over the course of time, the Equity and Inclusion Campaign, a coalition of more than 150 Gulf Coast organizations, has taken more of a central role in coordinating the various coalition partners because many of the partners in the GCCW campaign are also members of the E&I Economic Development and Workers' Rights working group. The E&I Campaign has twice held a series of three-day meetings in Louisiana, Mississippi, and Alabama to educate local residents on the details of the Gulf Coast Civic Works Act and to gather input from them about what they would like to see included in the 2009 version of the bill. The campaign has also sponsored numerous trips for Gulf Coast residents to Capitol Hill to advocate firsthand with congressional staffers. The most recent E&I trip was June 2–3, 2009. In addition, the E&I Campaign has held multiple meetings in Louisiana, Mississippi, and Alabama on the content of the bill. The vetting process E&I coordinated led to a much stronger bill, as local residents had the opportunity to include their suggestions in the language for the bill. (See Appendix 6 for the full list of the suggested revisions.)

CHAPTER 4

CIVIC WORKS FOR A TWENTY-FIRST-CENTURY NEW DEAL

From the very beginning, advocates for the Gulf Coast Civic Works (GCCW) Act saw it as a pilot project that could be replicated in communities throughout the nation. The early adopters felt that if implemented nationwide, their civic works model could reduce poverty by providing living-wage jobs and paid training programs, as well as rebuild American infrastructure. At the same time, advocates of the GCCW Act saw it as a way to "do democracy" because citizens would play an active role in community development.

Now that Congress has passed President Barack Obama's stimulus package, which includes billions for public works to create jobs and build infrastructure, the question remains, Where does the GCCW Act fit in? As stated in Chapter 3, the goal of the campaign was to have President Obama sign an executive order in the early days of his administration to create the structure of GCCW and then have Congress in the second stimulus package provide the necessary funds to the Office of the Federal Coordinator for Gulf Coast Rebuilding. Theoretically, the House Appropriations Committee could pass the structure for the project, but the campaign felt that the best way was for the president to create the structure and for the Appropriations Committee to provide the funds.

At first, there was hope that this plan might work. Several of our coalition partners had meetings with senior-level members of the Obama transition team. This optimism seemed to be validated when the Center for American Progress (CAP), led by President-elect Obama's transition cochair John Podesta, released its December report entitled "How to

Spend $350 Billion in a First Year of Stimulus and Recovery." In the report, CAP encouraged Congress and President Obama to include $1 billion for Gulf Coast Civic Works into the second stimulus package. However, in late January 2009 when the stimulus package was released, the project was not included in the congressional appropriations language, nor was an executive order anywhere in sight.[1]

With the chances of the act being included in the second stimulus package diminished, the campaign renewed its focus on passing a bill through Congress. On May 6, the Gulf Coast Civic Works Act of 2009 (House Resolution [HR] 2269) was reintroduced into the House of Representatives by Representatives Zoe Lofgren (D-CA), Joseph Cao (R-LA), Charlie Melancon (D-LA), Gene Taylor (D-MS), John Conyers (D-MI), Barbara Lee (D-CA), John Lewis (D-GA), Peter Stark (D-CA), and Charlie Rangel (D-NY). At the time of its introduction, more than 100 organizations signed on as supporters of the bill.

Revisions to the Gulf Coast Civic Works Act

There were several major changes to the Gulf Coast Civic Works Act of 2007, with the most important being that the Regional Authority was removed and replaced by the Office of the Federal Coordinator for Gulf Coast Rebuilding. The campaign received feedback from the Louisiana Recovery Authority, Senator Mary Landrieu (D-LA), Senator Roger Wicker (R MS), and many others that the Regional Authority would add another layer of bureaucracy and that a more efficient and streamlined approach would be to have the oversight of the project under the Office of the Federal Coordinator. With Gulf Coast Civic Works under the Office of the Federal Coordinator for Gulf Coast Rebuilding, the latter would provide oversight and transparency, give logistical and administrative assistance, and allocate funding to the local communities through a resident-driven grant-making process.

The Office of the Federal Coordinator was created by President George Bush and was set to expire on February 28, 2009. However, the GCCW campaign, Oxfam America, and the Louisiana congressional delegation called for the Office of the Federal Coordinator to be maintained, but with some key changes, such as the office reporting directly to the president rather than being under the Department of Homeland Security. Representative Charlie Melancon (D-LA) argued that "rebuilding the Gulf Coast is a complex and critical mission that deserves the full weight of the White House behind it"; Senator David Vitter (R-LA) said that the coordinator needed to have more autonomy and authority so that projects could get completed. Vitter noted, "It has often proved difficult for the coordinator to get all involved parties on the same page, and this had hindered progress," which highlights a point made earlier about the importance of getting the federal government to work together with local and state partners.[2]

On February 20, 2009, Obama decided to extend the Office of Federal Coordinator for Gulf Coast Rebuilding and to send two cabinet members to the region. However, it is yet unclear what Obama's vision is for the region and what specific actions he will pursue. If in the future, as part of GCCW, the coordinator reports directly to the president, this arrangement will be comparable to the structure of the New Deal public works. Even though President Obama may not sign off on each project, as Franklin Roosevelt previously did, Obama would be involved in the direction of the overall recovery. Under HR 2269, the Office of the Federal Coordinator will also have a sixteen-person commission from the region that will serve as the regional coordinating body for administering and planning projects for Gulf Coast Civic Works. Thus, at each level of planning, funding, administration, and oversight, local community groups will participate in the decisionmaking process and will have an increased voice in comparison to current policies.[3]

A second major change to the bill was its emphasis on green jobs. Environmental restoration has always been a part of the act, particularly the Civic Conservation Corps, but a year and a half into the campaign advocates began to frame the larger message to focus on "green jobs." One of the key campaign messages has become to restore the coastal environment by encouraging cutting-edge green building techniques and technologies to minimize carbon emissions and energy needs and by training workers for the growing green economy. Language has been added to the GCCW Act of 2009 that reflects this change. This focus on green jobs came about when the project began working with Dr. Beverly Wright of the Dillard University Deep South Center for Environmental Justice. Wright first heard about the act when one of the campaign's coalition partners, Sharon Gauthe of Bayou Interfaith Shared Community Organizing, spoke at a Dillard conference entitled "Race, Place, and the Environment After Katrina" in May 2008. From this connection, Dillard and the GCCW Project began working to bring green jobs and civic works together. As stated in Chapter 3, this effort culminated in a jointly sponsored conference held in New Orleans in November 2008, which was attended by eighty students and faculty from twenty-seven colleges. Out of this conference came the new language in the revised bill focusing on infrastructure projects that utilize emerging green building technologies and a proposal to use the green building rating system developed by the U.S. Green Building Council (USGBC). This integration of civic works and green jobs has taken on even more importance since the election of President Obama, who has been advocating for green jobs as part of his infrastructure and job-creation program.

A third change to the bill was a focus on protecting vulnerable populations. The revised version stated that rules and regulations will "ensure [that] hiring, planning and implementation adequately involve and look to protect the rights and interests of vulnerable populations, including women, low-income people, people of color, immigrants, the disabled, and the elderly." One way the act attempts to protect the rights of vulnerable populations is through job training. When students and faculty met with the Louisiana Recovery Authority and the New Orleans Workforce Investment Board, it became apparent to the GCCW advocates that the job-training section of the act needed to be stronger. These discussions and further research revealed that there was a need for 90,000 additional trained workers in Louisiana in the fields of construction in 2009. To meet this need for trained workers and to ensure that vulnerable populations were protected, four components were added to HR 2269: (1) it gives priority in gaining admission to job-training programs to Gulf Coast residents, including women and disadvantaged workers; (2) it provides funding for workforce intermediary tasks, such as child care and transportation, which will help to include women and people of color who have historically been excluded from good paying construction jobs; (3) it provides outreach to limited-English-proficient communities; and (4) it requires that at least 20 percent of the total hours worked by civic workers in apprenticeable occupations be performed by apprentices participating in programs of training and apprenticeship.[4]

In summary, the GCCW Act of 2009 is the compilation of the best thinking from what has and has not worked in the Gulf Coast. From 2007 to 2009, residents, community activists, and policymakers have vetted this bill. The GCCW Act has developed into a powerful tool for community development for the following reasons:

1. It allows citizens to participate in decisions that affect their lives.
2. It supports equitable economic development (e.g., provides for first-source hiring, protects people of color, women, and immigrants).

3. It provides for long-term development through job training and hiring of local contractors.
4. It focuses on green jobs.
5. It provides a dynamic, hybrid model of federal oversight and local control.

Civic Works as a National Model

Civic Works can serve as a national model to provide living-wage jobs and job training, to decrease poverty, to rebuild infrastructure using green technology, and to revitalize our democracy by giving citizens a way to participate in decisions that shape their lives. This belief that the GCCW Act could serve as a national model is based in historical precedent. New Deal public works projects were successful at creating good jobs and rebuilding infrastructure. From the beginning, Gulf Coast Civic Works was seen as pilot project for the rest of the nation and a New Deal for the Gulf Coast. Furthermore, advocates of the campaign researched the New Deal and based some of the GCCW's principles on the New Deal's public works projects. For example, the idea of providing strong oversight and having a close partnership between the federal government and the local communities was taken straight from the New Dealers.

Advocates for the act believe that it could be part of the solution for the crisis of the American worker. As stated in Chapter 1, conservative policies have contributed to income and wealth inequality since the 1980s, while globalization and technology have reduced the number of living-wage jobs in America. The crisis has come to a head as the economy continues to deteriorate, with unemployment rates nearing double-digit numbers.

As stated earlier, HR 2269 would provide relief to the Gulf Coast by providing a minimum of 100,000 prevailing-wage jobs and training opportunities for local and displaced workers. If expanded to the national level, an American civic works project would provide millions of living-wage jobs to workers, jobs that could not be outsourced or shipped overseas. Civic works are a stimulus package directed straight at Main Street because these jobs will put money in the pockets of everyday Americans. Civic works would increase purchasing power and stimulate the economy, creating the workforce and resources necessary to rebuild our deteriorated public infrastructure and restore our environment.

An American civic works model would also provide the necessary job training that our citizens need. The reality is that millions of American workers need to be trained. Unfortunately, the job-training programs in the United States rank toward the bottom of those in industrialized nations. In 2006, the Department of Labor spent $5.2 billion on job training and employment assistance, which was down from $6.1 billion in 1986. When we factor in the increase in population, this spending cut reduced what the United States provides to worker training and employment services from $63 per worker to $35; if inflation is taken into consideration, the cuts are even greater.[5]

In addition to creating a minimum of 100,000 prevailing-wage jobs and training opportunities for local and displaced workers, the bill would also reinvest in infrastructure and restoration of the coastal environment utilizing emerging green building technologies. The revised bill calls on all civic works projects to use the green building rating system Leadership in Energy and Environmental Design (LEED) developed by the USGBC, which measures and evaluates a building's energy and environmental performance. If taken to the national level, an American civic works project would encourage cutting-edge green building techniques and technologies to minimize carbon emissions and energy needs and prepare workers and businesses for this growing industry. Van Jones, author of *The Green Collar Economy,* argues that a Green New Deal can create 5 million green jobs during the next ten years through government and private investment. Jones states: "So when you think about the green economy, don't think about Buck Rogers. Think about Joe Sixpack—putting on a green hard hat and going off to fix America. Think about Rosie the Riveter—manufacturing solar arrays and wind turbines." A national civic works project could be a driving force in creating the green-collar economy.[6]

In addition to creating green jobs and building infrastructure, the Gulf Coast Civic Works Act provides President Obama with a way to engage citizens in democracy. Obama has been searching for a way to get tens of thousands of supporters involved in democracy, and this project just may be one of the ways to engage them. This focus on democracy is represented in the term *civic works,* as the government seemed to be unresponsive to the needs of ordinary citizens in the post-Katrina aftermath. This project grew out of the need for people's voices to be part of the solution. The Gulf Coast Civic Works Act, with its resident led Local Advisory Councils, is a way to ensure that the projects selected are the ones really needed and wanted by the community. At the same time, the Local Advisory Councils ensure that local communities benefit from the jobs and job training.

In fact, the development of the act itself has become a product of democracy, as regular citizens have had multiple opportunities to provide input for the language of the bill. Average Americans often feel that they have little input into decisions that affect their lives, particularly in an era where obtaining access to decisionmakers means making large campaign contributions. For example, 81 percent of the people who make campaign contributions of $200 or more to congressional campaigns have yearly incomes of $100,000 or more, and 95 percent of these $200-plus contributors are white. Romano Mazzoli, a retired Democratic representative from Kentucky, believes that "people who contribute get the ear of the members, and the ear of the staff. They have access—and access is it. Access is power. Access is clout. That's how things work." That is why Roger Tamraz, president of Oil Capital, Ltd., confessed at a 1997 Senate hearing on campaign finance abuses that he had not registered to vote because his $300,000 in campaign contributions were "a bit more than a vote." To neutralize this advantage, a national civics works project would provide average citizens with a tangible way to influence decisions. Moreover, a national civic works project would ensure that small and medium businesses were given their fair share of contracts. No longer would the large corporations receive the vast majority of contracts because of their strong connections to the political decisionmakers. A national civic works project would help to level the playing field.[7]

Another aspect of the GCCW Act that makes it appealing as a national model is that it is a hybrid. It is not solely a "big government" response; rather, it integrates the liberal idea of federal funding with the conservative idea of local control. This federal oversight role would provide a strategy to infrastructure spending. No longer would money be spent on projects that had little relation to one another. At the same time, this focus on having local communities take ownership of the rebuilding process would leverage the community's strengths by investing in resident-led development, creating a flexible organization that would cut through the bureaucracy by providing funds directly to the communities through a grant-making and participatory decisionmaking process.

President Obama's Public Works Plan

Ten days before President Obama was to take office, he laid out his vision to rebuild America in the twenty-first century. In a speech at George Mason University, Obama stated that to have a strong economy, America had to "put people to work repairing crumbling roads, bridges and schools by eliminating the backlog of well-planned, worthy and needed infrastructure projects," as well as "retrofit America for a global economy." This retrofit of America would include such things as a new "smart" electric grid, broadband lines in rural America, and investment in science and technology.

As President Obama's public works agenda moves into its implementation phase, currently without the civic works model, it will be important to see if his administration has learned the key lessons of the New Deal.

Oversight and Accountability

Obama and the Democratic Congress seem to understand the need for strong oversight of public works projects to safeguard against waste and corruption. When Representative Dave Obey (D-WI), chair of the House Appropriations Committee, announced the details of the American Recovery and Reinvestment Act, he stated that "a historic level of transparency, oversight and accountability will help guarantee taxpayer dollars are spent wisely and Americans can see results for their investment." Obama's statements have been even stronger: "The days of giving government contractors a blank check are over."[8]

To ensure oversight and accountability, the American Recovery and Reinvestment Act created a new accountability and transparency board that would review oversight of the recovery money and provide an early warning system to detect problems. The new board, which has been entitled the Recovery Accountability and Transparency (RAT) Board, includes inspectors from across the government, and they have been tasked with putting in place preventive measures to avoid fraud. Interestingly, this is not something the inspectors generally do; they are skilled at discovering fraudulent behavior through criminal investigations or audits, but they are not trained in preventing fraud. Obama has emphasized that the RAT Board will use the Web site Recovery.gov to monitor stimulus spending and contracts. It is hoped that citizen watchdogs and journals will examine this site closely and ferret out any suspicious activity. Even though these steps do show a concern about oversight, it is unclear whether they will be successful, particularly when the RAT Board must oversee an amount of money that is seventy times greater than the size of the Department of the Interior's annual discretionary budget. In hearings on the work of the RAT Board, Representative Dan Burton (R-IN) estimates that if 7 percent goes to waste—the amount that Burton estimates is misused in government spending—$55 billion of Obama's stimulus package would be wasted.[9]

Federal Government and Community Management

With so much at stake, what appears to be missing from the American Recovery and Reinvestment Act is a strong role for the community and for the federal government in the management of the projects. A major concern is that community members and the federal government will have very little say in what governors and city officials do with the money. The funds for Obama's stimulus package will flow through the existing system of providing federal money to the states and then to the counties and cities. For example, the act provides approximately $150 billion for infrastructure spending, with state and local politicians selecting the projects. David Leonhardt, a *New York Times* writer who focuses on the economy, is equally concerned about Obama's decision to fund "mostly a stew of spending on existing programs, whatever their warts may be." Leonhardt believes that Obama should have done "a lot more to change *how* the government spends its money." Leonhardt states: "In the current system, the federal government sends money to states without any real effort to evaluate whether it will pay for worthy projects. States rarely do serious analyses of their own. They build new roads before fixing old ones. They don't consider whether those new roads will lead to faster traffic or simply more traffic. They spend millions of dollars on legislators' pet projects and hulking new sports stadiums. In the world of infrastructure, cost-benefit analysis is still a science of the future."[10]

This lack of innovation in the Obama plan regarding how the government spends its money has led to some early problems. In some cases, the formulas that the federal government is using to distribute the stimulus money to schools winds up giving that money to wealthy districts rather than poorer districts because the formulas favor states that spend more per student and are based on population. For example, Utah, which has a $1.3 billion deficit and is facing huge educational cuts, is receiving $1,250 per pupil, whereas Wyoming, which has no budget deficit and is facing no educational cuts, is receiving $1,684 per pupil. Clearly, these well-worn federal formulas are not fully taking into account who is in most need of the money.[11]

In contrast, the New Dealers were deeply involved in how the government spent its money. As we saw in Chapter 2, Roosevelt set up new and creative ways to vet and select projects. Without the federal government's playing a stronger role in the management of Obama's public works projects, there is an increased chance that projects will not end up meeting the true needs of the people. Although Obama has pledged to avoid using money for pet projects, the structure he has decided on may actually do just that. Providing the necessary management and oversight will be key for the Obama administration in keeping Americans supporting public works because most people have little faith that politicians will do the right thing. For example, when Americans were given the choice between receiving tax cuts and having the government spend on projects such as infrastructure, Americans preferred the former over the latter 55 to 42 percent, not because they did not believe in spending projects, but because they believed that spending projects would go toward pet projects rather than toward uplifting the economy.[12]

Furthermore, an area not mentioned by Representative Obey or President Obama is the coordination of the projects with local and state partners at all stages of public works projects. Obey did mention that funds would be distributed "through existing formulas to programs with proven track records," but this is not the same thing as having a tight coordination among federal, state, and local levels. President Obama and Congress may need to create a body that helps state and local actors work through all the legal and logistical questions that arise in the conduct of large-scale public works projects.[13]

The Model for Building and Rebuilding

In relation to how these public works will be built, President Obama and the Democratic Congress have initially offered a contract model for doing so. Soon after taking office, Obama announced that 90 percent of the jobs created or saved would be in the private sector. As stated earlier, Americans are more comfortable with a contract model, as it supports private industry and fits into capitalist ideology. The reality is that many Americans currently do not trust the government to create an efficient program, particularly one that is operated by the government rather than by private contractors. As long as the economic downtown is short, the contract model for public works will most likely be the only model used to stimulate the economy. However, if the downturn is long and deep, the people may demand a more aggressive response, and a government-hiring model may well be a possibility. Just as the partial nationalization of the banks was justified by the financial crisis, a government-hiring model would be justified in the same way. A key lesson from the New

Deal is that government-run infrastructure projects are more effective at putting large-scale numbers of people to work. If Obama chooses to move to a government-run model, it will demonstrate a progressive shift away from the more centrist approach that he articulated in his almost-two-year campaign.[14]

The Sufficiency of the Stimulus

There is also a question about whether Obama's $787 billion stimulus package is large enough to fix the economy and create enough jobs. The stimulus package will provide 64 percent, or $504 billion, for new public spending and 36 percent, or $283 billion, for tax cuts. Economist Paul Krugman argues that the American economy, which under normal times would produce $30 trillion of goods and services during 2009–2010, is projected to fall more than $2 trillion below its capacity; thus, the stimulus package is not large enough, even when the multiplier effect is added in. Krugman states, "The bottom line is that the Obama plan is unlikely to close more than half of the looming output gap, and could easily end up doing less than a third of the job." Because of this gap, Krugman concludes that "the Obama plan just doesn't look adequate to the economy's need." Even President Obama's chair of the Council of Economic Advisers, Christina Romer, and Vice President Joe Biden's chief economist, Jared Bernstein, have concluded that the effect of the stimulus will not solve the problems of the economy. Romer and Bernstein predict that without the act unemployment will be at 8.8 percent in the first quarter of 2010 and that with the stimulus unemployment will be at 7 percent. Because Obama's first stimulus package will not fix the economy, there is already talk of the need for another stimulus package in late 2009 or early 2010.[15]

Not only will the American Recovery and Reinvestment Act not fix the economy, but it also will not fully repair the public infrastructure. Out of the $787 billion plan, approximately $150 billion are dedicated to infrastructure projects. Some of the major projects include $27.5 billion for highway and bridge construction, $11 billion for a smart electricity grid, $8.4 billion for mass transit, $8 billion for high-speed railroads, $7.2 billion for the expansion of broadband Internet, $6 billion for clean water projects, and $4 billion for weatherizing and repairing public housing. Robert Yaro, president of the Regional Plan Association, an organization that has developed long-term planning for Connecticut, New Jersey, and New York for almost 100 years, calls Obama's plan "a drop in the bucket."[16]

Governor Edward Rendell of Pennsylvania, who, along with Governor Arnold Schwarzenegger of California and Mayor Michael Bloomberg of New York, is a founding member of Building America's Future and has been advocating for the last several years for more public infrastructure spending, has said the Obama recovery bill is a good first step but is not even close to what is needed to fix our crumbling infrastructure. When the bill was first announced, Rendell highlighted the crisis of Pennsylvania's bridges, with 25 percent (about 5,500) being structurally deficient and 18 percent (about 4,000) being functionally obsolete. He argued that "anybody who thinks—if the president-elect thinks, or the team thinks—that this is the answer to America's infrastructure needs is in a different universe." This view was echoed by Mark Dettle, the public works director in Santa Cruz, California, who stated, "Every million dollars helps but the stimulus money is not going to fix all of the infrastructure needs of the city, the county, the state, or the nation."[17]

The bottom line is that Obama's plan does not provide enough money to fix America's infrastructure because just 19 percent of the spending for the stimulus package goes for public works. As stated earlier, the need for public infrastructure is $1.6 trillion from 2009 to 2013, and Obama's plan provides only $150 billion for 2009–2010. Moreover, much of the infrastructure money is going to high-tech projects rather than the traditional infrastructure projects that were highlighted earlier.

When it comes to how the projects are funded, Obama has followed in the path of the New Dealers as the money will be given to the states and cities as grants, not loans. Offering the funds as grants will speed up the enactment of the stimulus package because the states and cities will definitely spend the money, whereas states may not use the money if it is given as a loan. However, historical precedent has not stopped Senate Republican leader Mitch McConnell of Kentucky, who argues that the stimulus package should be given as loans to the states because he believes doing so will reduce wasteful spending. And even though wasteful spending needs to be reduced, it can be done through oversight and management of the projects, not through loans. Clearly, loans would greatly affect the states' willingness to use the funds and would slow down the recovery.[18]

Equity

Finally, the Obama administration would be wise to learn the New Deal lesson that public works projects must take into consideration issues of equity. Unfortunately, the existing federal model for building infrastructure will most likely perpetuate race and social class disparities. PolicyLink, a national research and action institute focusing on economic and social equity, argues that the way infrastructure has been built in the past has led to urban neighborhoods with outdated and dilapidated schools and other public facilities and rural unincorporated areas lacking sidewalks, safe roads, streetlights, and basic sewer systems. This question about equitable development must be raised with this $787 billion stimulus package and with any future package. As stated in Chapter 2, the questions that must be asked are (1) who gets the jobs, (2) what infrastructure projects will be built, and (3) which communities will benefit from the infrastructure projects.[19]

Leading experts, such as Robert Reich, secretary of labor under President Bill Clinton, have already expressed concern that women, people of color, and the poor will not have equal access to the jobs created by the stimulus plan. Reich warns that "if construction jobs will go to mainly white males who already dominate the construction trades, many people who need jobs the most—women, minorities, and the poor and long-term unemployed—will be shut out."[20]

Moving from Obama's Public Works to Civic Works

The Obama stimulus plan is now in place. However, the financial system is still in crisis, with Bank of America receiving an additional $20 billion loan in mid-January 2009 and AIG (American International Group) receiving $30 billion in capital injection in March 2009. With these latest bailouts coming on top of the already $300 billion of taxpayer money provided to banks, there is a sense that we have seen only the tip of this economic disaster iceberg. Gross domestic product decreased an annual rate of 6.3 percent in the fourth quarter of 2008 and 5.7 percent in the first quarter of 2009.[21]

With talk of the need for another stimulus package by next year, or sooner, public works appear to be with us for the foreseeable future, and there will be time for experimentation. In light of what has been learned in the Gulf Coast, and the two-year vetting process of the Gulf Coast Civic Works Act, I suggest the following changes to the Obama-led effort in order to make it a more effective and an equitable civic works project. First, I recommend the creation of a civic works agency, which could provide strong oversight and management on the front end of the projects to safeguard against waste and corruption. With a civic works agency involved in the early phases of the projects, as was the case in the New Deal, rather than after the fact, corruption and waste will be greatly minimized. By reducing corruption and waste, the civic works agency will play a fundamental role in maintaining public support because citizens will not support politicians' pet projects and corrupt spending practices. As with the Gulf Coast Civic Works Act and the New Deal public works projects, I recommend that the new civic works agency secure a role for representatives from community organizations, as they have a keen understanding of the reality on the ground.

Second, I advise the civic works agency to provide the necessary coordination among federal, state, and local officials as well as support for state and local actors to work through all the legal and logistical questions that arise in large-scale civic works projects. Janet Napolitano, President Obama's Homeland Security secretary, took a step in this direction when she issued a directive to her department to examine the possibility of colocating state and Federal Emergency Management Agency (FEMA) recovery efforts. Secretary Napolitano noted that Louisiana's and FEMA's recovery efforts are currently operating out of different locales. Similarly, a civic works agency can ensure that the federal government works closely with local and state partners to conduct large-scale projects.

Third, I recommend that the Obama administration immediately implement a pilot project based on a government-hiring model. If the economy continues to worsen, lessons learned from this pilot project could be used later to quickly and efficiently put people to work rebuilding our infrastructure.

Fourth, I suggest that the next stimulus package add $150 billion for infrastructure, so that the total spending on public infrastructure would be $300 billion for 2009–2010. Then, in 2011–2012, I would double it again; that is, spend another $300 billion on infrastructure. As stated earlier, the need is $1.6 trillion for five years—or $320 billion a year—and this $600 billion investment during these four years will get us closer to meeting the need. Some may question the price tag, particularly when the United States faces a more than $1 trillion deficit. Yet this level of investment is necessary because it is the best way to create millions of good jobs and rebuild America. Conservatives argue that Obama should center his stimulus plan on tax breaks, but many leading economists argue that the evidence points in the direction of public works over tax cuts. Economists point to the success of the New Deal public works and the failure of President Bush's $168 billion in tax cuts and rebates in 2008, which did so little to stimulate job growth. Moreover, the United States needs to rebuild its infrastructure to ensure long-term economic growth and social well-being, and a $150 billion investment does not come close to meeting the need.

Fifth, in order to ensure that equity issues are at the forefront, I recommend that training programs reach out to women, people of color, and the poor, three groups that might normally be overseen and marginalized. In the revised version of the GCCW Act, vulnerable populations were protected and apprenticeship and training programs were set in place. Similar language should be included for the current infrastructure projects so that women, people of color, low-income people, people with disabilities, and immigrants have access to these middle-class jobs. Another way to ensure equity is to require contractors to provide a minimum of 20 percent of the jobs to people with incomes at or below 200 percent of the federal poverty level and to the long-term unemployed. Lastly, a way to employ more women is to expand the notion of civic works to include such areas as child care and care for the elderly because infrastructure projects in the past have mainly employed men.[22]

In addition, to ensure that neglected communities get their fair share of infrastructure projects, I advise that Local Advisory Councils, similar to those in the GCCW Act, be created so that residents will play an active role in deciding what gets built in their communities and who does the building. These Local Advisory Councils would (a) conduct need assessments for infrastructure projects, (b) identify local businesses to be prime contractors and subcontractors, (c) put forward recommendations to the federal government about which projects are supported by the community, and (d) coordinate community resources, such as Workforce Investment Boards, job-training providers, nonprofit organizations, and faith-based organizations, to carry out civic works projects.

This model flattens the whole structure and gives communities much more control than they normally have over economic decisions. Civic works are an alternative model to the standard top-down approach, in which politicians choose large companies like Bechtel and Halliburton to come into a community and do the work. The Local Advisory Councils will allow the residents a democratic voice, encourage civic participation, and ultimately foster self-sufficient and sustainable communities.

CHAPTER 5
THE EXPERTS WEIGH IN ON CIVIC WORKS

In this chapter, a group of ten experts in the field of public policy, community organizing, and economic development provide their perspectives on what a civic works project would mean for the nation, as well as for the Gulf Coast. Their ideas are designed to add further depth and analysis to the proposition of rebuilding America through civic works.

The first set of articles—by Howard Zinn, Jason Scott Smith, Robert Leighninger Jr., Jeannette Gabriel, Angela Glover Blackwell, and Emily Ryo—focuses on President Barack Obama's public works projects and the possibility they have to rebuild America. Zinn's article, "A Great Opportunity," talks about the need for Obama to provide bold policy, such as a massive public works project, to fix the current economic crisis and to avert future crises. Zinn argues that if Obama does not do this, then citizens should rise up and demand it. In "Obama's New Deal?" Smith explores what is at stake for the Republican Party and wonders whether its response to Obama's policies will be like that of President Dwight Eisenhower, who accepted New Deal reforms, or like that of Barry Goldwater, who rejected them.

In "The New Deal Assault on the First Great Depression: A Mosaic, not a Monolith," Leighninger demonstrates that New Deal public works projects were not all the same, and he argues that today's models should not be as well. Leighninger then goes on to focus on four key lessons from the New Deal: (1) target the stimulus to the people who will spend their salaries immediately, (2) provide strong federal oversight, (3) ensure adequate funding, and (4) focus on building infrastructure.

Gabriel, in "Creating Jobs and Reviving Dreams: How a National Jobs Program Can Save Obama's America," also focuses on the lessons from the New Deal. Gabriel argues that a national jobs program is needed to combat the economic crisis and that a bold, systemic response like the Works Projects Administration is the best vehicle for moving the country forward because it would help the most economically disfranchised.

The final two authors in this set pick up on this theme of helping the most economically disfranchised. In "Community Colleges: Connecting People to Jobs and Creating a *New* New Deal," Blackwell argues that the most economically disfranchised must be trained for these infrastructure jobs, and the best way to do train them is through community colleges. Ryo argues, in "Poverty Alleviation Through Public Works," that Obama's public works projects should emphasize skill development and job training while at the same time building infrastructure that is of use to the poor. In addition, Ryo suggests that the poor need to be integrated into other economic opportunities, such as public transportation, child care, housing and food support.

The second set of articles—by David Bowman, Julie Kuklinski, Stephen Bradberry, and Jeffrey Buchanan—focuses on how the Gulf Coast Civic Works Act relates to Obama's public works plan. Bowman, in "Civic Works: The Case for a Strong Workforce Training Component," continues with a focus on the importance of job training. Bowman makes the case that the GCCW Act will provide Louisiana residents with the opportunity to gain basic skills and literacy while working at a prevailing wage. Julie Kuklinski, in "Civic Works: Training Today's Rosie the Riveter," continues this focus on job preparation, but focuses on how GCCW will provide women, who have normally been marginalized in the field of construction, with the necessary training to be successful. In "Community Organizing After Hurricane Katrina: Lessons Learned," Bradberry encourages the GCCW campaign to go down deeper into its base so that HR 2269 becomes part of daily conversation. Buchanan's provocative article, "Helping End the Human Rights Crisis in the Gulf Coast: Sound Policy, Smart Politics," makes the case that the GCCW Act will help to end the human rights crisis in the Gulf Coast.

A Great Opportunity

Howard Zinn
    Howard Zinn is a professor emeritus of political science, Boston University, and is the author of twenty books, including *A People's History of the United States.*

This current financial crisis is a major way station on the way to the collapse of the American Empire. The first important sign was 9/11, with the most heavily armed nation in the world shown to be vulnerable to a handful of hijackers. And now another sign: Both major parties rushing to get an agreement to spend $700 billion of taxpayer money to pour down the drain of huge financial institutions that are notable for two characteristics: incompetence and greed.

There is a much better solution to the current financial crisis. But it requires discarding what has been conventional "wisdom" for too long: that government intervention in the economy ("big government") must be avoided like the plague, because the "free market" will guide the economy toward growth and justice.

Let's face a historical truth: We have never had a free market. We have always had government intervention in the economy, and indeed that intervention has been welcomed by the captains of finance and industry. They had no quarrel with big government when it served their needs. It started way back when the Founding Fathers met in Philadelphia in 1787 to draft the Constitution. The first big bailout was the decision of the new government to redeem for full value the almost worthless bonds held by speculators. And this role of big government, supporting the interests of the business classes, continued all through the nation's history.

The rationale for taking $700 billion from the taxpayers to subsidize huge financial institutions is that somehow that wealth will trickle down to the people who need it. This has never worked. The alternative is simple and powerful. Take that huge sum of money and give it directly to the people who need it. Let the government declare a moratorium on foreclosures and give aid to home owners to help them pay off their mortgages. Create a federal jobs program to guarantee work to people who want and need jobs and for whom the free market has not come through.

We have a historic and successful precedent: Roosevelt's New Deal put millions of people to work rebuilding the nation's infrastructure and, defying the cries of "socialism," established social security. That can be carried further, with "health security"—free health care for all.

All that will take more than $700 billion. But the money is there. In the $600 billion for the military budget once we decide we will no longer be a warmaking nation. And in the swollen bank accounts of the super-rich by taxing vigorously both their income and their wealth.

When the cry goes up, whether from Republicans or Democrats (it was Bill Clinton who promised that "the era of big government is over"), that this must not be done because it is big government, the citizenry should just laugh. And then agitate and organize on behalf of what the Declaration of Independence promised: that it is the responsibility of government to ensure the equal right of all to "life, liberty, and the pursuit of happiness."

This is a golden opportunity for Obama to distance himself from the fossilized Democratic Party leaders, giving life to his slogan of "change." He has announced some proposals that go in the right direction, in job creation, in tax policy. However, the depth of the economic crisis requires much bolder steps, not only to deal with the current crisis, but also to change the underlying conditions that will create future crises. For instance, the deterioration of the nation's infrastructure and the drastic loss of jobs call for a massive public works program to do what "the market" has failed to do. If Obama does not show such boldness, it will be up to the citizenry, as it always has been, to raise a shout that will be heard in the White House and the halls of Congress and that cannot be ignored.

Obama's New Deal?

Jason Scott Smith
    Jason Scott Smith is an assistant professor of history, University of New Mexico, and he is the author of *Building New Deal Liberalism: The Political Economy of Public Works, 1933–1956.*
Barack Obama's plan for massive economic stimulus through investing in job creation and infrastructure recalls the example set by Franklin Roosevelt's New Deal. Indeed, seventy-six years after FDR took on the challenge of fighting a global economic meltdown by using the power of government to put people back to work, we face a similar task.

Economically, most people agree that Obama's proposed plan makes sense. Republicans, like Federal Reserve chair Ben Bernanke and Harvard economist Kenneth Rogoff, who advised John McCain's presidential campaign, agree with Democrats, like Nobel Prize winner Joseph Stiglitz and former labor secretary Robert Reich, that government spending on infrastructure is what our economy needs. The historical example of the New Deal provides a clear path that might be followed, as well as an important clue as to why some on the political right still resist the example of commonsense solutions to our economic crisis.

During the Great Depression, through Harold Ickes's Public Works Administration and Harry Hopkins's Works Progress Administration, the federal government spent huge sums of money in all but three of the nation's 3,071 counties. The WPA's 1935 appropriation of $4.88 billion alone was the equivalent of 135 percent of federal revenues, or about 6.7 percent of the nation's gross domestic product, in that year. Together, these public works agencies put people to work while constructing projects like New York's Triborough Bridge, as well as roads, sewers, hydroelectric dams, and hundreds of airports. Believing in socially useful infrastructure, these New Dealers built in order to improve the nation and to invest for the future. For example, the New Deal built new schools in almost half of the nation's counties. These public works programs were led by an uncommonly smart set of public servants. Hopkins, Ickes, and their subordinates were talented public administrators, blessed with an ability for tapping the legal and engineering expertise they needed when facing a national emergency. Furthermore, these New Dealers were not afraid of market capitalism: Ickes's PWA, for instance, built its projects by accepting bids from such private contractors as Bechtel and Brown & Root (recently a subsidiary of Halliburton) and carefully monitoring these firms' performance.[1]

Why should anyone oppose Obama's plan? Why should we stand back and do nothing? The answer is simple: The New Deal's public works programs were not only the correct policy response to economic crisis; they were also smart politics. Indeed, Hopkins was once reported to have declared that the secret to the New Deal's success was that it could "tax and tax, spend and spend, and elect and elect." This approach to governance, coupled with inept Republican opposition, gave the Democratic Party the presidency from 1933 to 1953. Indeed, when Dwight Eisenhower took back the presidency for Republicans in 1953, he spent much of his eight years in office quietly accepting and ratifying the New Deal's domestic reforms. So much so, in fact, that Barry Goldwater, when confronted by Eisenhower's massive program of federal highway construction, belittled Ike, charging that he was merely a "dime store New Dealer."

Today's conservatives who see themselves as the heirs to Goldwater's antigovernment philosophy correctly sense the political dangers for their ideology if the Republican Party were to acquiesce to an Obama stimulus that would follow in the steps of FDR and Eisenhower: Obama's plan would lead to economic recovery, but at the high cost of their worldview's legitimacy. Rather than make this point directly, however, these critics have instead cloaked their arguments in the rhetoric of the free market. Amity Shlaes, for example, has tried to argue that government spending would serve only to crowd out public investment and delay recovery. Shlaes and her allies, however, are not so much the ideological heirs of conservatives like Goldwater as they are the direct descendants of FDR's predecessor, Herbert Hoover. When Hoover stood back and did little to counter the Great Depression between 1929 and 1933, his inaction "crowded out" private investment, and it collapsed by a factor of 87 percent while the nation's GDP plummeted by one-third.[2]

During the Depression, we tried doing nothing, as Hooverites like Shlaes recommend, and we learned that this did not work. It is abundantly clear that we need to do something, and something big. Economists on the left and the right are in general agreement that a major fiscal stimulus via infrastructure spending is both necessary and smart policy. Ideologues on the far right who oppose this approach thus face a difficult choice: Do they want to be like Ike and endorse commonsense reforms, or do they want to cling to an outmoded ideology that does not work, like Hoover did?

For those who are not held captive by obsolete theories, however, our current moment presents a chance to draw on the best aspects of the New Deal's achievements—bold spending on public works construction that stimulates economic recovery, generates jobs, provides socially useful infrastructure, leverages input from local communities, and safeguards taxpayer money through careful oversight. If Obama's plan is carried out in this fashion, it can, as FDR once said, provide "a smashing answer for those cynical men who say that a democracy cannot be honest and efficient."

The New Deal Assault on the First Great Depression: A Mosaic, Not a Monolith

Robert Leighninger Jr.

Robert Leighninger Jr. is a faculty associate at the School of Social Work at Arizona State University, and he is the author of *Long-Range Public Investment: The Forgotten Legacy of the New Deal* and *Building Louisiana: The Legacy of the Public Works Administration.*

There is a lot of discussion of public works as a source of economic stimulus, and there is general agreement that such a benefit is possible. There is also a belief that tax cuts provide the same stimulus and are easier to provide and more politically popular. Public works, however, have two huge advantages over tax cuts: When you spend the money, you know that a good part of it will go directly into the economy in the form of purchases of building materials, *and* you will get something of lasting benefit in return. This is not just a theoretical argument, as economics often is; there is a track record of the effects of long-range public investment in the form of public works that goes back three-quarters of a century. This record is in the form of schools, university buildings, roads, bridges, tunnels, airports, parks, hospitals, courthouses, fire and police stations, city halls, museums, recreational facilities, and other structures built by the many public works programs of the New Deal. The evidence is all around us.

There were at least a dozen New Deal agencies that built things. Each had its own goals, structure, leadership, accomplishments, and failures. One of the glories of the New Deal was the amazing variety of its policy responses to the Great Depression. The Works Progress Administration (WPA) is often thought of as the only New Deal building program, and many projects that were constructed by other agencies are attributed to it. But there were many other programs.

The Public Works Administration (PWA) was created earlier than the WPA and in general built larger projects—for example, the Triborough Bridge, the Alameda County Courthouse, and Reagan National Airport. The Tennessee Valley Authority constructed a series of dams and reservoirs providing electrical power, security from flooding, and improved commerce to an entire seven-state watershed.

Critics say that public works projects take too long to plan and execute to provide any immediate economic stimulus. Other New Deal programs went to work quickly. The Civilian Conservation Corps (CCC) took young men off the streets and rails and sent them out to plant trees; stop soil erosion; fight forest fires; provide greater accessibility to our national parks, monuments, and forests; establish a skiing industry; and build whole systems of state parks nationwide. They were paid $30 a month, $25 of which were sent back to their struggling families. The Civil Works Administration (CWA) put 4 million people to work in a matter of weeks not only doing labor-intensive projects like building sidewalks, but also filling white-collar jobs in libraries and clinics and painting murals on public buildings.

One agency never mentioned in the current rediscovery of the New Deal, but one with special relevance to the Gulf Coast Civic Works Project, is the Resettlement Administration. It presided over ninety-six new communities and three new cities built by itself and two other agencies, the Federal Emergency Relief Administration (FERA) and the PWA. The communities brought together displaced farmers and others to start new lives. One of the first challenges of these communities was to get the new inhabitants to know each other and work together. In Katrina-ravaged New Orleans, existing communities were driven into exile. Their members already know each other and would like to come back if there are homes to come back to. An organization that could find these exiles, provide them with temporary housing, and give them the tools, materials, and supervision to work alongside skilled craftsmen could help them rebuild their communities quickly and enthusiastically. If the original community was disadvantageously located, community members could be resettled in a better place. If they were reunited with friends and family, being in a new location should not be a problem.

The projects in President Obama's economic stimulus bill are broader than the New Deal public works programs, including cyber-infrastructure inconceivable then, grants to states for education and health, and tax cuts. These are different times with different needs and different political structures to build on. There are also many ways to approach our problems. The New Deal was not a monolithic effort. There were many programs from which many lessons, good and bad, can be drawn. The four most important ones, I think, are these: First, public jobs can provide economic stimulus if they go to the people who will spend their salaries immediately. Tax cuts to rich people and corporations do not automatically produce investment. They already have plenty of money and see no point in investing when returns are so uncertain. Increased consumption can inspire investment as it did during the New Deal. Millions were desperate for basic food and clothing; money returned to the economy immediately with attendant multipliers. Those who produced and sold the food and clothes had more money to spend; even car sales went up after the CWA had been in operation a few months. Today we need more careful targeting; those known as the "working poor" should be high on the list.

Second, federal oversight, which was exercised relentlessly by the PWA and to a lesser extend by the WPA, will be necessary to reestablish public trust in an age accustomed to fraud and pork-barrel excesses. President Obama seems to recognize this, though no oversight machinery has been reported yet.

Third, we must make sure the commitment is sufficient to get the job done. Nobel laureate Paul Krugman and others are already saying Obama's numbers are not big enough. Roosevelt pulled the plug on the CWA, even though it was enormously effective, because he was frightened of how much it was costing. He started the recession of 1937 by again cutting public works programs. Had he hung on in 1934, we might not be debating whether World War II was required to end the Depression.

Fourth, we cannot be certain if tax rebates or salaries from public jobs will be spent. But if the money goes to public works, at least we have something to show for the expenditure, something that will pay dividends for decades.

Creating Jobs and Reviving Dreams: How a National Jobs Program Can Save Obama's America

Jeannette Gabriel

Jeannette Gabriel is public policy director for a nurses union (JNESO, IUOE-AFL-CIO) in New Jersey and also is an independent historian working on the Workers Alliance of America, the union that represented WPA workers and the unemployed during the Great Depression.

As the economy crumbles and the unemployment rate soars, government intervention in the economy has shifted from being an ideological position to being a necessity. Bank failures and mass bailouts have led to calls for nationalization of the financial system. In response to this looming crisis, the Obama administration has begun to investigate options for a federal government jobs program. There are critical issues to be addressed in what this government jobs program will look like. Will it be a bold response to a systemic crisis like the Works Projects Administration of the Great Depression? Or will it be a continuation of the current bailout plans that give the private sectors massive amounts of government money to do what they wish?[1]

One of the critical questions is, Will the central purpose of the jobs program be to develop infrastructure, or will it be to sustain and develop a demoralized workforce? These are two fundamentally different goals that will affect the structure of the jobs program. If the government chooses to prioritize infrastructural development, then the priority may be to provide jobs to already skilled workers who have been affected by the economic downturn—like the PWA program of the 1930s. However, if the main focus is to sustain and develop the workforce, then the government needs to think carefully about how to involve the most economically disfranchised groups within the society like the WPA program of the 1930s did. The WPA proved to be much more effective at assisting the groups most affected by the Great Depression—blacks and immigrants—the same groups that today are in desperate need.

Massive unemployment is not just a problem of the past. In February 2009, the official unemployment rates were 7.6 percent nationally. As during the Great Depression, the impact of the economic downturn has disproportionately affected African Americans and Latinos. The overall unemployment rate is 11.6 percent for blacks, 9.2 percent for Latinos, and only 6.6 percent for whites. But these are only the official numbers. Actual unemployment rates are much higher when the numbers of "marginally attached workers" who are not actively looking for work are included in the statistics. The current overall unemployment rate is 13.9 percent. Considering that in 2006 almost four out of ten blacks over the age of sixteen were jobless, one can only imagine how disastrous the impact of the recent job losses has been on black and immigrant communities.[4]

The only way to respond to this growing crisis is by developing mass job-training programs run by the government. The private sector has again and again shown its inability to engage in long-term infrastructural development. In addition, the recent display of flagrant greed by the financial sector indicates that the task of rebuilding the nation cannot be done effectively by private contractors, but only by the government. One of the possibilities for the Obama administration is to allocate training to the craft unions and offer jobs through that structure. The majority of jobs developed for the PWA program were given to craft union workers because they were already skilled and the construction industry had been devastated by the Depression. But this program did not work to stimulate the economy, so the Roosevelt administration decided to refocus its energies on the broader population of unemployed with the WPA program. This approach had two major positive impacts. One was to provide newfound opportunities for blacks and undocumented immigrants—or "aliens," as they were known at the time. The second was to offer jobs, not just for those working in infrastructural development, but also for white-collar professionals, artists, writers, actors, and teachers. These programs captured the imagination of the country and uplifted the workforce, not just by providing a paycheck, but also by providing hope for a better future. We now have an opportunity to uplift the nation once again. This is an opportunity for visionary thinking—not just about the roads and houses of our country, but also about the very soul of the nation.

Recent calls for a government jobs program have been focused on the devastated Gulf region that was pummeled by Hurricanes Rita and Katrina. It seems that the need for infrastructural rebuilding and federal government support throughout the Gulf region could revive public interest in a government jobs program. If the government could make an initial commitment to rebuilding the Gulf region, then possibly a campaign could be extended to address the crumbling urban areas. But now as unemployment escalates, it becomes more apparent that the task before us is larger than initially conceived. The economy is hemorrhaging jobs, and the private sector's free-market solutions have clearly failed. At the same time, the short-term glutinous legacy of right-wing policies has devastated our inner cities and rural areas.

Over time many Americans have lost faith in our government because it has prioritized the wealthy elite and the corporations. Instead of appreciating new immigrant communities for their hardworking contributions to the nation, our government has raided communities and criminalized innocent people. Instead of confronting systemic racism, the government has destroyed African American communities by using the CIA to ship drugs directly into the inner city and locked up millions in the largest prison industrial complex in the world. Instead of offering opportunities for advancement, the government has been complicit in maintaining a system where blacks and immigrants are mired in poverty. But this does not have to be our future. There is a different model of the U.S. government as a progressive and representative force. We have an opportunity before us to develop a comprehensive government jobs program that can reverse the mistakes of the past and provide a path to economic equality for all.[5]

Community Colleges: Connecting People to Jobs and Creating a *New* New Deal

Angela Glover Blackwell

Angela Glover Blackwell is founder and CEO of PolicyLink, a national research and action institute advancing economic and social equity.

As Americans grapple with an economic crisis that invites comparisons to the Great Depression, a central question is, How does the country design a New Deal for the twenty-first century? Community colleges can play a key role in creating jobs for a new generation of Americans searching for opportunity in an evolving economy. With blue-collar and smokestack jobs drying up, and the cost of four-year colleges soaring, many people are turning to community colleges to get ahead. Enrollments are growing at more than twice the rate of that at four-year schools. The Bureau of Labor Statistics has estimated that 63 percent of the 18.9 million new jobs that will be created by 2014 will require some postsecondary education.

Infrastructure jobs are at the core of the Obama administration's economic recovery plans. Many of these jobs will require technological expertise to reconstruct roads, fortify transit and water systems, and expand alternative energy sources and telecommunications networks. Even trade unions have begun to extend their on-the-job training programs and traditional apprenticeships into the classroom as equipment and tasks become more sophisticated.

This new, more demanding economy will not automatically set aside space at the table for low-income people, many of whom are people of color. Community colleges have historically provided a bridge to opportunity for disadvantaged groups. Seventy-five percent of all African Americans, Latinos, and Native Americans who pursue higher education start their journey in a community college.

However, years of neglect and financial cutbacks have severely limited the ability of community colleges to provide the high-quality training and workforce education programs that are proven on-ramps to good jobs in the infrastructure sector. A substantial and immediate infusion of new federal dollars would help provide states and municipalities with the resources they need to make community colleges engines for a revved-up twenty-first-century economy. To prevent graft and abuse, state and local governments can require that community colleges use the new infusion of government funds to complement infrastructure projects that are explicitly committed to hiring workers from low-income communities. Mandating that every infrastructure project set aside 1 or 2 percent of the total cost for job-training purposes would ensure a well-trained, ready-to-work labor force.

In California, 40 percent of all residents aged twenty-five and older have no college experience, but that figure may be changing as state officials, business executives, community groups, and college administrators begin to see the light. With an extensive network of 110 community colleges, California awarded about 6,300 community college certificates in infrastructure-related fields in 2007, as programs connecting low-income people to emerging infrastructure jobs have grown.

For example, Pacific Gas and Electric Co. (PG&E), through its PowerPathway program, is collaborating with community college districts in San Francisco, San José, and Fresno to train low-income youth and adults for entry-level line-worker jobs. The seven-year-old program has produced 400 apprentices, and company officials say they hope to add another 115–120 new line-workers a year. PG&E is supplementing its community college program with a similar program at a four-year school, California State University East Bay.

In 2007, the Silicon Valley Leadership Group started a program to train students for work in the green sector installing solar panels. A collaboration between industry and community colleges in the Bay Area, the program helps students to secure certification in the solar photovoltaic industry. One-third of California's 772 solar companies are in the Bay Area in an industry that employs approximately 17,000 people statewide. Over the next year, the industry is expected to add about 5,000 new jobs in California, almost half in the Bay Area.

Other efforts are under way to prepare students to work in water infrastructure, a growing field. For example, Project: WaterWorks, a collaboration of water agencies, economic development agencies, and community colleges in the San Diego area, offers a number of certificate and degree programs that prepare graduates for entry-level jobs in water management and treatment positions. With sixteen community colleges in California offering for-credit courses in wastewater treatment, water technology, and reclaimed water, this infrastructure sector is poised to become a growth industry in the state.

California is a model for how to build a twenty-first-century economy. Infrastructure jobs cannot be outsourced and add—rather than extract— value from the community and tap the resources that we have in abundance: our young people and underemployed adults.

Poverty Alleviation Through Public Works

Emily Ryo
    Emily Ryo is a sociology doctoral student at Stanford University; her research
    focuses on inequality, poverty, immigration, and the sociology of law.
Public works have a long history as a poverty alleviation tool. According to the World Bank, "As early as the fourth century B.C., Indian rulers were advised that when natural calamities struck, subjects should be employed in building forts or waterworks in return for food." Most recently, with President Barack Obama calling for vast public works spending, as an antidote to the failing economy, there has been a significant renewal of support for public works programs in the United States. Although public works have been a popular policy instrument for poverty reduction, very few countries have actually attempted to assess the poverty impact of public works programs. Much of the existing empirical data on the efficacy of public works programs as an antipoverty strategy come from studies of public works programs in developing countries. In this essay, I offer three basic lessons drawn from these studies on maximizing the poverty-reducing potential of public works programs in the United States.[6]

Lesson 1. Many public works programs are implemented on a short-term basis to address joblessness and transient poverty resulting from natural disasters or adverse economic shocks. Such programs often provide only temporary employment at low wages for unskilled and semiskilled workers on labor-intensive projects. However, for public works to operate as a long-term solution to *chronic* poverty, they must emphasize skill development and job training that can aid the poor in becoming more employable in the private sector in the future. Furthermore, skills imparted through such training must be those in demand by the local labor market. This is a lesson that has been confirmed, for instance, by the public works program in Limpopo, South Africa, where the participants reverted to unemployment when their jobs ended because the technical training they had received did not impart skills that were in short supply in the South African economy.[7]

Lesson 2. In addition to providing direct income gains to the poor, public works projects can generate indirect benefits to the poor in the form of durable assets and infrastructures (e.g., school buildings, community centers, health clinics). Too often, however, public works projects fail to engage in careful, long-term planning that focuses on broader, indirect benefits to the poor. For example, a common criticism of the rural public works in India has been that the assets created through these programs have been "privatized," with benefits going to the nonpoor without charge. Studies suggest that decentralized management with active participation of community-based organizations and local authorities is critical to ensuring that public works projects build and maintain infrastructures that are of value to the poor.[8]

Lesson 3. For optimal results, public works must be integrated within a wider and continuing program of economic opportunity for the poor. Public works typically incur vast start-up and ongoing costs; these costs will tend to be lower if the participants are literate, healthy, and readily able to get to work. From this perspective, educational services, food and housing subsidies, and access to public transportation, for example, are essential complements to public works programs. On the benefits side, there are obvious limits to public works as an antipoverty tool. Public works are based on the fundamental idea that the most abundant asset of the poor is their labor, but many of the poor (e.g., the elderly, disabled, working mothers) are limited in their capacity to work or cannot work without making undesirable tradeoffs (e.g., worse child care for greater household income). What this segment of the poor needs is not just full-time employment through public works, but also expanded safety net schemes that complement opportunities for flexible work.[9]

In 1784, Thomas Jefferson wrote to George Washington, "A most powerful objection always arises to propositions of [public works]. It is that public undertakings are carelessly managed and much money spent to little purpose." More than two centuries later, the same objection is commonly heard today: Critics intone that public works lead to large bureaucratic structures that generate "make-work" jobs and crowd out the private sector. However, well-designed public works programs that prioritize job training, collaborate closely with community-led organizations and local authorities, and work in tandem with other antipoverty initiatives can play a significant role in transferring much-needed social and economic benefits to the most needy.[10]

Civic Works: The Case for a Strong Workforce Training Component

David Bowman
> David Bowman is the director of research and special projects at the Louisiana Recovery Authority in the Disaster Recovery Unit.

In the wake of a national recession and rising unemployment rates, an influx of government investments in infrastructure will not only promote employment, but also, and more importantly, allow for the modernization of our infrastructure throughout the Gulf Coast. Keynesian theory promotes government investments in times of high unemployment, but in the case of the extremely devastated Gulf Coast, the benefits of rebuilding critical infrastructure are just as important for the long-term economic vitality of the region.

The Gulf Coast, particularly Louisiana, is unique in many ways, including natural resources, culture, and labor force. Outside of the metropolitan area of New Orleans, oil and gas, chemicals, agriculture, and fisheries are vital economic sectors. The city proper, however, has relied heavily on the tourism and hospitality industry and on an abundance of low-wage jobs. Louisiana as a whole and New Orleans in particular have suffered from low educational attainment rates and a correlated low labor force participation rate. A public works program that does not take these factors into consideration may boost the economy in the short term, but in the long term it will not have the desired effect of moving native Louisianans into the mainstream workforce.

For this reason, Myers-Lipton's second key lesson learned is critical: "The federal government must work together with local and state partners at all stages of the public works project." In Louisiana, because of our low literacy rates and low labor force participation rates, the workforce training aspect is critical to any successful jobs program. And in order for any program to work appropriately, there will need to be flexibility in the use of these rebuilding dollars. Flexibility should include the supports necessary to make both workforce training and workforce participation viable. For many of our citizens, the lack of reliable transportation or child care, including after-school programs, prevents participation. Others lack the basic literacy that is increasingly necessary to maintain a job in the new economy.

The Gulf Coast Civic Works provides an opportunity to provide a literacy component even while the participant may be working an "unskilled" job. The combination of literacy and job experience could provide the needed boost that keeps participants in the workforce following the program. The recovery of the Gulf Coast and New Orleans is not a three-year or even a five-year task; it is easily a fifteen-year task. Having said that, we will need to think early about transitioning from a construction-based economy to more long-term sustainable opportunities that build on the existing strengths of our region; this can be done only if we give participants the basic skills required to retool, i.e., basic literacy, numeracy, and life skills.

Could we have a civic works program in Louisiana that does not build our workforce? I am certain the answer is yes. We would likely cannibalize our existing workforce from our much-needed construction, shipbuilding, and oil and gas industries, driving up wages and exacerbating the challenges of our existing workforce shortage. Or we would end up temporarily bringing in workers that would rebuild. Many of these would eventually leave, and we would still leave many of our most vulnerable (many of whom are still displaced) either unable to return or unable to maintain the post-Katrina increase in rents and utilities. In the end, we would have rebuilt our infrastructure without lifting our most vulnerable out of poverty. We would also be denying the fifth lesson learned: "Take into consideration issues of equity."

A strong workforce component and workforce supports will admittedly increase the costs of projects in the short term. But this investment in our human capital will pay dividends in the long term. These costs can be reduced through creative partnerships with local governments and nonprofit organizations that can provide some of these needed supports. For example, picture AmeriCorps volunteers establishing after-school programs so that parents can work a full day or pursue training.

Or nonprofits working together to provide interim housing solutions for program participants, after-hours tutoring, or counseling. These types of partnerships are often lost once a federal funding stream is established and the focus shifts to implementation.

A just society is one that provides opportunities for all of its citizens. If we are to move toward a world in which every able adult is offered the pride, satisfaction, and inclusion that come with the ability to contribute to society based on his or her talents, we must take full advantage of the opportunities to build individual capacity. The Gulf Coast Civics Works initiative is one such opportunity that we should not let pass.

Civic Works: Training Today's Rosie the Riveter

Julie Kuklinski

Julie Kuklinski is the director of the Women in Construction Program at Moore Community House in Biloxi, Mississippi.

Remember Rosie the Riveter? This cultural icon represented the 6 million women who entered the workforce during World War II in the military factories and support services, including steel and lumber mills, foundries, and shipyards. These nontraditional occupations provided women the opportunity for upward mobility and self-esteem.

Today, the United States needs to train the next generation of Rosie the Riveters. As many working women recognize, policy leaders do not consider women's socioeconomic advancement as vital to our nation's economic security because too many jobs are segregated by gender and pay too little. Clearly, we are not taking full advantage of the economic potential of half of our population and are not addressing the issues that women face. The United States needs to provide women an opportunity to obtain careers in jobs that have been historically denied because this has proved successful in providing them access to quality and affordable child care and transportation, fair wages with benefits, and an increase of reproductive education.

In the Gulf Coast, the best method to do this is to enact the Gulf Coast Civic Works Act. This pilot program will provide investment in public infrastructure and will create 100,000 jobs and training opportunities on the Gulf Coast so that we can rebuild our communities. It will also demonstrate how women are viable assets to our nation's economic security.

The Gulf Coast region is often cited as one of the least resourced areas in the country. The hurricanes in the recent past have exacerbated an already difficult economic environment. Today, we see too few families, particularly mothers and children and women of color, returning to their homes, often ancestral homes, because of a number of factors: lack of affordable housing, jobs, child care, and adequate schools. Those families residing in the area tend to be poor, to be less likely to have health insurance, and to earn substandard wages.

According to the Self-Sufficiency Standard developed by Wider Opportunities for Women, a woman in Mississippi who is the sole breadwinner for her two children would have to earn almost $10 per hour to make ends meet, which is almost twice the state minimum wage. According to the Institute on Women's Policy Research, Mississippi has been ranked at or near the bottom of the fifty states during the last ten years in terms of women's poverty and health.[11]

These high poverty rates among women can be attributed mostly to the continued segregation of women in the workplace and their confinement to low-paying and low-quality jobs. To reverse this phenomenon, women must be prepared to compete for and succeed in jobs that pay higher wages and offer good benefits. Jobs in the trades, such as in construction, offer these kind of employment, often at three times the wages than those jobs in which women without strong educational backgrounds are usually concentrated.

Based out of Biloxi, Mississippi, Moore Community House (MCH) responded by creating a program to train women for these higher-paying jobs. To meet the overall organizational mission, Women in Construction (WinC) was established as an MCH program in June 2007. The mission of this program is to create a climate across the Gulf Coast that empowers women to pursue careers that will earn wages to promote self-sufficiency within the field of trades. The WinC program is the only construction training program for women available on the Mississippi Gulf Coast. It is a vital resource for women seeking sustainable careers and a living wage. Continued support through the Gulf Coast Civic Works Act will enable WinC to expand its programming, reach a greater amount of women, enhance leadership development among the students, and further strengthen this community as it redevelops. A funding commitment covering basic operating expenses in WinC's early years will provide this already strong and valuable fledgling program the stability it needs to serve the community for many years to come.

The indirect benefit of the Gulf Coast Civic Works Act will affect the lives of women in a significant number of ways. First, it will enable women who are otherwise unemployed or earning substandard wages to develop long-term skills that will help them and their families be self-sufficient for years to come, while at the same time contributing to the area's tax base. Second, the innovative design of the project will take into consideration the special needs of women and their families to make the project a success, which can then be replicated throughout the Gulf Coast and the entire country. Third, in order for the project to be successful, it will be necessary to involve many parts of the community in this effort, ranging from government and employers to postsecondary education leaders, with the result being that we will have begun to reshape traditional notions of what is and is not women's work. Lastly, the project will make an important contribution to the revitalization of the Gulf Coast community through the trainees' ability to participate in the rebuilding of key sites through both the construction and the sustainable development training tracks.

Not only is the WinC program a ready-to-go project, but we have seen a strong coalition of organizations on the Gulf Coast region supporting one another through resource sharing while working toward the shared goal of expanding upon the rich culture and potential of every single person on the Gulf Coast. The potential is there, the need is great, but keep in mind that resources are running thin. The Gulf Coast Civic Works Act responds to such a humanitarian crisis and is built upon the heart of a region that has not given up hope. This piece of legislation will show how governmental investment in public infrastructure can and will support local initiatives already in place and create 100,000 jobs on the Gulf Coast. This legislation will also show the rest of the nation that we can rebuild our local communities and country as a whole.

Community Organizing After Hurricane Katrina: Lessons Learned

Stephen Bradberry
    Stephen Bradberry is the coordinator of national campaigns for the Association of Community Organizations for Reform Now (ACORN).
The science of community organizing in the United States of America is one of working with people to access the tools necessary to, as much as possible, fully experience life, liberty, and the pursuit of happiness. The work of community organizing is listening to people, identifying commonalities and forming relationships, and moving those people from sitting on the sofa complaining about what they see on the news and experience

in their day-to-day lives to becoming leaders, voicing their concerns to those who determine the events governing local, city, state, and national affairs. The art of it all is the ability to work with people across regional, racial, or other determinants of who is to be considered a friend or foe toward creating an America that is fair and equitable in its consideration of who gets access to the tools necessary for the fullest expression possible of life, liberty, and the pursuit of happiness.

Following the hurricane season of 2005, residents of the Gulf Coast of the United States found themselves the victims of decisions being made about the future of their lives, livelihoods, and well-being without their input. Shortly after the disasters struck (there were two hurricanes that year—Katrina and Rita), local, state, and federal representatives provided the framework for recovery through exclusion. Here are just three examples:

- On September 8, 2005, James Reiss, the appointed chair of the Infrastructure Committee for the Bring New Orleans Back Committee, was quoted in an article entitled "Old Line Families Plot the Future" as saying, "Those who want to see this city rebuilt want to see it done in a completely different way: demographically, geographically, and politically, I'm not just speaking for myself here."[12]
- On September 10, 2005, Louisiana representative Richard Baker (R) was quoted in the *Wall Street Journal* saying: "We finally cleaned up public housing in New Orleans. We couldn't do it, but God did."[13]
- On September 28, 2005, Alphonso Jackson, secretary of Housing and Urban Development, was quoted in the *Houston Chronicle* as saying, "New Orleans is not going to be as black as it was for a long time, if ever again."[14]

It is important to appreciate the gravity of these statements. New Orleans, prior to the 2005 hurricane season, was demographically close to 70 percent African American, economically working class, and politically Democratic. As such, these previous statements made by key decisionmakers at the city, state, and national levels spoke directly to an intention to generate a recovery effort that would exclude the voice of the majority of people to be impacted by the results of that recovery.

Initial organizing efforts focused on providing emergency response and reestablishing the right to return. The efforts of local organizations were heroic in that not only did they maintain, or in many cases increase, their workload, but they also did so under the duress of staff and leadership who were experiencing many of the same obstacles as the people they served. As groups and organizations across the Gulf Coast region (Louisiana, Alabama, and Mississippi) began to look up from the emergency response and focus on recovery, there was a realization that a regionwide program would be necessary to ensure a fair and equitable recovery.

That regionwide plan began to take shape as two concurrent collaborative campaigns developed along the Gulf Coast for the purpose of winning passage of the GCCW Act: The Gulf Coast Civic Works Campaign, led by ACORN, and the RFK Center for Justice and Human Rights focused on organizing in the region; and the Gulf Coast Civic Works Project out of San José State University focused on organizing students across the United States. As the GCCW campaign grew, there came an awareness of the need to develop parallel policies in the areas of housing, education, and so on. Simultaneously, the Equity and Inclusion (E&I) Campaign began working with organizations across the Gulf Coast to form a coalition focused on developing policy in the areas of housing, education, health care, workers' rights, and economic development. In 2008, the GCCWP, the GCCW campaign, and E&I merged efforts; by the end of 2008, more than 200 community-, faith-, and student-based organizations had joined the campaign to pass the GCCW Act.

In early 2009 as the new president, America's first African American president, Barack Obama works though the beginning of his presidency, it is necessary for the success of the campaign to implement an act of *Sankofa. Sankofa*, in the Ghanaian language of Akan, means to reach back and grasp the essence of the past before moving forward. According to Charles Payne, the author of *I've Got the Light of Freedom: The Organizing Tradition and the Mississippi Freedom Struggle*, one of the major factors in the success of the voter registration campaign in 1960s Mississippi resulted from the efforts of the Student Non Violent Coordinating Committee to establish relationships within communities that allowed it to organize people into going down to the courthouse to register to vote.

The "essence" in this case is the mobilization of people within communities based upon established relationships that provide support and security. In this current campaign, the organizational relationships have been built. It is now time to go deeper, down into the memberships and constituencies of these community-, faith-, and student-based organizations. The movement of the campaign among these individuals, reached through their organizations, is the vehicle through which the science, art, and work of organizing can take place. In 2009, as the United States of America ponders how to recover from the debacle of the 2007 housing crises and the 2008 economic crises, the Gulf Coast Civic Works Act provides a unique organizing opportunity for a community-led American recovery starting with the recovery of the American Gulf Coast.[15]

Helping End the Human Rights Crisis in the Gulf Coast: Sound Policy, Smart Politics

Jeffrey Buchanan

> Jeffrey Buchanan is a human rights advocate currently serving in the Information Office at the RFK Center for Justice and Human Rights, in Washington, DC. He is also a Taproots Fellow with the Center for Community Change. He helped cofound the Gulf Coast Civic Works Campaign.

In 2007 the Opportunity Agenda found that eight in ten Americans agree that "we should strive to uphold human rights in the U.S. because there are people being denied their human rights in our country." In fact 77 percent of people believe the federal government should work on making regular progress on human rights. The federal response to Hurricane Katrina, which a majority of Americans viewed as violating human rights, is a prime example of why our nation must strive to uphold such principles and what can happen to leaders who fail to uphold them.[16]

The federal response to Hurricane Katrina was a shocking blow to our national psyche, decimating public confidence in President George W. Bush and ushering in sweeping electoral shifts in 2006 and 2008. Pollster John Zogby noted that voters in his polling after Hurricane Katrina saw a "structural failure of our system of government" and "hungered" for more responsive federal leadership that could muster necessary resources and have the flexibility to work with nongovernmental organizations, faith-based organizations, and local governments to adequately confront a crisis.[17]

Vulnerable populations, including women, low-income, African American, and immigrant communities, suffered well-documented abuses at the hands of numerous levels of government before, during, and after the storm. Hundreds of thousands of residents who evacuated the Gulf Coast after Hurricanes Katrina and Rita remain unable to return home. The slow pace of recovery in low-income neighborhoods has resulted in the collapse of institutions, including housing, schools, transportation, health care, and public safety. These challenges, along with persistent poverty, abusive labor practices, environmental degradation, and inadequate flood protection, all add up to an American human rights crisis along the Gulf Coast.[18]

Community organizers and advocates responded by demanding that the federal government step up to ensure the rights of their communities and that their voices be heard in the recovery, demands backed up by the United Nations' Guiding Principles on Internal Displacement.[19] These principles outline how to treat with dignity people forced to flee their communities after a disaster, defining their rights to housing, health care, and food as well as their rights to participate in recovery decisions and to have jobs or income to support their family. The principles declare that the federal government has a duty to create conditions that allow displaced people to voluntarily return home to live with safety and dignity, ensuring a right to return. Though the guiding principles are not legally binding, they are composed of relevant international human rights and humanitarian laws, including the 1948 Universal Declaration of Human Rights, of which the United States was a passionate endorser.[20]

The United States violated many of these principles, as elaborated in a 2006 brief to the UN Human Rights Committee and subsequently in a comprehensive report by the Institute for Southern Studies. In defense of these claims, U.S. officials in 2007 told the UN Human Rights Committee that they did not believe that Katrina's displaced survivors, whom they evasively labeled *evacuees,* deserved such protections.

The Gulf Coast Civic Works Act aims to implement these principles to confront the recovery challenges after our nation's largest displacement. The program utilizes a hybrid model of partnerships between local communities and the federal government similar to the one pictured by Zogby and a rights-based framework to create 100,000 jobs and training opportunities for rebuilding infrastructure, restoring the environment, and conserving energy. The policy aims to empower the region's greatest assets—the disaster's survivors—with the resources they need to help realize their human rights and revitalize their communities.

A renewed vision of community participation allows representative community based organization seats at the table to determine how recovery funds are spent to address the most pressing unmet needs facing their community, whether it be rebuilding schools, housing, health centers, libraries, day care centers, fire stations, or flood control; restoring wetlands and watersheds; or weatherizing homes, retrofitting buildings, or installing solar panels to conserve energy. Innovative partnerships with community and faith-based organizations would not only leverage their institutional knowledge and scale up their previous successes but also build capacity for future community development. Low-income families could find new ladders of economic opportunities thanks to increased funding for job training in critical recovery-related industries and first-source hiring for displaced survivors and local residents and apprenticeship requirements. Funding would finally address the interrelated challenges that kept thousands of displaced families from returning.

Even though there may be no magic bullet to overcome the immense social and economic realities along the Gulf Coast, an adequately funded civic works program would be a major step in beginning to address abuses. With such wide support for human rights and a new model of robust and flexible federal leadership in a crisis, support for civic works may be not only good policy but also good politics.

CHAPTER 6
AN ECONOMIC BILL OF RIGHTS

In *Social Solutions to Poverty,* I concluded by challenging readers to select one of the forty-plus poverty strategies discussed in the book and
to get busy implementing it. As I said in the beginning of this book, if
I had taken up my own challenge, I would not have chosen civic works.
At the time I wrote the book, conservatives controlled the entire federal government, so a civic works project had little chance of becoming
enacted. However, in late August 2005 all of that changed when Hurricane Katrina blew threw the Gulf Coast. Hurricane Katrina exposed
to the nation and the world our secret—that the United States leads the
industrialized nations in poverty rates and that our public infrastructure
is literally crumbling.

Many Bush administration insiders argue that the federal government's
inept response to Hurricane Katrina caused the downfall of George W.
Bush and created an opening for the Democrats, which ultimately led to
the Democrats taking control of both houses of Congress and Barack
Obama getting elected president. In a March 12, 2009, article in *The Nation,* Melissa Harris-Lacewell, associate professor of politics and African
American studies at Princeton, and James Perry, executive director of
the Greater New Orleans Fair Housing Action Center, argue this same
point: "Katrina is the wedge that opened the door for Democrats, and
this new Democratic administration and Congress owe a particular debt
to the people of the Gulf Coast." Fortunately for the Gulf Coast Civic
Works (GCCW) campaign, Harris-Lacewell and Perry go on to say that
"President Obama and his party must repay that debt. They can begin
by passing the Gulf Coast Civic Works Act (HR 4048). This bill uses

job creation and infrastructure investment to promote economic growth along the Gulf Coast."[1]

Roosevelt, Truman, and King and Economic Rights

In some way, civic works chose me; I did not choose civic works. It was just the solution that made the most sense following Hurricanes Katrina and Rita. At the same time, I had decided after writing *Social Solutions to Poverty* that Dr. King's call for an economic bill of rights provided the correct framework to end poverty in America. King's vision of the Beloved Community lifted my soul, but it was his policy suggestions based within a framework of an economic bill of rights that gave me practical solutions. However, King was not the first to call for an economic bill of rights; that distinction goes to President Franklin Roosevelt.

As World War II neared its conclusion, Roosevelt began to refocus his efforts at home, calling for the United States to develop an economic bill of rights. Based on Roosevelt's four freedoms—freedom of speech and expression, freedom of religion, freedom from want, and freedom from fear—he argued that the Bill of Rights had provided Americans with the ability to pursue life and liberty, but not happiness. He believed that the rise of industrial capitalism made the pursuit of happiness impossible because all could not attain economic security in this system. To correct this situation, FDR proposed a second bill of rights, but instead of focusing on political rights, it would focus on economic rights. Roosevelt enumerated these economic rights by stating that a second bill of rights should include

> the right to a useful and remunerative job in the industries or shops or farms or mines of the nation; The right to earn enough to provide adequate food and clothing and recreation; The right of every farmer to raise and sell his products at a return which will give him and his family a decent living; The right of every businessman, large and small, to trade in an atmosphere of freedom from unfair competition and domination by monopolies at home or abroad; The right of every family to a decent home; The right to adequate medical care and the opportunity to achieve and enjoy good health; The right to adequate protection from the economic fears of old age, sickness, accident, and unemployment; The right to a good education.[2]

Regrettably, Roosevelt died before implementing these economic rights, so it was left to his successor, Harry Truman.

In his 1945 State of the Union Address, President Truman announced that he planned to implement FDR's economic bill of rights so that all Americans would have the right to a living-wage job, a decent home, and health insurance. Later that year, Truman supported the passage of the Full Employment Act of 1945, which declared that all Americans were "entitled to an opportunity for useful and remunerative, regular, and full-time employment" and that government needed to provide the necessary expenditures to reach full employment. Conservatives were opposed, and they argued that the bill was socialistic. By the time the Employment Act of 1946 passed, its name had been changed, its major provisions had been eliminated, and the language had been weakened to just "promote" maximum employment. A housing bill suffered the same fate as the employment bill. Truman argued that the free market would not build enough homes for low-income people and that it was therefore necessary for the federal government to play an active role in ensuring all Americans a decent home. Originally, the housing bill proposed that the federal government would build hundreds of thousands of new homes, with many targeted for low-income people. However, by the time the housing act passed Congress, these provisions were greatly weakened. Lastly, conservatives, with the help of the American Medical Association (AMA), worked to defeat national health insurance, which doctors argued would reduce the quality of health care and take away their professional independence. Unfortunately, the AMA failed to recognize that its "reduction of the quality of health care" argument was meaningless for Americans who did not have access to adequate medical care because they did not have the money to pay for it.[3]

In the mid-1960s, Dr. Martin Luther King would pick up on Roosevelt and Truman's plan for an economic bill of rights. King argued that blacks' equality with whites would not be achieved unless there was fundamental change in American society. King characterized the changes up to 1966—including the Civil Rights Act of 1964 and the Voting Rights Act of 1965—as "surface changes," and he called on the civil rights movement to transform itself into a human rights movement because he felt that the former had done little to change the poverty of black Americans.[4]

To solve poverty in America, King made three policy proposals: a public works New Deal–like program assuring full employment, a guaranteed income at middle-class-income levels for the poor, elderly, and disabled, and the construction of 5 million new low-income housing units in ten years. Under King's proposal of public works and a guaranteed income, black Americans, as well as whites and other people of color who lived in poverty, would be lifted into the middle class and would be able to provide for themselves adequate housing, food, clothing, and health care. King's pronouncement on public works is still relevant today: "We must develop a federal program of public works, retraining, and jobs for all— so that none, white or black, will have cause to feel threatened. At the present time, thousands of jobs a week are disappearing in the wake of automation and other production efficiency techniques. Black and white, we will all be harmed unless something grand and imaginative is done. The unemployed, poverty-stricken white man must be made to realize that he is in the very same boat with the Negro. Together, they could exert massive pressure on Government to get jobs for all. Together, they could form a grand alliance."[5]

King argued that the richest nation in the world had the financial means to provide full employment for those who were able to work and to guarantee an income for those who were not. King recognized that public works and a guaranteed income would cost the United States money, but he declared: "It didn't cost the nation one penny to integrate lunch counters. It didn't cost the nation one penny to guarantee the right to vote. But now we are dealing with issues that cannot be solved without the nation spending billions of dollars and undergoing a radical redistribution of economic power." King would also state, "If our nation can spend $35 billion dollars a year to fight an unjust, evil war in Vietnam, and $20 billion dollars to put a man on the moon, it can spend billions of dollars to put God's children on their own two feet right here on earth." Dr. King dedicated the last two years of his life to this goal of ending poverty through public works and a guaranteed income.[6]

With the assassination of Dr. King, and then of Robert Kennedy, the issue of poverty faded into the background of mainstream debate. However, America was shocked out of its slumber in late August 2005 when the issue of poverty, as well as race, gripped the nation and world as we watched our brothers and sisters of the Gulf Coast, especially in New Orleans, suffer so greatly as they waited for assistance at the Superdome, at the Convention Center, and on rooftops for five days without adequate food, water, or shelter. Interestingly, the media had become so unaccustomed to covering our poverty crisis that they did not have the language to describe the social suffering they were seeing. What word the media did come up with was *refugee,* as if somehow the winds of Katrina blew away the citizenship of Gulf Coast residents.

As a result of Hurricane Katrina, the predominantly black city of New Orleans was hit hard, but the social suffering extended to the Vietnamese

American communities in New Orleans East and Biloxi, the Native American communities in Louisiana and Mississippi, and white communities all along the Gulf Coast. Katrina was a defining moment in U.S. history: It exposed the hidden face of poverty. Today, 37 million people, or 13 percent of the total population, are in poverty. Incredibly, 18 percent of American children live in poverty.[7]

As described earlier, a group of students and faculty started a movement to bring a modern-day New Deal to the Gulf Coast. Today, this campaign has grown to 200 community, faith, environmental, student, and human rights organizations advocating for the Gulf Coast Civic Works Act. For many of the organizers of the campaign, the act is a pilot project that can be replicated in other parts of the nation. For still others, this movement for a national civic works project is an attempt to fulfill the vision of Roosevelt, Truman, and King, which is to ensure that all Americans have a living-wage job. Because of the nation's economic and infrastructure crisis, now is the time to fulfill this vision.

The Imperative to Rebuild

As stated throughout this book, America must rebuild. It must do so because the average American worker is in trouble. American workers have faced stagnating or declining wages since the 1980s, but now with the economic downturn, workers are in crisis, as they have suffered massive layoffs and record home foreclosures. One result has been the rise of "tent cities" in Nashville, Tennessee; Sacramento and Fresno, California; Seattle and Olympia, Washington; and St. Petersburg, Florida. As Mayor Kevin Johnson of Sacramento says, "We're seeing an expanded definition of the homeless population, meaning homeowners and families that were intact who've lost their jobs and homes." In addition, America must rebuild because its infrastructure is in need. Bridges are falling, levees and dams are collapsing, and students are attending dilapidated schools. And even though these examples are the most extreme, the reality is that the entire American infrastructure is in need of repair. This infrastructure crisis is a threat to the nation's economy, health, and national security. It is time to rebuild America.[8]

Clearly, the nation is moving in this direction. People across the political spectrum now support the rebuilding of America through public works, as can be seen in the recent outpouring of support by business groups, labor unions, environmentalists, politicians, and, most important, the American people. In fact, big business and big labor have joined forces to promote public works projects. Bob Baugh, executive director of the Industrial Union Council of the American Federation of Labor–Congress of Industrial Organizations (AFL-CIO), reports, "The nation's building trades and manufacturing workers have been knocked flat on their backs by the economic downturn." Recently, the AFL-CIO has joined forces with Consolidated Edison of New York, a large utility company, and the National Wildlife Federation to launch "Rebuilding America," a campaign to promote public works to solve America's economic and infrastructure crises. As part of the campaign, Rebuilding America wrote an open letter to Senate majority leader Harry Reid (D-NV) during the debate over Obama's stimulus package, asking him to double the amount of money going toward energy efficiency. The Rebuilding America campaign argued that an "allocation of $20 billion in the pending economic recovery package would retrofit 4 million buildings in the next two years, create an immediate job development program, and help put America on track to dramatically decrease energy use in our built environment."[9]

Even the probusiness U.S. Chamber of Commerce has come out in full support of public investment in infrastructure. After the passage of Obama's stimulus bill, the Chamber of Commerce took out newspaper ads stating that, even though this was a "great opening act," it's time for "the feature performance." The Chamber of Commerce urged Congress and the president to develop a long-term investment plan for American infrastructure. The Chamber of Commerce argued: "Congress and the Obama Administration must take action to finish the job by developing long-term plans for maintaining, modernizing, and expanding the nation's infrastructure. Without proper investment and attention to these networks, the nation's economic stability, potential for job growth and competitiveness are threatened."[10]

Another group that supports public works to rebuild America is the climate change community. For example, the Sierra Club supports the effort to rebuild America but argues that it must be done with "high performance homes and buildings: Smarter, greener buildings that eliminate global warming emissions, reduce utility bills, and generate renewable energy." In a similar vein, Jonathan Rose, a board member of the Natural Resources Defense Council, states that the effort to rebuild America needs to lay the foundation for a new climate-based prosperity "focusing on the transformational benefits of investing in clean, smart energy systems, light rail systems, wind, solar, and energy efficiency."[11]

As stated earlier, the support for rebuilding America through public works has a powerful ally in the president. Soon after Obama was elected president, he responded to the deteriorating economic situation by announcing plans to rebuild America. A week after Obama pushed through his stimulus package, he spoke to a joint session of Congress for the first time, stating, "We will rebuild, we will recover, and the United States of America will emerge stronger than before." Clearly, Obama is a major supporter of rebuilding America through public works. And perhaps most important, the American people support this effort to rebuild America. In a 2008 poll, 95 percent of voters felt it was important to modernize and upgrade the country's bridges, roads, and energy facilities; 87 percent agreed that the economic health of the nation was at risk without appropriate investment in infrastructure.[12]

However, as noted throughout this book, public works can take many forms. As stated in Chapters 2 and 4, public works projects could be designed in a top-down, governor-and-mayor-directed, big-contractor-focused way, with modest oversight and great waste. This is not the model the nation should choose. Rather, the civic works model that has been supported and vetted in the Gulf Coast provides the nation with an example that is resident-led, provides strong oversight, ensures that the federal government works closely with local and state partners, guarantees that local contractors are included, and provides for equitable development.

A Permanent Civic Works Agency

At some point, the country will need a permanent civic works agency. New Dealers talked extensively about the need to create a permanent public works agency that during bad economic times would be in full swing and that during good times would be used less, but would be active in gathering data for future projects if the economy entered a recession or depression. Thus, a permanent American civic works agency would avoid having to start from scratch every time there was an economic downturn. Also, with some civic works projects going on even in good times, full employment could be achieved, which would put upward pressure on wages and help to reduce poverty.

Of course, many conservatives will oppose this idea for a permanent national civic works agency. Unfortunately, these conservatives do not want to deal with the reality that capitalism does not create enough good-paying jobs for all Americans to pursue happiness. Dr. King noted this when he stated, "We also know that no matter how dynamically the economy develops and expands it does not eliminate all poverty." A clear example of this occurred during the Clinton presidency when the United States experienced one of the greatest economic expansions in the nation's history. In 1999, at the end of this expansion, unemployment was 4.2 percent annually, but overall poverty was at 11.8 percent and children's poverty was still at 16.9 percent. So even after a great economic expansion, poverty remained high. The problem was not that the American economy could not produce enough jobs; it obviously did. The problem has been that the American economy produces too many poverty-level jobs. Clearly, America needs a permanent civic works agency to create millions more living-wage jobs even after the economic crisis ends. These civic works jobs, which cannot be offshored, will be beneficial to the pocketbooks of the civic workers and will push up wages because businesses will be encouraged to match these higher salaries. This permanent civic works agency will take the nation one step closer to Roosevelt's, Truman's, and King's dream for an economic bill of rights.[13]

Twelve Lessons on Social Action

In the "Sociology 164: Social Action" course, which generated the Gulf Coast Civic Works Project, the students continually reflect on the various actions they are taking in the community. To end this book, I will do the same. Twelve lessons have emerged from this campaign. They are think big; act humbly; frame the "change idea" in a historical context; focus the demand on a specific target; get face-to-face with people in power; ensure that a campaign has movement; emphasize commonalities when working in coalition; develop media skills; be persistent; do not worry about money; recognize that democratic space is necessary for the long haul; and develop a bigger vision than the campaign.

Think Big

Do not be afraid to think big. How can we end poverty in America and in the world? How can we stop war? How can we end violence against women? These types of visionary questions are at the heart of many religious traditions and have inspired humans for thousands of years. Most likely, they will inspire you, your friends, and your colleagues.

Since you are asking big questions, your answers will be big as well. Overcome your fear that you can really make a difference, and share your big questions and solutions with others. See what their reaction is. A key lesson from the Gulf Coast Civic Works Project is that a group of students and faculty 2,100 miles away from the Gulf Coast can work in solidarity with residents from the region to build a major movement to change America.

Act Humbly

When sharing your "big idea" with community members, do so humbly. Know that people have been thinking about these issues for a long time. And know that people, especially those from different socioeconomic backgrounds, ethnic and racial backgrounds, gender and sexual orientations, or regions of the country, will be sensitive when someone comes and offers a solution to "their problem."

In this project, the students and faculty always started the initial conversation by saying that we humbly offer this idea, that many of us are not from the region, and that we have done everything possible to include the voices of the people from the Gulf Coast in the language of the bill and in our advocacy efforts. Since the students and faculty have not imposed a solution, have been sensitive to the history of the region, and have included local residents at all levels of the project, people generally have been open to hearing more about it.

Frame the "Change Idea" in a Historical Context

The project has been successful in framing civic works and the activities of the campaign in a historical context The project has tried to convey that this federal legislation is neither radical nor new; instead, it is a practical solution deeply rooted in the American context. Practically, this has meant that the campaign has used the language of "A New Deal for the Gulf Coast" and has highlighted the many accomplishments of the New Deal public workers.

Another example of how the campaign has tried to frame our change idea in a historical context is when the project adopted the language of "Louisiana Winter," a reference to Mississippi Freedom Summer. The hope was to ground this return trip to the Gulf Coast in American history and to say to the nation that there is nothing odd or radical about students working for justice in the Gulf Coast. In fact, we tried to make the point that this is what American students do when a perceived injustice has occurred.

The raised fists are a key symbol of the GCCWP. (Courtesy of Mark Macala)

In addition, the students framed their change idea in a historical context by choosing raised fists to symbolize their movement. The raised fist has historically represented the struggle for power and justice. At San José State, raised fists have increased symbolic value because of the actions taken by Tommie Smith and John Carlos, the two Olympic athletes who raised their fists in Mexico City against racism and poverty in a struggle called the "Olympic Project for Human Rights." In this same way, students in the Gulf Coast Civic Works Project referred to the campaign as "this generation's human rights struggle."

This reference to human rights connected these current students to the struggles of Smith and Carlos. It also connected them to the larger civil rights struggle of the 1960s, as well as to Dr. Martin Luther King, who by 1965 had moved away from the language of civil rights and toward the language of human rights, which included economic deprivation and poverty. In the case of the Gulf Coast, human rights also included the internationally recognized rights of displaced persons to return home after a natural or social disaster.

Focus the Demand on a Specific Target

The GCCW campaign has always remembered one of the key lessons of community organizing: A demand must be directed at a specific target within an institution. Many times, people who want to bring about change will hold an event or a demonstration and not tie their specific demand to a target. This type of event may educate the general population, but it rarely leads to change. What leads to change is directing the group's energy at a specific target that has the institutional power to bring about the change the group desires.

A key part of this process is choosing the target. In the case of the Gulf Coast Civic Works campaign, the targets generally have been specific members of Congress and the president. As described in this book, the campaign has focused its energy on Speaker of the House Nancy Pelosi (D-CA) and key members of Congress such as Senator Mary Landrieu (D-LA) and Representative Bennie Thompson (D-MS). And even though the request may be a bit different depending on a person's role within an institution, the campaign has had a laserlike focus in asking its targets to use their institutional power to help enact the Gulf Coast Civic Works Act. For example, the campaign asked Senator Landrieu to introduce a companion bill to HR 2269 into the Senate, asked Representative Thompson and other representatives to cosponsor the GCCW Act in the House, and asked President Obama to sign an executive order authorizing GCCW Projects.

So to bring about change, take time to think about who has the institutional power to do so, and then develop a series of group actions directed at that person (e.g., phone-in and e-mail campaigns, rallies at her or his office). Importantly, the target should be consistently presented with the group's specific demand.

Get Face-to-Face with People in Power

The students and faculty have discovered that if they can get in front of their target (a person in a position of institutional power), there is a good chance they will be able to persuade her or him to support the GCCW Act. This happened again and again. One of the most powerful examples occurred with Representative Bennie Thompson, chair of the Department of Homeland Security, who had publicly stated in January 2007 that he was going to take the lead in the effort to pass a modern-day civic works project for the Gulf Coast. However, after almost two years Thompson had not even signed on as a cosponsor of the bill. Finally, we had the opportunity to talk to Thompson directly at the Democratic National Convention in August 2008. When asked in person if he would support the bill, he was immediate and direct in his response: "Yes" he said, and then he pointed to one of his staff members in the audience and told us to tell him that Thompson was signing on as a cosponsor. It was that simple. When we cut through all the staff and we were face-to-face, he immediately signed on. Not only is this type of action important to do for the practical reason of gaining supporters; it is also very empowering to get a member of Congress to agree to a campaign's position in a face-to-face meeting.

Students travel to the state capitol in Sacramento, California, to speak face-to-face with people in power. (Courtesy of Scott Myers-Lipton)

Ensure That a Campaign Has Movement

The necessity of having movement in a campaign is something spelled out in many community organizing books. To meet this goal, the project worked diligently to develop a series of well-planned events to keep up the momentum. The project created spring, fall, and winter events. Each of these events fit into a yearlong calendar that drove the movement. They included the following:

- January: Louisiana Winter
- February: Mardi Gras
- April: Post-Katrina National Summit
- August: Katrina anniversary event
- October: Dillard conference "Rebuild the Gulf Coast: Rebuild America"
- November: Campus Sleep-out

Interestingly, these events continue to develop over time. For example, the November event that spawned the GCCW Project was initially entitled "Poverty Under the Stars," but then it morphed into a national campus sleep-out under the banner "A New Deal for the Gulf Coast." For the third annual event, the focus of the sleep-out had changed again to "American Tent City." Although all of these events dealt with poverty, homelessness, and the GCCW Act, each event was responding to the social conditions of the time, which was necessary to keep the movement fresh.

Emphasize Commonalities When Working in Coalition

The Gulf Coast Civic Works campaign has built a powerful coalition of more than 200 organizations. The campaign has brought together groups such as the Association of Community Organizations for Reform Now, the largest low- to moderate-income community-based organization in the country and known for direct confrontation with the power elite, and All Congregations Together and Bayou Interfaith Shared Community Organizing, two coalitions of faith-based communities from New Orleans and the bayou, respectively. The campaign found that when it focused on what organizations shared, the smaller issues, such as different organizational cultures and social change perspectives, became less important. Perhaps this proved true because all the coalition members realized that the Gulf Coast was in crisis and that the region needed "all hands on deck" if a solution was going to be enacted. In practical terms, this led the more progressive elements in the coalition to understand that they would have to play a background role at times, particularly in talking with conservative lawmakers.

Coalition members communicated weekly, and many times daily, to ensure that everyone was on the same page with the message and strategy. Several times throughout the campaign, there was a need for a frank discussion when one coalition member felt that another member had done something outside of what was agreed to or had done something that was potentially harmful to the campaign. Honesty was a key part in resolving these issues, as both parties spoke truthfully about what was said and what their intention was. When people realized that there was no intent to harm, these issues generally died down quickly.

Develop Media Skills

The GCCW Project has received an incredible amount of TV, radio, and newspaper coverage. Of course, a campaign has to develop creative events that have a hook in order for the media to be interested. For the GCCW Project, the hook has generally been that students are *doing something* at an event. For example, students were planting 1,836 flags with the names and ages of the Katrina victims, they were reading off the names of the Katrina victims with the flags behind them, they were pitching tents for a campus sleep-out, they were marching through campus, or they were protesting with masks on in front of a trailer similar to one provided to Gulf Coast residents by the Federal Emergency Management Agency to dramatize the high levels of formaldehyde in the trailers.

In addition to creating events that were visually appealing, the project developed a three-part strategy when working with the media. Initially, letters were sent to the various assignment desks four weeks before an event; the letter described the who, what, why, and where of the event. A week before the event, the project would follow up with an e-mail to the assignment desks as well as to the specific reporters we had contacts with. Then, two to three days before an event, phone calls would be made to the assignment desks, asking whether they would be covering the event. This three-part strategy was extremely successful at getting the media to the events.

Be Persistent

This project has been successful because there was an extremely committed core group of ten to fifteen students, faculty, nonprofit leaders, and community organizers who would not let the issue die. As the nation moved on after the hurricanes, this group of activists kept the Gulf Coast in the news and offered the GCCW Act as one of the key solutions for the region.

Of course, almost everyone was unpaid. The people at the nonprofits simply added this project to their job responsibilities. People in the campaign who were not from the Gulf Coast were asked what motivated them to work for free for more than two years on a project that affected people thousands of miles away. I believe that people did it because they were intrinsically motivated by a vision of a more just America and wanted to correct a wrong of biblical proportions. This core commitment allowed people to work long hours, miles from the scene of the disaster and crisis, and continue to be motivated.

This does not mean that all people will stay dedicated to the campaign. Many will do something, and a few will stay and do a lot. This is what has happened with the Gulf Coast Civic Works Project. The campaign has engaged hundreds of students from all over the nation. However, most came into the project, did a few things, and then left. Of course, an organization should do everything possible to develop ways to keep people involved and engaged. However, at some level this "in-and-out" movement is the nature of social change work. Many will come through, a few will become committed, and all should be recognized for doing something positive. The leadership should help people who make a longer-term commitment understand that this in-and out movement is the nature of community work, which will help them not to become discouraged when others move on.

Do Not Worry About Money

Do not worry about where the money will come from; just start to plan the activity. If the idea is a good one, the money will come. I know that this lesson relies on a huge deal of faith, but every time the project needed money, it came. For example, when the project needed money for air flights and housing for fifty students to attend the Dillard University conference, the money came. We had no idea where it would come from, just the faith that if we asked enough people—as well as the right people—the money would appear ... and it did.

Recognize That Democratic Space Is Necessary for the Long Haul

It is difficult to sustain a movement over the long haul without democratic space in which to meet. By democratic space, I mean an area that is accessible to all; where rallies and demonstrations can occur; where the community is reminded of its core values such as equality and freedom; and where people feel empowered to express themselves and take action. At San José State, a key part of developing student activism in general and the GCCW Project in particular has been the Smith and Carlos statues. Every day as students walk by the statues, they are reminded that the university is not just about getting a good job and financial success; the university is also about developing the ability to stand up for what is right and just. This constant reminder has helped to change the culture of the campus, which is important for a society that celebrates conspicuous consumption.

Moreover, this democratic space has provided students and the community with a meeting space to take further social action. Almost all of the project events at San José have taken place at the Smith and Carlos statues. Importantly, the university has just built a monument to the life and work of union organizer and civil rights activist César Chávez. There are already plans by students and faculty to use this democratic space to advocate for social action.

Develop a Bigger Vision Than the Campaign

The larger vision behind the GCCW Project has been Dr. King's Beloved Community. In this community, the triple evils of poverty, racism, and war would be eliminated. This vision has inspired the faculty and students to end the social suffering in the Gulf Coast, particularly in relation to racism and poverty. Interestingly, Joseph Recasner, dean of students at the MLK Elementary School in New Orleans, saw the enactment of King's vision when he looked out at the diverse group of Louisiana Winter students who had come to the Lower Ninth Ward on Dr. King's birthday in January 2007. He reminded the students of the social suffering that was occurring in his community, but he asked them not to lose hope, as he saw in the students a living example of Dr. King's vision. Recasner told the large gathering of students, "As we look to the future and I look at your smiling and glowing faces, representing all colors of the rainbow— this is truly what Dr. King meant when he said that we should walk hand and hand, working and believing in a nation that promises freedom and justice." The Beloved Community is alive and well in this project, and it is what sustains and drives the project forward. At the same time, the commitment to King's community has made faculty and students think beyond this specific campaign. Ultimately, the students and faculty have created a "power organization," and people are already contemplating what to do after the passage of this specific bill. One of the things being explored is an initiative to promote civic works and rights.

The goal of this initiative would be to provide citizens and students with the tools and strategies to combat poverty, as well as promote human rights and community values along the Gulf Coast and in their own neighborhoods. The initiative would help expand and support an active multicultural national partnership of academics, students, policy experts, community organizers, environmentalists, and faith-based organizations to promote economic and social opportunity through civic works projects and to ensure that at-risk communities will have a say in how federal development dollars are spent in their neighborhoods. The initiative would provide the network with targeted research as well as vital media, educational, and advocacy support. In addition, the initiative would continue to train and cultivate its growing network of student advocates at San José State and across the country through various service-learning opportunities and events. Ultimately, the goal of this initiative would be to promote the idea of an economic bill of rights.

As I said earlier in the chapter, I concluded my first book by suggesting that readers select one of the poverty strategies presented and get busy implementing it. That is what I have done; I recommend you do the same. Time is of the essence, as the very soul of the nation is at stake.

APPENDIXES

APPENDIX 1: GULF COAST CIVIC WORKS ACT (HR 2269)

111TH CONGRESS
1ST SESSION
H. R. 2269

To establish the Gulf Coast Civic Works Commission within the Department of Homeland Security Office of Federal Coordinator of Gulf Coast Rebuilding to administer the Gulf Coast Civic Works Project to provide job-training opportunities and increase employment to aid in the recovery of the Gulf Coast region.

IN THE HOUSE OF REPRESENTATIVES

Ms. ZOE LOFGREN of California introduced the following bill; which was referred to the Committee on May 6, 2009

A BILL
To establish the Gulf Coast Civic Works Commission within the Department of Homeland Security Office of Federal Coordinator of Gulf Coast Rebuilding to administer the Gulf Coast Civic Works Project to provide job-training opportunities and increase employment to aid in the recovery of the Gulf Coast region.

Be it enacted by the Senate and House of Representatives of the United States of America in Congress assembled,

Sec. 1. Short Title.

(a) SHORT TITLE.—This Act may be cited as the "Gulf Coast Civic Works Act".

(b) TABLE OF CONTENTS.—The table of contents of this Act is as follows:

Title I—The Gulf Coast Civic Works Commission

Title II—The Gulf Coast Civic Works Project

Sec. 2. Purposes.

It is the purpose of this Act to—

(1) establish a Federal authority to implement the necessary equitable government response to the disaster experienced in the region for all Gulf Coast communities;

(2) provide a minimum of 100,000 job and training opportunities to those whose livelihoods have been affected by the devastation of the Gulf Coast region, particularly women and individuals who qualify as low income;

(3) create stronger and more sustainable communities better able to mitigate the physical, social, and economic impact of future disasters;

(4) assure that those who are most vulnerable to the direct effects of climate change are able to prepare for and adapt to those impacts by building resilience and reducing risk;

(5) strengthen the workforce by providing job training for thousands of workers that will enable them to rebuild communities and make an independent living;

(6) rebuild homes, public infrastructure, historic buildings, and community resources, to protect communities from future disasters and restore lives and faith in the Federal Government;

(7) promote sustainable development, energy conservation, environmental restoration, and encouraging emerging industries and green technologies;

(8) ensure equitable working conditions by providing workers with fair wages;

(9) utilize the recommendations of community organizations and coalitions in order to rebuild and strengthen communities; and

(10) strengthen partnerships between the public and private sector that will lead to increased economic growth in the region.

Sec. 3. Definitions.

In this Act:

(1) GREEN BUILDING; HIGH-PERFORMANCE BUILDING.— The term "green building" or "high-performance building" means a building that is designed to achieve integrated systems design and construction so as to significantly reduce or eliminate the negative impact of the built environment on the following:

(A) Site conservation and sustainable planning.

(B) Water conservation and efficiency.

(C) Energy efficiency and renewable energy.

(D) Conservation of materials and resources.

(E) Indoor environmental quality and human health.

(2) GULF COAST REGION.—The term "Gulf Coast region" means the areas of Louisiana, Mississippi, Texas, and Alabama that were devastated by Hurricanes Katrina and Rita.

(3) INFRASTRUCTURE PROJECT.—The term "infrastructure project" means the building, improvement, or increase in capacity of a basic installation, facility, asset, or stock that is associated with—

(A) a levee or other flood protection construction;

(B) a public facility such as a public schoolhouse, public college or university; police station, fire station, library, clinic, hospital, job center, shelter, or community center;

(C) a mass transit system;

(D) a public housing property that is eligible to receive funding under section 24 of the United States Housing Act of 1937 (42 U.S.C. 1437v);

(E) a road or bridge;

(F) a public utility system, structure, or facility; or

(G) a drinking water system or a waste water system.

(4) LEED CERTIFICATION.—The term "LEED certification" means the Leadership in Energy and Environmental Design green building rating system developed and adopted by the United States Green Building Council, which measures and evaluates the energy and environmental performance of a building.

(5) LIFE-CYCLE COST.—The term "life-cycle cost" means the cost of a building, as determined by the methodology identified in the National Institute of Standards and Technology's special publication 544 and interagency report 80-2040, available as set forth in the Code of Federal Regulations, title 15, part 230, including the initial cost of its construction or renovation, the marginal cost of future energy capacity, the cost of the energy consumed by the facility over its expected useful life or, in the case of a leased building, over the remaining term of the lease, and the cost of operating and maintaining the facility as such cost affects energy consumption.

(6) LOCAL DEVELOPMENT PLAN.—The term "local development plan" means the plan which may be prepared or adopted by a local advisory council with the consultation and assistance of the Commission staff and adopted by a town meeting.

(7) LOCAL ADVISORY COUNCIL.—The term "local advisory council" means the local council established in each municipality to develop and manage the Civic Works Project, as described in section 104.

(8) PERSON.—The term "person" means an individual, corporation, municipality, governmental agency or authority, business trust, estate, trust, partnership, association, joint venture, two or more persons having a joint or common interest, or any legal entity. A State agency or authority shall not be deemed a person within the meaning of this Act.

(9) REGIONAL POLICY PLAN.—The term "regional policy plan" means the plan prepared as described in section 105.

(10) STATE AGENCY.—The term "State agency" means any department, board, bureau, commission, institution, public higher education institution, school district, or other governmental entity of a State.

Sec. 4. Severability.

If any provision of this Act, or the application of such provision with respect to any person or circumstance, is held invalid, the remainder of this Act, and the application of such provision to any other person or circumstance, shall not be affected by such holding.

Title I—The Gulf Coast Civic Works Commission

Sec. 101. Establishment of Commission.

(a) IN GENERAL.—There is hereby established within the Department of Homeland Security Office of the Federal Coordinator of Gulf Coast Rebuilding the "Gulf Coast Civic Works Commission" (in this Act referred to as the "Commission").

(b) MEMBERSHIP.—

(1) IN GENERAL.—The Commission shall be composed of 16 individuals appointed by the President, by and with the advice and consent of the Senate, from among individuals who are citizens of the United States and residents or evacuees of the Gulf Coast Region, and shall have gender, age, ethnic and racial diversity reflective of the Gulf Coast Region, and shall have diverse experience and knowledge representative of all the issues related to complete recovery including, but not limited to: housing, worker and immigrant rights, infrastructure, social services, levee protection, and coastal restoration.

(2) NOMINATIONS BY GOVERNOR OF LOUISIANA.—Four members of the Commission shall be appointed under paragraph (1) from among individuals who are nominated for appointment by the Governor of Louisiana in consultation with community based Gulf Coast Region coalitions.

(3) NOMINATIONS BY GOVERNOR OF MISSISSIPPI.—Four members of the Commission shall be appointed under paragraph (1) from among individuals who are nominated for appointment by the Governor of Mississippi in consultation with community based Gulf Coast Region coalitions.

(4) NOMINATIONS BY GOVERNOR OF ALABAMA.—Four members of the Commission shall be appointed under paragraph (1) from among individuals who are nominated for appointment by the Governor of Alabama in consultation with community based Gulf Coast Region coalitions.

(5) NOMINATIONS BY GOVERNOR OF TEXAS.—Four member of the Commission shall be appointed under paragraph (1) from among individuals who are nominated for appointment by the Governor of Texas in consultation with community based Gulf Coast Region coalitions.

(6) POLITICAL PARTY AFFILIATION.—Not more than 8 members of the Commission may be affiliated with any 1 political party.

(c) CHAIRPERSON AND VICE CHAIRPERSON.—

(1) CHAIRPERSON.—The Commission shall annually elect a chairperson. The first set of officers shall be elected at the Commission's initial organizational meeting, which shall be conducted within 30 days of the effective date of this Act.

(2) VICE CHAIRPERSON.—The Commission shall annually elect a vice chairperson. The first set of officers shall be elected at the Commission's initial organizational meeting, which shall be conducted within 30 days of the effective date of this Act.

(3) ACTING CHAIRPERSON.—In the event of a vacancy in the position of Chairperson of the Commission or during the absence or disability of the Chairperson, the Vice Chairperson shall act as Chairperson.

(d) TERM OF OFFICE.—

(1) IN GENERAL.—Each member of the Commission appointed shall serve a term of 3 years.

(2) INTERIM APPOINTMENTS.—Any member appointed to fill a vacancy occurring before the expiration of the term for which such member's predecessor was appointed shall be appointed only for the remainder of such term.

(3) CONTINUATION OF SERVICE.—The Chairperson, Vice Chairperson, and each appointed member may continue to serve after the expiration of the term of office to which such member was appointed until a successor has been appointed and qualified.

(4) REMOVAL FOR CAUSE.—The Chairperson, Vice Chairperson, and any appointed member may be removed by the President for cause.

(5) FULL-TIME SERVICE.—The members of the Commission shall serve on a full-time basis.

(e) VACANCY.—Any vacancy on the Commission shall be filled in the manner in which the original appointment was made, provided—

(1) any member appointed to fill a vacancy in the Commission occurring prior to the expiration of the term for which his predecessor was appointed shall be appointed for the remainder of such term; and

(2) vacancies in the Commission so long as there shall be nine members in office shall not impair the powers of the Board to execute the functions of the Commission, and nine of the members in office shall constitute a quorum for the transaction of the business of the Commission.

(f) BASIC PAY.—

(1) CHAIRPERSON.—From the amounts appropriated under section 211, the Chairperson shall be paid at the rate of basic pay for level III of the Executive Schedule under section 5314 of title 5, United States Code.

(2) MEMBERS.—From the amounts appropriated under section 211, each member of the Commission, with the exception of the Chairperson, shall be paid at a rate of basic pay for level IV of the Executive Schedule under section 5315 of title 5, United States Code.

(g) INELIGIBILITY FOR OTHER OFFICES.—

(1) OTHER GOVERNMENT POSITIONS.—No person may serve as a member of the Commission while holding any position as an officer or employee of the Federal Government, any State government, or any political subdivision of any State.

(2) RESTRICTION DURING SERVICE.—No member of the Commission may—

(A) be an officer or director of any insured depository institution, insured credit union, depository institution holding company, Federal reserve bank, Federal home loan bank, investment bank, mortgage bank, or any other entity which enters into any contract with the Commission; or

(B) hold stock in any insured depository institution, depository institution holding company, investment bank, mortgage bank, or any other entity which enters into any contract with the Commission.

(3) CERTIFICATION.—Upon taking office, each member of the Commission shall certify under oath that such member has complied with this subsection and such certification shall be filed with the secretary of the Commission.

(h) CLARIFICATION OF NONLIABILITY.—

(1) IN GENERAL.—A director, member, officer, or employee of the Commission has no liability under the Securities Act of 1933 with respect to any claim arising out of or resulting from any act or omission by such person within the scope of such person's employment in connection with any transaction involving the disposition of assets (or any interests in any assets or any obligations backed by any assets) by the Commission. This subsection shall not be construed to limit personal liability for criminal acts or omissions, willful or malicious misconduct, acts or omissions for private gain, or any other acts or omissions outside the scope of such person's employment.

(2) EFFECT ON OTHER LAW.—This subsection shall not be construed as—

(A) affecting—

(i) any other immunities and protections that may be available to person to whom paragraph (1) applies under applicable law with respect to such transactions; or

(ii) any other right or remedy against the Commission, against the United States under applicable law, or against any person other than a person described in paragraph (1) participating in such transactions; or

(B) limiting or altering in any way the immunities that are available under applicable law for Federal officials and employees not described in this subsection.

(i) PRINCIPAL OFFICE.—The principal office of the Commission shall be located in the State of Louisiana. There may be established agencies or branch offices in the District of Columbia and in any municipality in the Gulf Coast region to the extent provided for in the by-laws of the Commission.

(j) PROPERTY OWNERS' RIGHTS AND PROTECTIONS.—

(1) NO AUTHORITY TO EXERCISE EMINENT DOMAIN.—The Commission shall have no authority to acquire interests in property by eminent domain.

(2) LOCAL INVITATION.—Notwithstanding any other provision of this title, the Commission may take no action in any municipality unless the local government of such municipality has adopted a resolution of invitation for the Commission's assistance.

(3) COMPLIANCE WITH LOCAL DEVELOPMENT PLANS.—The Commission shall have no authority to carry out projects which are not consistent with local development plans established by State or local government, or local advisory councils.

(k) TERMINATION.—Section 14(a)(2)(B) of the Federal Advisory Committee Act (5 U.S.C. App.; relating to the termination of advisory committees) shall not apply to the Commission.

Sec. 102. Capitalization of the Commission.

(a) IN GENERAL.—The Commission shall have capital stock subscribed to by the Government in such amount as the President may determine to be appropriate, to the extent provided in advance in an appropriation Act for any fiscal year.

(b) CERTIFICATES.—Certificates evidencing shares of nonvoting capital stock of the Commission shall be issued by the Commission to the President of the United States, or to such other person or persons as the President may designate from time to time, to the extent of payments made for the capital stock of the Commission.

(c) PUBLIC DEBT TRANSACTION.—For the purpose of purchasing shares of capital stock of the Commission, the Secretary of the Treasury may use as a public-debt transaction the proceeds of any securities issued under chapter 31 of title 31, United States Code.

(d) REPORTS.—

(1) IN GENERAL.—The Board shall submit to the Director of the Office of Management and Budget and to the Secretary of the Treasury quarterly reports and an annual report on the expenses of the Commission during the period covered by the report, the financial condition of the Commission as of the end of such period, the results of the Commission's operations during such period, and the progress made during such period in fulfilling the mission and purposes of the Commission, together with a copy of the Commission's financial operating plans and forecasts for the annual or quarterly period (as the case may be) succeeding the period covered by the report.

(2) PUBLIC AVAILABILITY.—Each report submitted to the Director of the Office of Management and Budget and to the Secretary of the Treasury under paragraph (1) shall be made available to the public.

(e) TERMINATION OF AUTHORITY TO ISSUE STOCK.—No shares of capital stock of the Commission may be issued after the end of the 10-year period beginning on the date of the enactment of this Act.

(f) REVENUE USED TO RETIRE STOCK.—Any net revenue of the Commission in excess of amounts required to meet on-going expenses and investments shall be paid to the Secretary of the Treasury to redeem the capital stock of the Commission and shall be deposited in the general fund of the Treasury.

Sec. 103. Officers, Employees, and Other Agents of the Commission.

(a) IN GENERAL.—The Commission may appoint such managers, assistant managers, officers, employees, attorneys, and agents, as are necessary for the transaction of its business, fix their compensation, provide benefits including pension and health care, define their duties, require bonds of such of them as the Commission may designate, and provide a system of organization to fix responsibility and promote efficiency.

(b) STAFF.—

(1) EXECUTIVE DIRECTOR.—The Commission shall have an executive director, and hire officers as required. The executive director shall be responsible for overall management of the Commission's operations, and supervising planning matters including the preparation and amendment of the local project plans, and the assistance to local advisory councils in their completion of local plans.

(2) CHIEF REGULATORY OFFICER.—The Commission shall appoint a chief regulatory officer to supervise the development of regional impact review process. The Commission shall also have a clerk whose duties shall include the keeping of the Commission's official records.

(c) STAFF DUTIES.—The executive director and other officers shall—

(1) coordinate project planning with the relevant Federal, State, regional and municipal authorities, laws and planning processes;

(2) work with State and municipal governments and nonprofit leaders to develop guidelines and regulations for districts of critical planning concern and regional funding priorities;

(3) assist residents and local officials in forming local advisory councils;

(4) assist local advisory councils in developing proposals of priority projects which have not yet been funded by prior Federal assistance for the Gulf Coast Civic Works Projects;

(5) evaluate the adequacy of the respective component of each local recovery plan submitted to the Commission for certification;

(6) monitor and publicly record the progress of each local advisory council in implementing the respective component of its local plan; and

(7) report to the Commission on the progress of each municipality in implementing the respective component of its local comprehensive plan.

(d) REMOVAL.—Any appointee of the Commission may be removed in the discretion of the Commission.

(e) CONTRACTS, SALARIES, AND WAGES.—No regular officer or employee of the Commission shall receive a salary in excess of that received by the members of the Commission, and—

(1) all contracts to which the Commission is a party and which require the employment of laborers and mechanics in the construction, alteration, maintenance, or repair of buildings, levees, or other projects shall contain a provision that not less than the prevailing rate of wages for work of a similar nature prevailing in the vicinity shall be paid to such laborers or mechanics;

(2) in the event any dispute arises as to what are the prevailing rates of wages, the question shall be referred to the Secretary of Labor for determination, and his decision shall be final. In the determination of such prevailing rate or rates, due regard shall be given to those rates which have been secured through collective agreement by representatives of employers and employees;

(3) where such work as is described in the two preceding paragraphs is done directly by the Commission the prevailing rate of wages shall be paid in the same manner as though such work had been let by contract; and

(4) insofar as applicable, the workers compensation laws of the United States shall extend to persons given employment under the provisions of this Act.

(f) POLITICAL TESTS PROHIBITED IN EMPLOYMENT.—

(1) APPOINTMENT.—In the appointment of officials and the selection of employees for the Commission, and in the promotion of any such employees or officials, no political test or qualification shall be permitted or given consideration, but all such appointments and promotions shall be

given and made on the basis of merit and efficiency. Any member of the Board who is found by the President of the United States to be guilty of a violation of this section shall be removed from office by the President of the United States, and any appointee of the Board who is found by the Board to be guilty of a violation of this section shall be removed from office by the Board.

(2) COMPENSATION.—In the selection of employees for works projects authorized by the Commission, made by an official, employee, or other authorized agent of the Commission, and in the determination of wages or salaries, no political test or qualification shall be permitted or given consideration, but all such selection, hiring, appointments and promotions shall be given and made on the basis of merit and efficiency.

(3) CONTRACTS.—In the authorization of contracts or agreements made or entered into by an official, employee, or other authorized agent of the Commission, and in the determination or rates or terms of payment for such contracts and agreements, no political test or qualification shall be permitted or given consideration, but all such contracts and agreements shall be given and made on the basis of merit, efficiency, and fiscal responsibility.

Sec. 104. Powers of the Commission.

(a) In addition to the regulatory and planning powers contained in this Act, the Commission shall have those powers necessary convenient to carry out the purposes and provisions of this Act, including the following powers:

(1) To sue and be sued, and complain and defend, by and through its own attorneys, in any court of law or equity, State or Federal.

(2) To make use of alternate dispute resolution mechanisms such as negotiation, mediation or arbitration.

(3) To prescribe bylaws that are consistent with law to provide for—

(A) the management and operational structure of the Commission;

(B) the manner in which general operations are to be conducted; and

(C) such other matters as the Commission determines to be appropriate.

(4) To fix the compensation and number of, and appoint, employees for any position established by the Commission.

(5) To apply for and receive Federal and private grants and loans and to expend such funds with the approval of the Commission.

(6) To conduct investigations necessary to ensure compliance with the provisions of the Act.

(7) To negotiate and enter into Civic Works Project agreements as described in sections 106 and 107.

(8) To appoint hearing officers and, where it deems appropriate, to delegate to such hearing officers the responsibility to hold public hearings under this Act and to assemble and report the record for decision by the Commission or its designee and recommend decisions to the Commission or its designee; however, any applicant or party aggrieved, following a hearing by a hearing officer, shall have the right to a public hearing before the Commission in accordance with the provisions of section 103 of this Act.

(9) To recommend to State and municipal agencies appropriate regulations for consistency with the regional policy plan.

(10) To promulgate and amend rules and regulations as appropriate to carry out its responsibilities under this Act.

(11) To appoint advisory boards, councils, subcommittees and panels as it deems appropriate to carry out its responsibilities under this Act.

(12) To recommend public acquisition of specified land areas for preservation or recreational purposes.

(13) To make use of the services of Federal, State, county and local employees as may be available to the Commission to carry out its responsibilities under this Act.

(14) To coordinate its regulatory functions with local, State, and Federal authorities and, where possible and appropriate, to conduct joint hearings with those authorities.

(15) To acquire funds and to manage such funds.

(16) To produce an annual report which will be included in the annual Executive Office report.

(17) To reimburse Commission members for reasonable expenses incurred in connection with their service on the Commission consistent with Department of Homeland Security administrative and budgetary procedures.

(18) To conduct studies in collaboration with local governments, nonprofit organizations, industry organizations, and other State and Federal agencies in order to create regional comprehensive workforce, infrastructure, and environment analysis and development plans.

(19) To assist local governments and community planning organizations in developing local comprehensive plans and, when requested, to assist local governments in carrying out their local planning and regulatory responsibilities.

(20) To review and comment upon local comprehensive plans.

(21) To conduct community outreach and public education.

(22) To conduct an annual public conference on workforce development, infrastructure development, and land use in the Gulf Coast and to invite to such conference any private, local, State, or Federal Governmental representatives it deems appropriate.

(23) To make grants to build the capacity of and support capital improvements for community colleges, vocational centers, nonprofit organizations, and other job-training facilities and programs serving the affected region.

(24) To make grants and provide technical assistance to municipalities for use in local planning activities.

(25) To provide technical assistance, administrative support, and compliance training for small businesses and job-training programs serving the affected region.

(26) To establish a process and procedures for participating entities to hire employees, pay wages, and develop capital facilities and developments of regional impact which are necessary to ensure balanced growth.

(27) To purchase or lease and hold such real and personal property as it deems necessary or convenient in the transaction of its business, and may dispose of any such personal property held by it.

(28) To fund the construction of new structures and facilities as necessary for the recovery of the Gulf Coast region.

(29) Coordinate national, State, district, county or municipal programs for the recovery and development of the Gulf Coast region.

(30) Formulate and periodically require reports of progress on all projects; and, where avoidable delay or malfeasance appears, to recommend appropriate measures for eliminating such problems, and, similarly, to recommend the termination of projects for cause.

(31) Prescribe rules and regulations to—

(A) assure that as many of the persons employed on all work projects as is feasible shall be persons affected or displaced by hurricanes Katrina or Rita;

(B) utilize and support as many of those individuals, communities, community organizations, faith-based organizations, and businesses within the region as is feasible, including the provision of child care to the children of working parents;

(C) govern the selection of such participating business and organizations on an open bid basis;

(D) ensure hiring, planning and implementation adequately involve and look to protect the rights and interests of vulnerable populations, including women, low-income people, people of color, immigrants, the disabled, and the elderly;

(E) develop, conduct, and administer training and assistance programs, in connection with any program under this title, including training and assistance programs for Federal wage requirement compliance, in order that business enterprises with limited capacity may achieve proficiency to compete, on an equal basis, for contracts and subcontracts;

(F) enter into contracts with private contractors, companies, and other public and private entities, in compliance with the hiring, bidding, wage requirements of this Act, to complete public projects;

(G) formulate and administer a system of uniform periodic reports of the employment on such projects of persons, businesses, organizations, and communities from the region; and

(H) investigate wages and working conditions and to make and submit to Congress such findings as will aid Congress in prescribing working conditions, rates of pay, and continuance or development of projects.

(32) To recommend and carry out useful projects designed to assure a maximum of employment and recovery in affected localities.

(b) NOTICE OF HEARING.—Whenever the Commission is required to provide notice of a public hearing pursuant to the provisions of this Act, the Commission shall give notice by publication in a newspaper of general circulation throughout the region once in each of two successive weeks, the first publication to be not less than fourteen days before the day of the hearing. Notice shall also be posted in a conspicuous place in the Commission's offices not less than fourteen days before the day of the hearing. Copies of all documents subject to notice and hearing shall be available for public inspection at the Commission's office during normal business hours.

(c) TERMINATION OF CONTRACT FOR CAUSE.—In the case of any service contract between the Commission and any other person, the Commission may terminate such contract for cause, whether by reason of breach of contract, violation of regulations or guidelines of the Commission, or otherwise, or bar any such person from entering into any other contract, after notice and an opportunity for an agency hearing on the record.

(d) AGENCY AUTHORITY.—

(1) STATUS.—The Commission, in any capacity, shall be an agency of the United States for purposes of section 1345 of title 28, United States Code, without regard to whether the Commission commenced the action.

(2) FEDERAL COURT JURISDICTION.—

(A) IN GENERAL.—All suits of a civil nature at common law or in equity to which the Commission, in any capacity, is a party shall be deemed to arise under the laws of the United States.

(B) REMOVAL.—The Commission may, without bond or security, remove any action, suit, or proceeding from a State court to the appropriate United States district court before the end of the 90-day period beginning on the date the action, suit, or proceeding is filed against the Commission or the Commission is substituted as a party.

(C) APPEAL OF REMAND.—The Commission may appeal any order of remand entered by any United States district court.

(3) SERVICE OF PROCESS.—The Commission shall designate agents upon whom service of process may be made in States comprising the Gulf Coast region and the District of Columbia.

(4) BONDS OR FEES.—The Commission shall not be required to post any bond to pursue any appeal and shall not be subject to payments of any filing fees in United States district courts or courts of appeal.

(d) REAL ESTATE AND OTHER PROPERTY.—In order to enable the Commission to exercise the powers and duties vested in it by this Act:

(1) The exclusive use, possession, and control of necessary real estate, together with all facilities connected therewith, and tools, machinery, equipment, accessories, and materials belonging thereto, and all laboratories and plants used as auxiliaries thereto; and all machinery, lands, and buildings in connection therewith, and all appurtenances thereof, and all other property to be acquired by the Commission in its own name or in the name of the United States of America, are hereby entrusted to the Commission for the purposes of the Act.

(2) The President of the United States is authorized to provide for the transfer to the Commission of the use, possession, and control of such other real or personal property of the United States, as he may from time to time deem necessary and proper for the purposes of the Commission as herein stated.

(e) FINANCIAL STATEMENTS AND REPORTS.—

(1) The Commission shall at all times maintain complete and accurate accounting of all costs and expenses associated with the holding and management of any asset or liability acquired by the Commission and in carrying out the activities of the Commission under this Act.

(2) The Board shall file with the President and with the Congress, in December of each year, a financial statement and a complete report as to the business of the Commission covering the preceding governmental fiscal year. This report shall include a statement of all costs associated with the Commission and its associated projects, including an itemized statement of the cost of administration, the cost of employee salaries and wages, the cost of materials, and the total number or employees and the names, salaries, and duties of those receiving compensation at the rate of more than $35/hour or $45,000 a year.

(3) The rules of the Office of the Inspector General and the Comptroller General of the United States shall apply to the activities and accounts of the Commission, including the regular oversight and audits of the Commission. In such connection, the Offices of the Inspector General and the Comptroller General, and their authorized agents, shall have free and open access to all papers, books, record, files, accounts, plants, warehouses, offices, and all other things, property and places belonging to or under the control of or used or employed by the Commission, and shall be afforded full facilities for counting all cash and verifying transactions with and balances in depositories.

(f) RESERVATION OF RIGHTS AND REMEDIES.—The government of the United States hereby reserved the right, in case of war or national emergency declared by Congress, to take possession of all or any part of the property described or referred to in this Act for the purpose of national security, defense, or for any other purposes; but, if this right is exercised by the Government, it shall pay the reasonable and fair damages that may be suffered by any party whose contract is hereby violated, after the amount of the damages has been fixed by the United States Courts of Claims in proceedings instituted and conducted for that purpose under rules prescribed by the court.

(g) RECOMMENDATIONS AND FURTHER LEGISLATION.—The President shall, from time to time, as the work provided for in the preceding section progresses, recommend to Congress such legislation as he deems proper to carry out the general purposes stated in such section, and for the special purpose of bringing about in the Gulf Coast region in conformity with the general purposes—

(1) the physical reconstruction and improvement of the devastated Gulf Coast region;

(2) the improvement of levees and other flood control systems;

(3) the economic and social well-being of the people living in the Gulf Coast Region;

(4) the creation of jobs and job training programs; and

(5) the economic development of the Gulf Coast region.

(h) LOCAL DEVELOPMENT PLANS.—

(1) ESTABLISHMENT OF LOCAL ADVISORY COUNCILS.—

(A) IN GENERAL.—

(i) DESIGNATION BY MUNICIPALITIES.—Not later than 30 days after the date of the adoption of a resolution of invitation described in section 101(d)(2), any municipality of over 25,000 people in the affected area may designate an entity to serve in an advisory capacity to the Commission.

(ii) OTHER MUNICIPALITIES.—For any municipality that does not designate an advisory entity under clause (i)—

(I) in each municipality of over 25,000 people in the Gulf Coast Region in which the Commission operates, the Commission shall provide for the establishment of a local advisory council; and

(II) in each municipality under 25,000 in the Gulf Coast Region in which the Commission operates, the Commission shall provide for the establishment of a local advisory council by combining, with the cooperation and consent of such municipalities, multiple municipalities that are, to the maximum extent practicable, located contiguously.

(B) MEMBERSHIP.—Each local advisory council shall consist of such local elected officials (including municipal officials), community groups (such as homeowners and community associations), and other interested, qualified, groups as the Commission may determine to be appropriate. Each local advisory council shall have gender, age, ethnic and racial diversity reflective of the communities they represent, and shall have diverse experience and knowledge representative of the issues related to complete recovery including, but not limited to: coastal restoration, infrastructure, social services, and worker and immigrant rights.

(C) CONSULTATION.—The Commission shall consult with each local advisory council to determine which Civic Works Projects to fund in each municipality. In addition to consultation with each local advisory council, the Commission shall consult with a broad range of local officials and community groups, including those that are not part of the local advisory council. The Commission shall hold public meetings, periodically and in advance of major decisions, in the affected municipality to receive input from the affected communities.

(D) LOCAL ADVISORY COUNCIL ASSESSMENTS.—Each local advisory council shall provide an assessment to the Commission which shall include the following:

(i) Review of the state of recovery and needs in their area, including—

(I) workforce development;

(II) workforce housing;

(III) employment;

(IV) disaster mitigation;

(V) infrastructure and public works, including roads, bridges, water systems, public transportation, schools, hospitals, childcare facilities, police and fire stations, training facilities, and municipal, parish, county and State facilities;

(VI) environmental restoration, including restoring wetlands, barrier islands, watersheds, fisheries, and forests; energy efficiency; art, architecture, and cultural needs; and

(VII) accessibility of work related services like childcare, transit, and healthcare;

(ii) Identification of community assets such as interested governmental, nonprofit, faith-based and private partners including—

(I) workforce intermediaries; identifying workers; helping residents find work and relevant available training opportunities; and identifying existing businesses workforce needs;

(II) training entities; and

(III) local and small and disadvantaged businesses as possible subcontractors on recovery contracts; and

(iii) A list of all known local, small or disadvantaged businesses interested in participating in subcontracting opportunities related to recovery projects to be considered by prime contractors in Civic Works Projects selected under section 106.

(E) PROJECT PROPOSALS.—Local advisory councils shall utilize consultation and assessment to create Civic Works Projects consistent with the purposes of this Act. The creation of Civic Works Projects must include community input through public hearings in the community with opportunity for notice and comment from the affected community.

(F) CIVIC WORKS PROJECT PROPOSALS.—The Commission will review bids submitted by contractors for development projects within the local advisory council's jurisdiction. Contracts with both subcontractors and prime contractors will be accepted or denied based on the sealed open bid process described in section 107, with priority given to local, small and disadvantaged businesses and businesses that employ local or displaced residents, women, minorities, immigrants, persons with disabilities, and that provide living wages for employees, and have policies for environmental protection and efficient use of energy.

(G) LOCAL OVERSIGHT.—Local advisory councils shall communicate with subcontractors and prime contractors to insure that development projects are being carried out consistent with local development plans, guidelines, and budgets. All contractors must adhere to requirements set forth by the local advisory councils and by the general guidelines set forth by the Commission. The Commission will make available technical support to the local advisory councils to ensure oversight.

(H) LOCAL COORDINATION.—Each local advisory council will coordinate existing community resources including but not limited to Workforce Investment Boards, job training providers, faith-based organizations, and nonprofit organizations to carry out projects under this Act. Where resources or capacity to carry out projects is not available, the local advisory council may apply to the Commission for funding to create new programs, agencies, or services.

(I) PROJECT FUNDING.—After each local advisory council has completed consultation, assessment and identified existing local resources as required by this Act, the local advisory council may apply to the Commission for funding to carry out the proposed project.

(2) LOCAL DEVELOPMENT PLANS.—In executing the redevelopment mandate under this title, the Commission—

(A) shall take into account and comply with any redevelopment plan established by State and local government officials; and

(B) may only solicit bids for such redevelopment that are based on and comply with a plan developed by local governments, if such a plan exists.

Sec. 105. Regional Coordination.

(a) ESTABLISHMENT OF REGIONAL TASK FORCES.—The Commission shall establish regional taskforces as are necessary to carry out the purposes of this Act and ensure local projects provide for regionally coordinated workforce, infrastructure, and sustainable land development along the Gulf Coast.

(b) PURPOSE OF TASK FORCES.—The purpose of a taskforce shall be to examine Civic Works Project funding and ensure local funding priorities help advance long term needs and planning of Federal, State, regional and nongovernmental bodies.

(c) REGIONAL POLICY PLAN.—The Commission shall in consultation with local advisory councils, the regional taskforces and any other committee established prepare a regional policy plan for the region which shall be designed to present a coherent set of regional planning policies and objectives to guide development throughout said region and to protect the region's communities, businesses, and resources, and which shall reflect and reinforce the goals and purposes set out in this Act.

(d) CONTENTS OF REGIONAL POLICY PLAN.—The regional policy plan shall include—

(1) identification of the region's critical resources and management needs, including its natural, coastal, historical, recreational, cultural, architectural, aesthetic, public infrastructure, workforce, and economic resources, available open space, and available regions for industrial, agricultural, aquacultural and development activity;

(2) a growth policy for the region including guidelines for the protection of workers, businesses, and regional resources and the provision of capital facilities necessary to meet current and anticipated needs;

(3) regional goals for the provision of fair, affordable housing, job creation, waste disposal, open space, recreation, coastal resources, capital facilities, economic development, historic preservation, and any other goals deemed appropriate and important by the commission; and

(4) a policy for coordinating regional and local planning efforts, including coordinating planning activities of private parties and local, State, or Federal Governmental authorities.

Sec. 106. Sealed Open Proposal Process.

(a) SELECTION OF CIVIC WORKS PROJECTS THROUGH COMPETITIVE SEALED PROPOSALS.—

(1) All Civic Works Projects shall be awarded by competitive sealed proposal except as otherwise provided.

(2) An invitation for proposals shall be issued and shall include a project description, goals, lists of prospective project governmental, nonprofit and private partners and roles and all contractual terms and conditions applicable to the Civic Works Projects.

(3) Adequate public notice of the invitation for proposals shall be given at least fourteen days prior to the date set forth therein for the opening

of proposals, pursuant to rules. Such notice may include publication by electronic on-line access or in a newspaper of general circulation at least fourteen days prior to bid opening.

(4) Proposals shall be opened publicly in the presence of one or more witnesses at the time and place designated in the invitation for proposals. The relevant information as may be specified by rules, together with the name of each proposing entity, shall be entered on a record, and the record shall be open to public inspection. After the time of the award, all proposals and proposal documents shall be open to public inspection.

(5) Proposals shall be unconditionally accepted. Proposals shall be evaluated based on the requirements set forth in the invitation for proposals, which may include criteria to determine acceptability, such as inspection, testing, quality, workmanship, delivery, and suitability for a particular purpose. Those criteria that will affect the costs and be considered in the evaluation for award shall be objectively measurable, such as discounts, transportation costs, and total or life-cycle costs.

(6) Withdrawal of inadvertently erroneous bids before the award may be permitted pursuant to rules if the bidder submits proof of evidentiary value which clearly and convincingly demonstrates that an error was made. Except as otherwise provided by rules, all decisions to permit the withdrawal of bids based on such bid mistakes shall be supported by a written determination made by the responsible officer.

(7) The agreement shall be awarded with reasonable promptness by written notice to the proposing entities whose proposals best meet the requirements and criteria set forth in the invitation for proposals.

(b) SOLICITATION OF PROPOSALS BY ELECTRONIC ON-LINE ACCESS. The Commission may invite proposals using electronic on-line access, including the internet, for purposes of acquiring contracts for public projects on behalf of the Commission or a Local Advisory Council.

(c) CANCELLATION OF INVITATIONS FOR PROPOSALS.—An invitation for bids or any other solicitation may be cancelled or any or all proposals may be rejected in whole or in part as may be specified in the solicitation when it is in the best interests of the Commission. The reasons for any cancellation or rejection shall be made part of the contract file.

(d) RESPONSIBILITY OF PROPOSING ENTITY AND OFFERORS.—

(1) A written determination of nonresponsibility of a proposing entity or offeror shall be made pursuant to rules. The unreasonable failure of a proposing entity or offeror to promptly supply information in connection with an inquiry with respect to responsibility may be grounds for a determination of nonresponsibility with respect to such proposing entity or offeror.

(2) Information furnished by a proposing entity or offeror pursuant to this section shall not be disclosed without prior written consent by the bidder or offeror.

(e) RULES AND REGULATIONS.—The Commission shall promulgate rules and regulations which are designed to implement the provisions of this section. The rules shall include provisions requiring the Commission or Local Advisory Council to keep certain public project records, even if duplicative, in accordance with generally accepted cost accounting principles and standards.

(f) FINALITY OF DETERMINATIONS.—The determinations required are final and conclusive unless they are clearly erroneous, arbitrary, capricious, or contrary to law.

(g) REPORTING OF ANTICOMPETITIVE PRACTICES.—When for any reason collusion or other anticompetitive practices are suspected among any proposing entity or offerors, a notice of the relevant facts shall be transmitted to the Attorney General of the United States or other appropriate authority.

(h) PROHIBITION OF DIVIDING WORK OF PUBLIC PROJECT.— It is unlawful for any person to divide a work of a public project into two or more separate projects for the sole purpose of evading or attempting to evade the requirements of this article.

Sec. 107. Sealed Open Bid Process.

(a) CONTRACTING OF CIVIC WORKS PROJECTS THROUGH COMPETITIVE SEALED BIDDING.—The following are requirements for the contracting of Civic Works Projects selected under section 106:

(1) All contracts for Civic Works Projects shall be awarded by competitive sealed bidding except as otherwise provided.

(2) An invitation for bids shall be issued and shall include a project description and all contractual terms and conditions applicable to the project.

(3) Adequate public notice of the invitation for bids shall be given at least 14 days prior to the date set forth therein for the opening of bids, pursuant to rules prescribed by the Commission. Such notice may include publication by electronic on-line access or in a newspaper of general circulation at least fourteen days prior to bid opening.

(4) Bids shall be opened publicly in the presence of one or more witnesses at the time and place designated in the invitation for bids. The amount of each bid and such other relevant information as may be specified by rules, together with the name of each bidder, shall be entered on a record, and the record shall be open to public inspection. After the time of the award, all bids and bid documents shall be open to public inspection in accordance with the provisions of title 5 of the United States Code, section 552.

(5) Bids shall be unconditionally accepted. Bids shall be evaluated based on the requirements set forth in the invitation for bids, which may include

criteria to determine acceptability, such as inspection, testing, quality, workmanship, delivery, and suitability for a particular purpose. Those criteria that will affect the bid price and be considered in the evaluation for award shall be objectively measurable, such as LEED certification, wages and benefits to employees or subcontractors, percentage of women, and minorities hired, number of residents and displaced residents hired, discounts, transportation costs, and total or life-cycle costs.

(6) Withdrawal of inadvertently erroneous bids before the award may be permitted pursuant to rules if the bidder submits proof of evidentiary value which clearly and convincingly demonstrates that an error was made. Except as otherwise provided by rules, all decisions to permit the withdrawal of bids based on such bid mistakes shall be supported by a written determination made by the responsible officer.

(7) The contract shall be awarded with reasonable promptness by written notice to the low responsible bidder whose bid meets the requirements and criteria set forth in the invitation for bids. In the event that all bids for a construction project exceed available funds, as certified by the appropriate fiscal officer, the responsible officer is authorized, in situations where time or economic considerations preclude re-solicitation of work of a reduced scope, to negotiate an adjustment of the bid price with the low responsible bidder in order to bring the bid within the amount of available funds; except that the functional specifications integral to completion of the project may not be reduced in scope, taking into account the project plan, design, and specifications and quality of materials.

(b) EXCEPTIONS.—The requirements described in subsection (a) shall not apply to:

(1) A Civic Works Project for which the agency of government receives no bids or for which all bids have been rejected.

(2) A situation for which the Commission determines it is beneficial to the public good for the Commission to act as the prime contractor and administer the specific Civic Works Project.

(3) A situation for which the Commission determines it is necessary to make emergency procurements or contracts because there exists a threat to public health, welfare, or safety under emergency conditions, but such emergency procurements or contracts shall be made with such competition as is practicable under the circumstances. A written determination of the basis for the emergency and for the selection of the particular contractor shall be included in the contract file.

(4) Nothing in this article shall be construed to affect or limit any additional requirements imposed upon the Commission for awarding contracts for Civic Works Projects.

(c) SOLICITATION OF BIDS BY ELECTRONIC ON-LINE ACCESS.— The Commission may invite bids using electronic on-line access, including the internet, for purposes of acquiring contracts for public projects on behalf of the Commission or a Local Advisory Council.

(d) CANCELLATION OF INVITATIONS FOR BIDS.—An invitation for bids or any other solicitation may be cancelled or any or all bids or proposals may be rejected in whole or in part as may be specified in the solicitation when it is in the best interests of the Commission. The reasons for any cancellation or rejection shall be made part of the contract file.

(e) RESPONSIBILITY OF BIDDERS AND OFFERORS.—

(1) A written determination of nonresponsibility of a bidder or offeror shall be made pursuant to rules. The unreasonable failure of a bidder or offeror to promptly supply information in connection with an inquiry with respect to responsibility may be grounds for a determination of nonresponsibility with respect to such bidder or offeror.

(2) Information furnished by a bidder or offeror pursuant to this section shall not be disclosed without prior written consent by the bidder or offeror.

(f) PREQUALIFICATION OF CONTRACTORS.—Prospective contractors may be prequalified for particular types of construction, and the method of compiling a list of and soliciting from such potential contractors shall be pursuant to rules to be promulgated by the Commission.

(g) TYPES OF CONTRACTS.—Subject to the limitations of this section, any type of contract which will promote the best interests of the agency of government may be used; except that the use of a cost-plus-a-percentage of-cost contract is prohibited. A cost-reimbursement contract may be used only when a determination is made in writing that such contract is likely to be less costly to the agency of government than any other type of contract or that it is impracticable to obtain the construction required unless the cost-reimbursement contract is used.

(h) COMMISSION TO SUBMIT COST ESTIMATE.—

(1) Whenever the Commission or Local Advisory Council proposes to undertake the construction of a public project reasonably expected to cost less than fifty thousand dollars ($50,000) by any means or method other than by a contract awarded by competitive bid, it shall prepare and submit a cost estimate in the same manner as other bidders; except that, for projects under the supervision of Commission or Local Advisory Councils undertaken by such means or method, the Commission or Local Advisory Council shall prepare a cost estimate. The Commission or Local Advisory Council itself may not undertake the proposed project unless it shows the lowest cost estimate.

(2) In preparing such cost estimate, the Commission or Local Advisory Council shall preserve a full, true, and accurate record of the cost of such project. Such records shall be kept and maintained by the responsible officer on behalf of the Commission or Local Advisory Council. To the

extent the Commission or Local Advisory Council contracts with any other Federal, State, or local government agency in connection with a public project, such other agency shall provide all necessary data or information to enable the Commission or Local Advisory Council to document a full, true, and accurate record of the cost of such project, which data or information shall be kept in an orderly manner by the Commission or Local Advisory Council for a period of at least six years after completion of the project. All such records shall be considered public records and shall be made available for public inspection.

(3) The Commission or Local Advisory Councils shall not be required to be bonded when performing the work on a public project.

(i) RULES AND REGULATIONS.—The Commission shall promulgate rules and regulations which are designed to implement the provisions of this section and section 108. The rules shall include provisions requiring the Commission or Local Advisory Council to keep certain public project records, even if duplicative, in accordance with generally accepted cost accounting principles and standards.

(j) FINALITY OF DETERMINATIONS.—The determinations required are final and conclusive unless they are clearly erroneous, arbitrary, capricious, or contrary to law.

(k) REPORTING OF ANTICOMPETITIVE PRACTICES.—When for any reason collusion or other anticompetitive practices are suspected among any bidders or offerors, a notice of the relevant facts shall be transmitted to the Attorney General of the United States or other appropriate authority.

(l) PROHIBITION OF DIVIDING WORK OF PUBLIC PROJECT.—It is unlawful for any person to divide a work of a public project into two or more separate projects for the sole purpose of evading or attempting to evade the requirements of this article.

Sec. 108. Environmental Protection.

(a) DESIGNATION OF CERTAIN AREAS.—The Commission may propose the designation of certain areas which are of critical value to the region as districts of critical planning concern that must be preserved and maintained due to one or more of the following factors:

(1) the presence of significant natural, coastal, scientific, cultural, architectural, archaeological, historic, economic or recreational resources or values of regional, statewide or national significance; or

(2) the presence of substantial areas of sensitive ecological conditions which render the area unsuitable for development; or

(3) the presence or proposed establishment of a major capital public facility or area of public investment.

(b) STANDARDS AND CRITERIA.—The Commission may propose standards and criteria specifying the types of development which are likely to present development issues significant to more than one municipality in the Gulf Coast region.

Title II—The Gulf Coast Civic Works Project

Sec. 201. Purposes.

The purposes of this title shall be—
(1) to create a minimum of 100,000 jobs for Gulf Coast residents and evacuees;
(2) to increase employment in the Gulf Coast region; and
(3) to build a skilled workforce for rebuilding and developing the lands, communities, and infrastructure impacted by hurricanes and flooding in the Gulf Coast region.

Sec. 202. Establishment; Contract Authority.

(a) ESTABLISHMENT.—The Commission shall establish and administer a Gulf Coast Civic Works Project to implement, manage, and coordinate numerous public works projects for the purposes described in section 201.
(b) CONTRACT AUTHORITY.—The Gulf Coast Civic Works Project is authorized to enter into such contracts or agreements with States as may be necessary, including provisions for utilization of existing State administrative agencies, and may acquire real property by purchase, donation, condemnation, or otherwise.

Sec. 203. General Activities.

The Commission shall carry out the Gulf Coast Civic Works Project established under section 202, which shall include the following activities:
(1) Identifying areas of the Gulf Coast region that are in need of recovery, rebuilding, and development projects.
(2) Cooperating with the local Gulf Coast community once a Civic Works Project request has been received and approved by the Commission, to ensure that Gulf Coast residents and evacuees will be hired by local employers or directly by the Commission to complete the work.
(3) Working in conjunction with local employers on Civic Works Projects and other recovery, rebuilding, and development projects, identify where a shortage of workers who are Gulf Coast residents and evacuees exists, and

identify the type of workers necessary for such projects to be more effective and efficient.

(4) Identifying such projects for which there is a shortage of qualified workers who are Gulf Coast residents or evacuees and, in conjunction with State and local workforce investment boards, establish additional job training programs where necessary, including areas where there is a concentration of Gulf Coast evacuees.

(5) Working in conjunction with other Federal, State and local agencies, the private sector and membership-based community groups to actively recruit Gulf Coast residents and evacuees to rebuild the Gulf Coast region through Civic Works Projects and other recovery, rebuilding, and development projects.

(6) Assisting Gulf Coast residents and evacuees employed or trained through the Commission to gain access and information to housing programs.

Sec. 204. Job-Training Partnerships.

(a) JOB-TRAINING PROGRAMS.—

(1) IN GENERAL.—From the amounts appropriated under section 211, the Commission shall, in conjunction with State and local workforce investment boards, community colleges, community-based organizations, schools, and other existing workforce development organizations, support job-training programs in effect at the date of the enactment of this Act or establish job-training programs and apprenticeships in order to recruit and train qualified workers for specific job vacancies in approved Civic Works Projects and other recovery, rebuilding, and development projects.

(2) PRIORITY.—The Commission shall work with the entities identified in paragraph (1) to set up local hiring halls through which Gulf Coast residents, including women and disadvantaged workers, shall have priority in getting admission into the job-training programs described in paragraph (1) and access to child care, if necessary. Such sums so deducted shall remain available until expended.

(b) CAPACITY BUILDING PARTNERSHIPS.—

(1) IN GENERAL.—The Commission may work in partnership with the entities identified in subsection (a)(1) and other public and private nonprofit organizations in order to assist such entities or organizations in carrying out workforce development or job-training programs by—

(A) providing technical assistance necessary and capacity-building support; and

(B) awarding grants in accordance with paragraph (2) to expand the entity's or organization's capacity to carry out workforce development or job-training programs, or to create new job-training or workforce development initiatives designated for the purposes of this Act.

(2) AUTHORITY TO ASSIST PUBLIC OR PRIVATE NONPROFIT ORGANIZATIONS.—

(A) IN GENERAL.—The Commission may make grants to the entities identified in subsection (a)(1) and other public and private non-profit organizations seeking to work in partnership with the Commission that—

(i) have experience with job-training or workforce development;

(ii) have been in effect at least 1 year prior to submitting an application for a grant under this subsection; and

(iii) meet such other criteria as the Commission may establish.

(B) USE OF FUNDS.—An entity or organization receiving a grant under this subsection may use such grant funds to make subgrants or enter into contracts with other organizations to implement, operate, or expand workforce development or job-training programs as described in subsection (a), or apprenticeship programs which meet the requirements described in section 205 or provide technical assistance and training to Gulf Coast residents and evacuees.

(3) APPLICATION FOR PARTNERSHIP.—

(A) Organizations seeking to work in partnership with the Commission shall submit an application to the Commission, or to such agency as designated by the Commission, outlining the details of—

(i) Civic Works Projects or other recovery, rebuilding, and development project;

(ii) the need for partnership; and

(iii) the need for and intended use of grants or other funds awarded under this title.

(B) The Commission shall set forth application guidelines and procedures for organizations seeking to work in partnership with the Commission.

Sec. 205. Apprenticeship Programs.

(a) IN GENERAL.—Subject to subsection (b), a contract between a contractor, subcontractor, or other employer and the Commission for a Civic Works Project or other recovery, rebuilding, and development project shall contain the following related to apprenticeship programs:

(1) A contract for a project described in this section for which the contract price exceeds $250,000 shall contain a provision stating that the contractor or subcontractor must be approved as a training agent by the Commission, if a program of apprenticeship and training for the apprenticeable occupations used by the contractor or subcontractor exists in the State or local community where the project is being implemented.

(2) A provision stating that at least 20 percent of the total hours worked on a project described in this section by workers in apprenticeable occupations

shall be performed by apprentices participating in programs of apprentice-ship and training. The workers may be employed by the contractor or any subcontractor on the works project.

(b) EXCEPTIONS.—Upon application by an contractor, subcontractor, or employer, the Commission may grant an exception to any or all of the requirements described in subsection (a) in any situation where the Commission concludes that compliance with such requirement would not be possible as the project could not be completed by workers in apprenticeable occupations.

Sec. 206. Job Creation.

(a) EMPLOYMENT.—After identifying Civic Works Projects and other recovery, rebuilding, and development projects in the Gulf Coast region the Commission shall work in conjunction with local employers and the heads of other Federal agencies on such projects to recruit and hire additional workers from the Gulf Coast region. In the event that contractors or other employers have a need for but do not have sufficient funding for additional workers the Commission may hire for such projects and, from the amounts appropriated under section 211, pay the wages of additional workers to work on such projects.

(b) PROJECT CREATION.—After identifying areas of the Gulf Coast region that are in need of recovery, rebuilding, and development projects where no such projects exist, the Commission may, subject to available funds, establish and fund such projects. In establishing any project under this subsection, the Commission shall hire all necessary developers, contractors, and employees to carry out such projects.

Sec. 207. First Source Hiring And Outreach.

(a) FIRST SOURCE HIRING REQUIREMENTS.—
(1) IN GENERAL.—Subject to paragraph (2), any contractor or other employer receiving funds under this Act, including any subcontractor or other entity in a subcontract with any such contractor or employer, shall comply with first source hiring requirements, which shall include—
(A) giving priority to Gulf Coast residents and evacuees when interviewing, recruiting, or hiring for any Civic Works Project or other recovery, rebuilding, and development project by —
(i) unless business necessity requires a shorter period of time, leaving open a position for not less than 25 days to give such residents and such evacuees an opportunity to interview for such position; or
(ii) filling its first available positions with such residents and such evacuees; and
(B) providing timely, appropriate notification of available positions to the Commission so that the Commission may train and refer an

adequate pool of Gulf Coast residents and evacuees to contractors or other employers.

(2) EXCEPTION.—Upon application by a contractor or other employer, the Commission may grant an exception to any of all of the requirements in any situation where it concludes that compliance with this subsection would not be possible in the timeframe provided.

(b) OUTREACH PARTNERSHIPS.—

(1) IN GENERAL.—The Commission shall work with the heads of Federal agencies, as well as State and local employment offices to conduct outreach to Gulf Coast residents and evacuees regarding employment in the Gulf Coast region, including which contractors and other employers are required to comply with first source hiring requirements. The Commission shall also contract with community groups, faith groups, and nonprofit organizations with connections to local communities in the Gulf Coast region to—

(A) conduct outreach to Gulf Coast residents and evacuees;

(B) work with contractors and other employers to identify interested candidates outside of the Gulf Coast region who wish to work in the region and enter job-training programs, if necessary, to work in the region; and

(C) set up local hiring halls described in subsection (c).

(2) LIMITED-ENGLISH PROFICIENCY COMMUNITIES.—The outreach conducted by the Commission under paragraph (1) shall include outreach to limited-English proficiency communities through multilingual meetings, translated flyers, outreach to ethnic medias, and other outlets. The Commission shall work with organizations servicing limited English proficiency communities to set up first source hiring halls as described in subsection (c) and to assist contractor and other employers in the Gulf Coast region in recruiting and hiring limited-English proficiency workers.

(c) LOCAL HIRING HALLS.—The Commission shall also contract with community groups, faith groups, and nonprofit organizations, as well as the entities identified in section 204(a)(1), with connections to local communities in the Gulf Coast region to set-up a central location or multiple locations (which may be referred to as "local hiring halls") in each community of the Gulf Coast region where—

(1) contractors and other employers receiving funding under this Act may recruit, interview, or hire Gulf Coast residents or evacuees for any Civic Works Project or other recovery, rebuilding, and development project; and

(2) Gulf Coast residents or evacuees may be provided access to child care while seeking employment or working.

Sec. 208. Wages.

(a) JOB TRAINING AND APPRENTICESHIP WAGES.—
(1) JOB TRAINING WAGES.—Job training programs established or funded under this Act shall ensure that trainees are paid in an amount of not less than $10 per hour
(2) APPRENTICESHIP WAGES.—Apprenticeship programs established or funded under this Act shall ensure that apprentices are paid not less than $15 per hour.
(3) ADJUSTMENT FOR INFLATION.—Beginning 1 year after the date of the enactment of this Act and each year thereafter, the minimum wages specified in paragraphs (1) and (2) shall be adjusted by the percentage increase during the 12-month period ending the preceding June in the Consumer Price Index for All Urban Consumers published by the Bureau of Labor and Statistics of the Department of Labor.
(b) EMPLOYEE WAGES.—The Commission shall ensure that all laborers and mechanics employed by the Commission or by contractors or subcontractors in the performance of construction or recovery projects will be paid wages at rates not less than those prevailing on similar work in the locality as determined by the Secretary of Labor in accordance with subchapter IV of chapter 31 of part A of subtitle II of title 40, United States Code (commonly referred to as the "Davis-Bacon Act").

Sec. 209. Other Projects.

(a) INFRASTRUCTURE AND PUBLIC WORKS DEVELOPMENT.—
In addition to the other activities described in this title, the Commission shall establish or coordinate infrastructure projects in accordance with local and regional comprehensive plans.
(b) ENVIRONMENTAL RESTORATION.—In addition to the other activities described in this title, the Commission shall establish or coordinate environmental restoration projects.
(c) CIVIC CONSERVATION CORPS.—In addition to the other activities described in this title, the Commission shall establish a conservation corps composed of individuals between the ages of 17 and 24 to focus on wetland restoration, forestation, and urban greenery.
(d) ENERGY EFFICIENCY AND CONSERVATION.—In addition to the other activities described in this title, the Commission shall establish or coordinate projects—
(1) to reduce greenhouse gas emissions created as a result of activities within the jurisdictions of eligible entities in a manner that
(A) is environmentally sustainable; and

(B) to the maximum extent practicable, maximizes benefits for local and regional communities;

(2) to reduce the total energy use of the eligible entities; and

(3) to improve energy efficiency in—

(A) the transportation sector;

(B) the building sector; and

(C) other appropriate sectors.

(e) WORK FORCE HOUSING.—In addition to the other activities described in this title, the Commission shall establish or coordinate housing improvement projects to assist workers in finding affordable housing.

(f) SUPPLEMENTAL SERVICES.—In addition to the other activities described in this title, the Commission shall establish or coordinate existing social service resources, including childcare and transportation services, as are necessary to ensure employment, training, and projects under this Act are carried out effectively and efficiently.

(g) YOUTH WORKS PROGRAM.—In addition to other activities described in this title, the Commission shall establish or coordinate existing resource for a Youth Employment Program, particularly for disadvantaged, at risk, and out-of-school youth between the ages of 12–19 years old, to provide summer and after school employment or skills training opportunities.

(h) ARTS, CULTURE, HISTORICAL RESTORATION AND HERITAGE.—In addition to the other activities described in this title, the Commission is authorized to provide grants for projects that reflect, promote, or maintain the architectural, artistic and cultural heritage of the affected region, including the chronicling of stories surrounding the 2005 and 2008 Hurricanes.

(i) GULF COAST ARTISTS GRANTS.—

(1) IN GENERAL.—The Commission may provide not more than 15 grants per year to eligible recipients for artistic and cultural projects which reflect, document, or preserve the history and culture of the Gulf Coast region. Grants shall be provided on the basis of the demonstrated merit of the applicant as determined by the Commission.

(2) ELIGIBLE RECIPIENTS.—To be eligible to receive a grant under paragraph (1), an individual shall—

(A) be a resident of the Gulf Coast region; and

(B) have demonstrated skill or talent in music, theater, writing, or the visual arts.

(3) AMOUNT OF GRANT.—The amount of the grants provided under this subsection shall be determined by the Commission.

(4) APPLICATION.—To receive a grant under this subsection, an eligible recipient shall submit an application to the Commission in such form and manner as the Commission shall determine.

(5) USE OF GRANT FUNDS.—A grant provided under this subsection shall be used on an artistic project that—

(A) showcases the history or culture of the Gulf Coast region; or

(B) has as its subject the effects of Hurricanes Katrina or Rita.

(j) CHRONICLE OF HURRICANES KATRINA AND RITA GRANTS.—

(1) AUTHORIZATION.—The Commission may provide not more than 5 grants to an eligible recipient for projects that chronicle the story of Hurricanes Katrina and Rita. Grants shall be provided on the basis of the demonstrated merit of the applicant as determined by the Commission.

(2) ELIGIBLE RECIPIENTS.—To be eligible to receive a grant under paragraph (1), an individual shall—

(A) be a resident of the Gulf Coast region; and

(B) have demonstrated skill or talent as a writer or film maker.

(3) AMOUNT OF GRANT.—The amount of the grants provided under this section shall be determined by the Commission.

(4) APPLICATION.—To receive a grant under this section, an eligible recipient shall submit an application to the Commission in such form and manner as the Commission shall determine.

(5) USE OF GRANT FUNDS.—A grant provided under this section shall be used on a project that chronicles, through the written word or through film, the story of Hurricanes Katrina and Rita from the perspective of survivors and evacuees.

Sec. 210. General Provisions and Guidelines.

In conducting works projects under this title, the Commission shall adhere to the following rules and guidelines:

(1) All public works projects shall be conducted in, and be for the benefit of, the lands of the Gulf Coast region, and the individuals, families, communities, and businesses of the Gulf Coast region.

(2) The Gulf Coast Civic Works Project shall employ a minimum of 100,000 Gulf Coast region residents and evacuees for all works programs and other related job opportunities.

(3) The Gulf Coast Civic Works Project shall make job opportunities, job training programs, and other beneficial projects known to the Gulf Coast communities through advertising and partnerships with regional agencies and employment organizations, and partnerships with community based organizations.

(4) Whenever possible, the Gulf Coast Civic Works Project shall purchase materials, equipment, supplies, and services from local businesses and producers.

(5) The Gulf Coast Civic Works Project shall maintain nondiscriminatory practices and shall not discriminate in hiring or employment decisions on the basis of race, gender, nationality, ethnicity, religion, or sexual orientation.

(6) No employee or trainee of the Gulf Coast Civic Works Project shall have financial interest in any public Commission engaged in business with the Gulf Coast Civic Works Project, nor in any Commission engaged in the manufacture, selling, or distribution of goods or materials used in construction projects authorized by the Commission, nor shall any employee or trainee have any interest in any business that may be adversely affected by the success of the Commission.

(7) Employees and trainees of the Gulf Coast Civic Works Project shall not be considered Federal employees for any purpose under the laws of the United States.

SEC. 211. Authorization of Appropriations.

(a) AUTHORIZATION OF APPROPRIATIONS.—There is authorized to be appropriated to the Commission such sums as may be necessary for fiscal years 2010 through 2014 to carry out this Act.

(b) PARTNERSHIPS.—The Commission shall make every effort to partner with State and local governments and private industry in the funding and administration of projects under this title.

APPENDIX 2:
ACTION ALERT: SENATE CALL-IN CAMPAIGN

ACTION ALERT   GULF COAST CIVIC WORKS ACT

WEDNESDAY, 11/19/08

Senate Call-in for the Gulf Coast Civic Works Project

The Gulf Coast Civic Works Project needs your help to introduce important legislation for job creation, infrastructure rebuilding, and environmental protection in the Gulf Coast. Our advocacy already helped to create the Gulf Coast Civic Works Act (HR 4048), introduced in the House of Representatives in 2007.

Now, we are calling on the Senate to introduce a companion bill into the upcoming session.

This Wednesday through Friday, hundreds of students from around the country will be making phone calls to Louisiana Senators Mary Landrieu and David Vitter asking them to introduce legislation.

We need your help! Please take two minutes to call or email the Senator's offices and let them know that you are part of the national campaign to pass legislation for the Gulf Coast. Thank you for your time!

WHEN: Wednesday, November 19 and Friday, November 21.

WHAT TO SAY: Hello, I am _____ and I am working on the Gulf Coast Civic Works Campaign. I am calling to ask Senator Vitter/Landrieu to introduce a companion bill to House Resolution 4048, the Gulf Coast Civic Works Act, which is co-sponsored by Charlie Melancon (D-LA) and Rodney Alexander (R-LA). This federal bill will create 100,000 good jobs and training opportunities for local and displaced workers to rebuild infrastructure and restore the environment. Please tell the Senator to introduce a companion bill to HR 4048. Thank you.

PHONE NUMBERS:
Senator Landrieu: (202) 224-5824
Senator Vitter: (202) 224-4623

EMAIL CONTACTS
Or email the Senators' Legislative Directors at:
Dionne Thompson at dionne_thompson@landrieu.senate.gov
Zak Baig at zak_baig@vitter.senate.gov

APPENDIX 3: DRAFT OF EXECUTIVE ORDER

Establishing the Gulf Coast Civic Works Commission and Authorizing Civic Works Projects

By the authority vested in me as President by the Constitution and the laws of the United States of America, and to further strengthen Federal support for the just, equitable and complete recovery and rebuilding of Gulf Coast region affected by the Hurricanes of 2005, it is hereby ordered as follows·

Sec. 1. Establishment of Gulf Coast Civic Works Commission.

(a) I hereby establish within the Department of Homeland Security Office of the Federal Coordinator for Gulf Coast Rebuilding the Gulf Coast

Civic Works Commission (the "Commission"), which shall be responsible for advising and assisting the Federal Coordinator for Gulf Coast Rebuilding (the "Coordinator") with respect to all workforce and infrastructure projects related to Gulf Coast recovery and rebuilding. The Commission shall serve also as the regional coordinating body for planning and administering Gulf Coast Civic Works Projects for the recovery of the Gulf Coast region, and shall have the responsibilities, duties, and powers established herein.

(b) The Commission shall be comprised of 16 individuals appointed by the President, by and with the consent of the Senate. Four members of the Commission shall be appointed from among individuals who are nominated for appointment by the Governor of Louisiana. Four members of the Commission shall be appointed from among individuals who are nominated for appointment by the Governor of Mississippi. Four members of the Commission shall be appointed from among individuals who are nominated for appointment by the Governor of Alabama. Four members of the Commission shall be appointed from among individuals who are nominated for appointment by the Governor of Texas. Not more than eight of the members of the Commission may be affiliated with any one political party. Each member of the Commission must be a resident of the towns or municipalities within the region he or she represents. Each member shall have one vote except the Coordinator, whose function shall be advisory except in the event of a tie vote. The Commission shall have gender, age, ethnic and racial diversity reflective of the Gulf Coast communities affected by the storms, and shall have diverse experience and knowledge representative of all the issues related to complete recovery and rebuilding including, but not limited to: housing, construction, economic development, worker and immigrant rights, infrastructure, social services, levee protection and coastal restoration. The heads of other executive departments and agencies and other senior officials shall be invited to attend Commission meetings when appropriate.

(c) The Commission shall have an Executive Director, and hire officers as required. The executive director shall be responsible for overall management of the Commission's operations. The Commission, executive director and other officers shall:

(i) coordinate project planning with the relevant federal, state, regional and municipal authorities, laws and planning processes;

(ii) work with state and municipal governments and community, environmental, faith-based and other non-profit leaders to develop guidelines and regulations for districts of critical planning concern and regional funding priorities;

(iii) ensure hiring, planning and implementation adequately involve and look to protect the rights and interests of vulnerable populations, including women, low-income people, people of color, immigrants, the disabled, and the elderly;

(iv) assist residents and local officials in forming Local Advisory Councils per sub-section (d) of this section;

(v) assist Local Advisory Councils in developing proposals of priority projects which have not yet been funded by prior federal assistance for the Gulf Coast Civic Works Projects per section 4 of this Order;

(vi) evaluate the adequacy of the respective component of each Gulf Coast Civic Works Projects proposal submitted to the Commission for review;

(vii) monitor and publicly record the progress of each Local Advisory Council; and

(viii) report to the Office on the progress of each local advisory board.

(d) Local Advisory Councils. Not later than 30 days after the date of the adoption of a resolution of invitation for assistance from the Commission, any municipality, county or parish of over 25,000 people within the Gulf Coast region may designate an entity to serve in an advisory capacity to the Commission. For any municipality, county or parish that does not designate an advisory entity under this section, the Commission shall provide for the establishment of a local advisory council, combining multiple municipalities, preferably in contiguous county or parishes, in the Gulf Coast Region in which the Commission operates.

(e) Limitation.

(i) The Commission shall have no authority to acquire interests in property by eminent domain.

(ii) Notwithstanding any other provision of this title, the Commission may take no action in any municipality unless the local government of such municipality, parish or county designated to oversee development of a community or area within the municipality, parish or county, has adopted a resolution of invitation for the Commission's assistance.

(iii) The Commission shall have no authority to carry out projects which are not consistent with local development plans established by state or local government or Local Advisory Councils.

Sec. 2. Purpose Statement.

The Commission shall carry out Gulf Coast Civic Works Projects ("Civic Works Projects") to provide a minimum of 100,000 job and training opportunities to those whose livelihoods have been affected by the devastation of the Gulf Coast region, particularly women, low-income people, and other vulnerable populations, and to further equitable revitalization of all communities impacted by the Gulf Coast hurricanes; realize the rights of people internally displaced by the Gulf Coast hurricanes to return and participate in their communities' recovery; protect Gulf Coast communities from future disasters, including building coastal communities' resilience from climate impact; workforce development by coordinating existing resources and programs; access to job-training and apprenticeship opportunities; development of adequate public infrastructure, including but not limited to levees, roads, transportation systems, and water supply; the provision of adequate public facilities, including but not limited to schools, police stations, firehouses, and community centers; coordination of the provision of adequate capital facilities with the achievement of other goals; the development of an adequate supply of fair affordable housing; conservation and preservation of natural undeveloped areas, wildlife, flora and habitats for endangered species; restoration of coastal resources; protection of groundwater, surface water, and ocean water quality and fisheries, as well as the other natural resources of the Gulf Coast; promotion of energy conservation and emerging industries with the goal of providing better environmental standards for the construction, rehabilitation, and maintenance of buildings and use of energy; and the preservation of historical, cultural, archaeological, architectural, and recreational values.

Sec. 3. Job-Training and Employment Programs.

The Commission shall, in conjunction with State and local workforce investment boards, community colleges, and other existing workforce development organizations, support existing job-training resources and establish job-training, apprenticeship and pre-apprenticeship, and community hiring halls where necessary in order to recruit and hire and where necessary train qualified workers for specific vacancies in recovery, rebuilding, and priority industries. The Commission shall work in conjunction with local employers to identify trades where a shortage of skilled workers exists.

    (a) Hiring Halls, Outreach and Capacity-Building Partnerships. The Commission may work in partnership and provide funding as is necessary to organizations described in subsection (a) of this section and other public and private nonprofit organizations in order to assist such organizations in developing and operating first source hiring halls through which Gulf Coast residents and displaced residents shall have priority in hiring and getting into job-training programs, to provide access to child care for working parents, to conduct outreach to workers eligible for first source hiring, and to work with contractors to identify interested candidates outside of the region who wish to return to work and, if necessary, enter job-training programs,

    (i) The Commission shall have as a priority the recruitment of women and disadvantaged workers who reside in the locality where the projects exist.

    (ii) The Commission shall ensure that Limited English Proficiency (LEP) communities are present and included through multilingual meetings, publications and partnerships with organizations servicing LEP communities including in regards to public meetings, outreach and hiring halls.

(b) First Source Hiring. Any contractor receiving Federal funds under this Order shall comply with first source hiring agreements for interviewing, recruitment, and hiring in order to initially provide displaced residents and residents from the disaster area with consideration for employment. The duration of the first source interviewing requirement shall be 25 days, unless the contractor receives approval from the Commission for reasons of business necessity or public interest emergency to hire in a shorter period of time. A contractor may establish its good faith efforts by filling its first available positions with job applicants obtained through the first source hiring procedures.

(i) Any contractor receiving Federal funds under this Order shall comply with requirements for providing timely, appropriate notification of available positions to the Commission so that the Commission may train and refer an adequate pool of residents from the disaster area to participating employers. Any contract for a Civic Works Project for which the contract price exceeds $250,000 shall contain a provision requiring the contractor or subcontractor to be approved as training agent by the Commission, if a program of apprenticeship and training for the apprenticeable occupations used by the contractor or subcontractor exists in the State or local community where the project is being implemented.

(ii) Hiring Decisions—Any contractor receiving Federal funds under this Order shall make the final determination of whether a potential employee is qualified for the position.

(iii) Exceptions—Upon application by employer, the Commission may grant an exception to any or all of the requirements in any situation where it concludes that compliance with this section would not be possible in the timeframe provided.

(iv) Subcontracts—Any subcontract entered into by any contractor receiving Federal funds under this Act shall require the subcontractor to comply with the requirements of and shall contain contractual obligations substantially the same as those set forth in this Order.

(c) Wages. Job training or apprenticeship programs established or funded under this Order shall ensure that trainees are paid in an amount of not less than $10 per hour, and that apprentices are paid not less than $15.

(d) Apprenticeships. A provision stating that at least 20 percent of the total hours worked on a project described in this section by workers in apprenticeable occupations shall be performed by apprentices participating in programs of apprenticeship and training. The workers may be employed by the contractor or any subcontractor on the works project.

(i) Exceptions to Apprenticeship Programs. Upon application by an contractor, subcontractor, or employer, the Commission may grant an exception to any or all of the requirements described in subsection (a) in any situation where the Commission concludes that compliance with such requirement would not be possible as the project could not be completed by workers in apprenticeable occupations.

Sec. 4. Civic Works Project Creation.

After identifying areas of the Gulf Coast region that are in need of Civic Works Projects, the Commission shall coordinate existing resources to ensure that projects are carried out in compliance with local and regional plans. Where no such projects exist, the Commission may, subject to available funds, establish and fund such projects. In establishing any project under this section, the Commission shall approve all necessary developers and contractors to carry out such projects based on a sealed open bid process for projects including:

(a) infrastructure and public works development; job-training facilities; environmental restoration;

(b) civic conservation corps composed of individuals between the age of 17 and 24, focus on wetland restoration, forestation, and urban greenery;

(c) energy efficiency and conservation;

(d) workforce housing;

(e) supplemental services such as childcare and transportation services, as are necessary to ensure that employment, training, and projects under this Order are carried out effectively;

(f) youth works program, targeting disadvantaged, at risk, and out-of- school youth between the ages of 12–19 years old, to provide summer and after school employment or skills-training opportunities; and

(g) Arts, Culture, Historical Restoration and Heritage grants for projects that reflect, promote, or maintain the architectural, artistic and cultural heritage of the affected region, including the chronicling of stories surrounding the 2005 and 2008 Hurricanes.

Sec. 5. Public-Private Partnerships.

(a) Local Advisory Council Proposals. The Commission may solicit, receive, consider, evaluate, and accept proposals for a Civic Works Project from local advisory councils for consideration utilizing a sealed open-proposal process. Proposals should be selected on their ability to fulfill the mission of this Order and in compliance with the needs and priorities of municipalities, state agencies, and local residents to be affected by the proposed project.

(b) Unsolicited Proposals. The Commission may receive, consider, evaluate, and accept an unsolicited proposal for a public-private initiative if the proposal is independently originated and developed in coordination with resident organizations in the community affected; benefits the public pursuant to the mission of this Order and in compliance with the needs and priorities of local residents to be affected by the proposed project; and includes sufficient detail and information for the Commission to evaluate the proposal in an objective and timely manner.

(c) Public-Private Agreement. After selecting a proposal for a Civic Works Project, the Commission shall enter into an agreement with the selected local advisory council or any configuration of public or private entities providing for the planning, acquisition, financing, development, design, construction, reconstruction, replacement, improvement, maintenance, management, repair, leasing, or operation of a Civic Works Project designated by this Order.

(i) After entering in the agreement, the Commission may solicit, receive, consider, evaluate, and accept bids to serve as prime contractor for the completion of a Civic Works Project from bidders utilizing a sealed open-bid process.

(ii) Proposals should be selected on their ability to fulfill the mission spelled out in this Order and to comply with the needs and priorities of municipalities, state agencies, and local residents affected by the project or contract.

(iii) The financing mechanism included in a contract may include the imposition and collection of user fees and the development or use of other revenue sources.

(iv) A agreement between the Commission and a local advisory council, public or private entity shall specify at least the following: The responsibility of each party to the contract to comply with or conform to each element of the project or contract and the timing of the assumption of responsibility; the type of property interest, if any, the parties will have in the facility; if and how the parties will share costs of development of the project; if and how the parties will allocate financial responsibility for cost overruns; liability for nonperformance; any incentives for performance; any accounting and auditing standards to be used to evaluate progress on the project; and other terms and conditions.

(v) The provisions of (c) shall not apply to:

(A) A situation for which the Commission determines it is beneficial to the public good and the purposes of this Order for the Commission, in conjunction with a municipality or State agency, to hire employees directly to work on such projects. In establishing any project under this subsection, the Commission shall hire all necessary developers, engineers, and employees to carry out such projects.

Sec. 6. Green Building Permits and Approval.

All construction projects receiving funding from the Board shall be required to comply with the following regulations for Green Building: The design, construction, operations, maintenance, renovation, and deconstruction of all major facilities that enter into the pre-design phase after the date of enactment of this Order, and the site of all such facilities, shall aim conform to, or exceed, the Gold rating of the most recent version of the USGBC LEED-NC Green Building Rating System for a new building and for major renovations OR the most recent version of LEED Green Building Rating System Version LEED-EB for an existing building. All such buildings shall be certified through the LEED certification process.

Sec. 7. Environmental Protection.

The Commission may propose the designation of certain areas which are of critical value to the region as districts of critical planning concern that must be preserved and maintained due to one or more of the following factors; the presence of significant natural, coastal, scientific, cultural, architectural, archaeological, historic, economic or recreational resources or values of state-wide, regional or national significance; the presence of substantial areas of sensitive ecological conditions which render the area unsuitable for development; or the presence or proposed establishment of a major capital public facility or area of public investment.

    (a) The Commission may propose standards and criteria specifying the types of projects or developments which are likely to present environmental issues significant to more than one municipality in the Gulf Coast region.

Sec. 8. Wages.

The Commissions shall ensure that all laborers employed by the Commission or by contractors or subcontractors in the performance of programs or projects initiated under this Order or funded by the Commission will be paid wages at rates not less than those prevailing on similar work in the locality as determined by the Secretary of Labor in accordance with subchapter IV of chapter 31 of part A of subtitle II of title 40, United States Code (commonly referred to as the Davis-Bacon Act).

Sec. 9. Continuing Authorities.

This order does not alter the existing authorities of United States Government departments and agencies. All executive departments and agencies are directed to assist the Commission and the Assistant in carrying out the purposes of this order.

Sec. 10. General Provisions.

(a) This order does not create any right or benefit, substantive or procedural, enforceable at law or equity by a party against the United States, its
departments, agencies or instrumentalities, its officers or employees, or any
other person.

(b) References in this order to State and local governments shall be construed
to include tribal governments (including those recognized by the United
States and the states of Alabama, Louisiana, Mississippi and Texas) and
United States territories and other possessions.

(c) References to the "Gulf Coast region" shall be construed to include the
areas impacted by Hurricanes in 2005 in the states of Alabama, Louisiana,
Mississippi and Texas including FEMA DR 1603, 1604, 1605, 1606, 1607,
1786, 1789, 1791, 1792 and 1794.

(d) References to "non-profit" shall be construed to include community,
economic development, environmental, faith-based, labor, workforce development and other not-for-profit private entities and collaborations operating
in the Gulf Coast region.

(e) References to the "United States" shall be construed to include United
States territories and possessions.

Sec. 11. Funding Partnerships.

The Commission shall make every effort to partner with Federal, State and local
governments, nonprofit and private industry in the funding and administration
of projects under this Order.

PRESIDENT OF THE UNITED STATES
THE WHITE HOUSE

APPENDIX 4:
NEW ORLEANS CITY COUNCIL RESOLUTION R-08

CITY HALL: November 20, 2008

BY: COUNCILMEMBER FIELKOW

WHEREAS, the public workers in projects such as the Works Project Administration (WPA), the Public Works Administration (PWA), and the Civilian Conservation Corps during the Great Depression built or repaired 103 golf courses,

800 state parks, 1,000 airports, 2,500 hospitals, 2,500 sports stadiums, 8,192 parks, 11,338 schools, 12,800 playgrounds, 124,031 bridges, 125,110 public buildings and 651,087 miles of highways and roads, as well as hired 238 bands and orchestras, arrested 20 million acres from soil erosion, stocked one billion fish in lakes and rivers, and planted three billion trees, and

WHEREAS, the efforts of the WPA and PWA during the Great Depression can still be seen in New Orleans through such city fixtures as Charity Hospital; the New Orleans Public Library in Bywater; the botanical garden and golf course at City Park; the Cabildo; Napoleon House; the Seventh Street Wharf; and the Audubon Zoo; and

WHEREAS, Hurricane Katrina damaged and destroyed over 200,000 Gulf Coast homes, and damaged or destroyed schools, hospitals, police and fire stations, roads, community centers, bridges, parks, and forest land, and left over 100,000 individuals in Louisiana and across the Gulf Coast unemployed; and

WHEREAS, the effects of Hurricanes Katrina, Gustav, and Ike underscore the need for environmental reform, including greener building practices, more efficient energy consumption, and a commitment to coastal conservation and restoration; and

WHEREAS, New Orleans continues to restore its core infrastructure so that residents can return and businesses can function effectively; and

WHEREAS, despite the federal government's response to this unprecedented disaster, individuals continue to struggle to regain and rebuild their lives; and

WHEREAS, the Gulf Coast Civic Works Act, HR 4048, will ensure that real progress is made toward rebuilding and sustaining the Gulf Coast region through the establishment of a federal authority to fund resident-led recovery projects; the creation of 100,000 good jobs and training opportunities for local and displaced workers to rebuild infrastructure and restore the environment; empowering residents to realize their right to return with dignity and safety; revitalizing the local workforce; and helping create more sustainable communities.

WHEREAS, the Gulf Coast Civic Works Act, HR 4048, rebuilds vital public infrastructure and restores the environment, specifically:
- Rebuilds and repairs public infrastructure including schools, police and fire stations, hospitals, parks, roads, water and sewer systems, and cultural centers
- Builds equitable flood protection and restores marshes and wetlands

- Serves as a national model for disaster recovery and infrastructure development

WHEREAS, the Gulf Coast Civic Works Act, HR 4048, creates jobs and provides job training, specifically:
- Creates a minimum of 100,000 jobs and training for Gulf Coast residents
- Creates a Civilian Conservation Corps for youth 17–24 to focus on wetland restoration, forestation, and urban greenery
- Provides 15 grants for artistic projects to highlight Gulf Coast culture and history

WHEREAS, the Gulf Coast Civic Works Act, HR 4048, takes action to jumpstart the economy, specifically:
- Establishes the Gulf Coast Recovery Authority to implement and coordinate the necessary federal response to the devastation of the Gulf Coast
- Coordinates existing federal programs to ensure effective and efficient recovery
- Creates opportunities for local businesses through competitive contract bidding

WHEREAS, the Gulf Coast Civic Works Act, HR 4048, spurs sustainable community development, specifically:
- Allows community groups and officials to determine what projects are needed in local advisory councils
- Focuses benefits on the regional economy through first source hiring provisions
- Strengthens workforce by providing jobs and needed skills training

WHEREAS, the Gulf Coast Civic Works Act, HR 4048, requires accountability, specifically:
- Requires oversight and community participation in all recovery projects

WHEREAS, the impact of Hurricanes Katrina, Gustav and Ike is a national tragedy that requires the attention of every American, regardless of party affiliation or state residence;

THEREFORE, BE IT RESOLVED THAT THE COUNCIL OF THE CITY OF NEW ORLEANS is supportive of efforts towards passage of HR 4048: the Gulf Coast Civic Works Act, to coordinate recovery projects, rebuild key infrastructure and ensure sustainable community development and is committed to working closely with local community groups, our Louisiana state and federal delegation, and the U.S. House of Representatives Committee on

Education and Labor to further strengthen this legislation as it moves through the Congress.

BE IT FURTHER RESOLVED, that the Clerk of Council forward a certified copy of this resolution to The Honorable C. Ray Nagin, Mayor of the City of New Orleans, the Louisiana State and Federal legislative delegation, the U.S. House of Representatives Committee on Education and Labor, and the President of the United States.

THE FOREGOING RESOLUTION WAS READ IN FULL, THE ROLL WAS CALLED ON THE ADOPTION THEREOF AND RESULTED AS FOLLOWS:
YEAS:
NAYS:
ABSENT:
AND THE RESOLUTION WAS ADOPTED

G:/CCRSRCH/RESOLUTS/07-159

APPENDIX 5: GULF COAST CIVIC WORKS CAMPAIGN INTERFAITH STATEMENT: SUPPORTING HUMAN RIGHTS IN GULF COAST RECOVERY IS A MORAL PRIORITY

As Hurricanes Ike and Gustav hit the Gulf Coast, internally displacing over one million people, we as a nation were reawakened to the needs of the Gulf Coast. Three years after Hurricanes Katrina and Rita struck and the levees breached, the slow pace of recovery and the new needs caused by Ike and Gustav's destruction have created a moral crisis along the Gulf Coast that demands a powerful response from people of faith.

While the nation has learned to better prepare for this latest hurricane, whether by inaction or injustice, we have still failed to protect the well-being of Gulf Coast survivors, new residents and their families, especially the children, the poor, the sick, and the vulnerable through just long-term rebuilding policies which fully support human rights. The collapse of local institutions, homelessness, internal displacement, poverty, abusive labor practices and environmental degradation mean they continue to suffer and struggle unduly. A spiritual wound remains open across the region, one felt in God's creation and every community across this country.

Our God is a God of justice, of humanity and of healing, and this moral injustice calls each of us to bold action in support of the common good. We must act to justly rebuild communities, restore the Gulf Coast, and empower families to overcome the devastation they suffered in our nation's worst natural disasters.

As people of faith and as Americans we believe in transcendent human dignity and place our trust in basic human rights. Many of the survivors of these disasters lack the resources to return to their communities to reunite with their families. Many families still have not recovered and have not been able to resume their lives with the dignity and safety that are their right. New residents who came to work in the recovery face hardships and abuses.

Gulf Coast communities continue to suffer from toxic trailers; closed schools, police stations, and hospitals; a shortage of affordable housing; crumbling roads and water systems; and workplace abuse.

As we have seen during Hurricane Gustav, an inadequate flood protection system and accelerating erosion of the wetlands left residents vulnerable to this and future disasters. Through years of improper stewardship, preventable coastal erosion has destroyed billions of dollars' worth of natural flood protection and threatens the homes, places of worship, schools, and businesses of those who live along the Gulf Coast. This also threatens the security of the majority of our nation's energy infrastructure, parts of which were once built above land and now reside below saltwater. The result is an American human rights and national security crisis that requires the attention all Americans, regardless of where they live, their faith, or their political party.

Together Hurricanes Katrina, Rita, Ike and Gustav killed more than 2,000 people. They destroyed thousands of homes, businesses, and places of worship, causing over $150 billion in damages and displacing hundreds of thousands of families. Members of diverse faith communions have responded generously, volunteering thousands of hours to rebuild lives across Alabama, Louisiana, Mississippi and Texas and giving millions in charitable donations. Faith groups have formed powerful new partnerships with local community leaders, non-profits, and other denominations, to lead some of the most successful efforts in the recovery.

We have learned that acts of faith and mercy alone, no matter how profound, cannot provide everything needed for a sustainable recovery. Gulf Coast families deserve a federal government that recognizes their needs by rebuilding their communities, supporting basic human rights of all communities, addressing poverty and displacement, and confronting coastal erosion. The government must empower local communities to take the lead in rebuilding their neighborhoods, renewing their lives, and restoring God's creation. We believe it is a moral obligation for the federal government to fulfill its promises for Gulf Coast recovery: empowering residents to return and participate in equitably rebuilding their communities.

Now we are joining community and faith leaders across Alabama, Louisiana, Mississippi and Texas and calling on people of faith to form a new partnership for a renewed and just federal Gulf Coast recovery policy to put all Gulf Coast communities, regardless of race, ethnicity or income, on the path to an economically, socially and environmentally sustainable recovery.

We ask national leaders of both parties, Democrats and Republicans, as they discuss the future of our nation, to honor the third anniversary of Hurricanes Katrina and Rita and the survivors of Hurricanes Ike and Gustav by pledging to fulfill these obligations in the next Administration and Congress, including:

- Passing policy based on the Gulf Coast Civic Works Act for a resident-led partnership to rebuild vital public infrastructure, restore the environment, and create good jobs and economic opportunities for residents and returning displaced families to help create stronger, safer, and more equitable communities;
- Increasing funding for federal, state, and local partnerships in the Gulf Coast to create more affordable housing and promote home-ownership for returning families, workers, and residents moving out of unsafe FEMA trailers; and
- Supporting federal funding to restore the coastal wetlands and barrier islands that form the Gulf Coast's natural barriers to flooding and to build improved levee systems to create a comprehensive flood control system which could protect all Gulf Coast communities from another Category 5 storm.

Signed, 108 diverse leading religious officials

APPENDIX 6: SUGGESTED CHANGES FOR REVISED BILL AND EXECUTIVE ORDER

Workforce Development:

- Increase emphasis on training for existing jobs as well as job creation.
- Increase amount of funding to workforce development.
- Ensure access for constituents often overlooked, including LEP populations and young people, to programs.
- Provide summer job and training opportunities for youth ages 15–19.
- Add language encouraging the creation of apprenticeship opportunities.
- Incorporate schools, especially community colleges.

Equity and Workers' Rights:

- Add competitive bidding language for primary contractors.
- Add language about equity from CBC Gulf Recovery bill.

- Add language on nondiscrimination and access to programs for workers and contractors from disadvantaged groups.
- Add language protecting LEP communities.
- Ensure equitable access for minority faith-based organizations and non-discrimination in hiring in participating nonprofits.
- Add language on worker protections and limited levels of contracting.

Economic Development:

- Provide incentives or assistance for local small businesses to compete for contracts.
- Improve language for local businesses.
- Provide funding for workforce intermediary-type tasks (child care, travel to return home, etc.) in workforce development funding.
- Take steps to entice private industry and other relevant parties.

Structural Changes and Accountability:

- Put project under authority of Gulf Coast Recovery Coordinator Office.
- Add "green jobs" projects like retrofitting building or green energy type projects.
- Include government-run model language (WPA) to the contract model (PWA).
- Allow nonprofits to bid for contracts.
- Expand role of transportation and housing in the bill.
- Ensure rural development is addressed.
- Expand possibility of environmental projects beyond the youth program.
- Consider specifying that the Corporation is subject to the provisions of the Administrative Procedural Act (APA).
- Make board and decision-making more accountable to the community by increasing power of local advisory councils.
- Involve the Delta Regional Authority and Lower Mississippi Delta Development Commission as reporting agencies.
- Create a National Gulf Coast Civic Works Study Group charged with reviewing some best practices of past federal programs in the region.
- State specific procedures that would streamline bureaucratic regulatory and granting processes.
- Define: resident, living wage, trainee, apprentice, "resolution of invitation," community-based organization (schools and other educational institutions, faith-based organizations).
- Frame bill in postfinancial bailout language.

Notes

Notes for Chapter I

1. "Economy Rescue: Adding Up the Dollars," *CNNMoney.com*, January 5, 2009, http://money.cnn.com/news/specials/storysupplement/bailout_scorecard/#bailoutSub1_0 (accessed February 12, 2009).

2. Frank Langfitt, "September Job Losses Underscore Depth Of Crisis," *National Public Radio*, October 3, 2008, http://www.npr.org/templates/story/story.php?storyId=95357684&ft=1&f=1017 (accessed October 3, 2008); Associated Press, "Manufacturing Index Drops to 28-Year Low," *National Public Radio*, January 2, 2009, http://www.npr.org/templates/story/story.php?storyId=92583860 (accessed January 2, 2008); David Goldman, "Worst Year for Jobs Since '45," *CNNMoney.com*, January 9, 2009, http://money.cnn.com/2009/01/09/news/economy/jobs_december/index.htm (accessed January 9, 2009); Edmund Andrews, "Economy Shed 598,000 Jobs in January; Rate Rises to 7.6 Percent, More Than Forecast," *New York Times*, February 6, 2009, http://www.nytimes.com/2009/02/07/business/economy/07jobs.html?hp (accessed February 6, 2009); U.S. Department of Labor, Bureau of Labor Statistics, "Employment Situation Summary," June 5, 2009, http://www.bls.gov/news.release/empsit.nr0.htm (accessed June 11, 2009); Sudeep Reddy, "The Other Unemployment Rate: 13.9 Percent," *Wall Street Journal*, February 6, 2009, http://blogs.wsj.com/economics/2009/02/06/the-other-unemployment-rate-139 (accessed February 6, 2009); "Number of Americans Receiving Unemployment Benefits Hits Record High," *CNN Wire*, January 29, 2009, http://www.nydailynews.com/money/2009/01/29/2009-01-29_number_of_americans_receiving_unemployme.html (accessed February 6, 2009); Jeannine Aversa, "More States See Double-Digit Jobless Rates," *Finance and Commerce*, March 11, 2009, http://www.finance-commerce.com/article.cfm/2009/03/12/More-states-see-doubledigit-jobless-rates-About-51-million-people-are-drawing-state-unemployment-ins (accessed March 14, 2009).

3. James Park, "The U.S. Needs Manufacturing Jobs—so Does the Middle Class," *AFL-CIO Now Blog*, June 20, 2006, http://blog.aflcio.org/2007/03/02/manufacturing-job-losses-continue-hit-black-workers-hardest (accessed December 6, 2008); Scott Myers-Lipton, *Social Solutions to Poverty: America's Struggle to Build a Just Society* (Boulder, CO: Paradigm Publishers, 2006); Katherine S. Newman, *Falling from*

Grace: Downward Mobility in the Age of Affluence (Berkeley and Los Angeles: University of California Press, 1999); Alan S. Brown, "Strength in Numbers," *Mechanical Engineering* (September 2008), http://www.memagazine.org/contents/current/features/strength/strength.html (accessed November 28, 2008).

4. David T. Collins and Mike H. Ryan, "The Strategic Implications of Technology on Job Loss," *Academy of Strategic Management Journal* (2007), http://www.alliedacademies.org/public/journals/JournalDetails.aspx?jid=13 (accessed February 14, 2009).

5. U.S. Department of Labor, Bureau of Labor Statistics, "Labor Force Statistics from the Current Population Survey: Characteristics of Minimum Wage Workers, 2007," http://www.bls.gov/cps/minwage2007tbls.htm (accessed December 31, 2008); U.S. Government Info, "Federal Hourly Minimum Wage History," http://usgovinfo.about.com/library/blminwage.htm (accessed December 31, 2008); U.S. Department of Labor, Bureau of Labor Statistics, "CPI Inflation Calculator," http://data.bls.gov/cgi-bin/cpicalc.pl (accessed December 31, 2008); U.S. Census Bureau, Housing and Household Economic Statistics Division, "Poverty Thresholds for 2007 by Size of Family and Number of Related Children Under 18 Years," http://www.census.gov/hhes/www/poverty/threshld/thresh07.html (accessed January 7, 2008).

6. Michael Katz, *The Undeserving Poor: From the War on Poverty to the War on Welfare* (New York: Pantheon Books, 1989); Harold Kerbo, *Social Stratification and Inequality: Class Conflict in Historical, Comparative, and Global Perspective* (New York: McGraw-Hill, 2003); D. Stanley Eitzen and Maxine B. Zinn, *Social Problems* (New York: Allyn and Bacon, 2006).

7. Myers-Lipton, *Social Solutions to Poverty*.

8. Ruth Milkman and Bongoh Kye, "The State of the Unions in 2008: A Profile of Union Membership in Los Angeles, California, and the Nation" (Los Angeles: UCLA Institute for Research on Labor and Employment, 2008); "The Union Advantage," *Change to Win*, http://www.changetowin.org/no_cache/why-organize/the-union-advantage.html?sword_list%5B%5D=Advantage (accessed December 14, 2008).

9. Edmund L. Andrews, "Report Finds Tax Cuts Heavily Favor the Wealthy," *New York Times*, August 13, 2004, http://www.nytimes.com/2004/08/13/politics/campaign/13tax.html?ex=1250136000&en=6f84660636ae70cd&ei=5090&partner=rssuserland (accessed September 9, 2005).

10. Chuck Collins and Felice Yeskel with United for a Fair Economy and Class Action, *Economic Apartheid in America: A Primer on Economic Inequality and Insecurity* (New York: New Press, 2005); Frank Levy and Peter Temlin, "Inequality and Institutions in Twentieth-Century America," Massachusetts Institute of Technology Working Paper Series (Cambridge, MA: MIT, 2007), http://web.mit.edu/ipc/publications/pdf/07-002.pdf (accessed September 15, 2008).

11. Collins and Yeskel, *Economic Apartheid in America*; Jeanne Sahadi, "CEO Pay: 364 Times More Than Workers," *CNNMoney.com*, August 29 2007, http://money.cnn.com/2007/08/28/news/economy/ceo_pay_workers/index.htm (accessed January 7, 2009).

12. Collins and Yeskel, *Economic Apartheid in America*.

13. Ibid.

14. Hollis Stambaugh and Harold Cohen, *I-35W Bridge Collapse and Response*

(Minneapolis, MN: U.S. Fire Administration, 2008), www.usfa.dhs.gov/downloads/pdf/publications/tr_166.pdf (accessed February 12, 2009).

15. American Association of State Highway and Transportation Officials, "Bridging the Gap: Restoring and Rebuilding the Nation's Bridges," July 2008, http://www.transportation1.org/BridgeReport/bridge-collapse.html (accessed October 5, 2008); Associated Press, "Nearly Half of U.S. Rural Bridges Found Lacking," *New York Times,* September 27, 1989, http://query.nytimes.com/gst/fullpage.html?res=950DE4D6123EF934A1575AC0A96F948260 (accessed October 5, 2008); Joann Loviglio, "U.S. Bridges Falling Down?" *ABC News,* July 28, 2008, http://abcnews.go.com/US/wireStory?id=5467344 (accessed November 3, 2008); Bernard L. Schwartz, "Redressing America's Public Infrastructure Deficit: Testimony Before the House Committee on Transportation and Infrastructure," *New American Foundation,* June 19, 2008, http://www.newamerica.net/publications/policy/redressing_america_s_public_infrastructure_deficit (accessed October 7, 2008); American Association of State Highway and Transportation Officials, "Facts and Figures About the U.S. Transportation System: Condition of the Nation's Bridges," http://www.transportation.org/?siteid=93&pageid=2493 (accessed October 7, 2008); American Association of State Highway and Transportation Officials, "Subcommittee on Public Affairs: Frequently Asked Questions," http://www.iowadot.gov/subcommittee/faq.aspx (accessed November 10, 2008).

16. American Society of Civil Engineers, "Report Card for America's Infrastructure," http://www.infrastructurereportcard.org/fact-sheet/bridges (accessed June 11, 2009).

17. Michael E. Dyson, *Come Hell or High Water: Hurricane Katrina and the Color of Disaster* (New York: Basic Civitas Books, 2006).

18. "Des Moines Businesses Complain About Weak Levee," *Sioux City Journal,* July 17, 2008, http://www.siouxcityjournal.com/articles/2008/07/17/news/latest_news/e47d6e60a849b123862574890076dc4.txt (accessed October 8, 2008).

19. Glenn Silber and Malia Zimmerman, "After the Flood," *Hawaii Reporter,* March 14, 2008, http://www.hawaiireporter.com/story.aspx?c8d20fc2-02a6-492b-8766-731aaca30128 (accessed February 12, 2009); American Society of Civil Engineers, "Report Card for America's Infrastructure," http://www.infrastructurereportcard.org/fact-sheet/dams (accessed June 11, 2009).

20. Holly Deyo, "Blackout 2003 Revisited," *Millennium-Ark,* January 21, 2008, http://standeyo.com/NEWS/08_Sci_Tech/080121.blackout.2003.html (accessed October 10, 2008).

21. American Society of Civil Engineers, "Report Card for America's Infrastructure," http://www.infrastructurereportcard.org/fact-sheet/energy (accessed June 11, 2009); Allan J. DeBlasio, Terrance J. Regan, Margaret E. Zirker, Kristin Lovejoy, and Kate Fichter, "Learning from the 2003 Blackout," *U.S. Department of Transportation Federal Highway Administration* 68, no. 2 (September–October 2004), http://www.tfhrc.gov/pubrds/04sep/04.htm (accessed October 8, 2008); Jason Leopold, "Three Years After Blackout, Power Problems Persist," *Truthout,* August 17, 2006, http://www.truthout.org/article/three-years-after-blackout-power-problems-persist (accessed November 8, 2008); Associated Press, "Experts Warned of Weak Power Grid," *Wired,* August 15, 2003, http://www.wired.com/science/discoveries/news/2003/08/60057 (accessed October 12, 2008).

22. ACLU of Northern California, "California Judge Finalizes Historic Education Settlement in ACLU Lawsuit," March 23, 2005, http://www.aclu.org/rightsofthepoor/edu/13461prs20050323.html (accessed October 15, 2008); ACLU of Northern California, "Landmark Lawsuit on Behalf of Public School Students Demands Basic Education Rights Promised in State Constitution," May, 17, 2000, http://www.aclu.org/racialjustice/edu/15951prs20000517.html (accessed October 15, 2008).

23. ACLU of Northern California, "Landmark Education Case Will Hold State Responsible for Pervasive Substandard Conditions in Public Schools," May 17, 2000, http://www.aclunc.org/news/press_releases/landmark_education_case_will_hold_state_responsible_for_pervasive_substandard_conditions_in_public_schools.shtml (accessed October 15, 2008).

24. American Society of Civil Engineers, "Report Card for America's Infrastructure," http://www.asce.org/reportcard/2009/??? (accessed June 11, 2009); Joe Agron, "Growth Spurt: Thirtieth Annual Official Education Construction Report," *American Schools and Universities* (May 2004), http://www.asumag.com/mag/405asu21.pdf (accessed January 8, 2009).

25. American Society of Civil Engineers, "Report Card for America's Infrastructure," http://www.infrastructurereportcard.org/fact-sheet/schools (accessed June 11, 2009); Agron "Growth Spurt."

26. Building America's Future, "Why Invest," 2008, http://investininfrastructure.org/initiatives/stimulus.html (accessed October 18, 2008).

27. Ibid.

28. Bernard Schwartz, "Why the Promise of Prosperity Requires Public Investment," *Schwartz Center for Economic Policy Analysis,* May 2008, www.newschool.edu/cepa/publications/books/08_SCEPA_BOOK5_02.pdf. (accessed October 20, 2008); Mort Kondracke, "Bridge Collapse Shows Nation Needs Infrastructure Work," *Real Clear Politics,* August 07, 2007, http://www.realclearpolitics.com/articles/2007/08/bridge_collapse_shows_nation_n.html (accessed January 8, 2009).

29. "Economy Rescue," *CNNmoney.com*

30. U.S. Department of the Treasury, "Statement by President Bill Clinton at the Signing of the Financial Modernization Bill," November 12, 1999, http://www.treas.gov/press/releases/ls241.htm (accessed January 9, 2009).

31. Robert Kuttner, "The Dangers of Deregulation," *Boston Globe,* March 17, 2007, http://www.boston.com/news/globe/editorial_opinion/oped/articles/2007/03/17/the_dangers_of_deregulation (accessed October 23, 2008); William C. Wheaton and Gleb Nechayev, "The 1998–2005 Housing 'Bubble' and the Current 'Correction': What's Different This Time?" *Journal of Real Estate Research* 30, no. 1 (2008): 1–26.

32. Souphala Chomsisengphet and Anthony Pennington-Cross, "The Evolution of the Subprime Mortgage Market," *Federal Reserve Bank of St. Louis Review* 88, no. 1 (January–February 2006): 31–56; Kuttner, "The Dangers of Deregulation", Veena Trehan, "The Mortgage Market: What Happened?" *USA Today,* December 7, 2004, http://www.usatoday.com/money/perfi/housing/2004-12-07-subprime-day-2-usat_x.htm (accessed February 1, 2009).

33. Mara Lee, "Subprime Mortgages: A Primer," *National Public Radio,* March 23, 2007, http://www.npr.org/templates/story/story.php?storyId=9085408 (accessed

February 2, 2009). Michelle J. Nealy, "On the Losing End," *DiverseEducation.com*, May 1, 2008, http://www.diverseeducation.com/artman/publish/printer_11077.shtml (accessed February 2, 2009); News Services, "Mortgage Application Denial Rate Inches Up," *Washington Post*, September 13, 2007, http://www.washingtonpost.com/wp-dyn/content/article/2007/09/12/AR2007091202541.html (accessed February 2, 2009).

34. Edmund L. Andrews, "Greenspan Concedes Error on Regulation," *New York Times*, October 23, 2008, http://www.nytimes.com/2008/10/24/business/economy/24panel.html?_r=2&hp&oref=slogin (accessed October 23, 2008); Paul Krugman, "Blindly into the Bubble," *New York Times*, December 21, 2007, http://www.nytimes.com/2007/12/21/opinion/21krugman.html (accessed December 22, 2008).

35. Stacie Young, "The Foreclosure Crisis in the Chicago Area: Fact, Trends, and Responses," *Federal Reserve Bank of Chicago*, August 20, 2008, www.chicagofed.org/community_development/files/Foreclosure_CrisisDocFinal_102708_bg.doc (accessed January 9, 2009); "U.S. Foreclosure in August Most in Three Years," *Capital Times*, September 12, 2008, http://www.newser.com/archive-us-news/1G1-184848953/us-foreclosures-in-august-most-in-three-yearsnews.html (accessed January 9, 2009); Vikas Bajaj and Louise Story, "Mortgage Crisis Spreads Past Subprime Loans," *New York Times*, February 12, 2008, http://www.nytimes.com/2008/02/12/business/12credit.html?pagewanted=1 (accessed February 1, 2009); Dan Levy, "U.S. Foreclosures Top Quarter-Million for 10th Straight Month," *Bloomberg.com*, February 12, 2009, http://www.bloomberg.com/apps/news?pid=20601087&sid=aG4wgV6SHqOI&refer=home (accessed March 14, 2009).

36. Steve Kroft, "The Bet That Blew Up Wall Street," October 26, 2008, http://www.cbsnews.com/stories/2008/10/26/60minutes/main4546199.shtml (accessed January 11, 2009).

37. BBC News, "Buffett Warns on Investment 'Time Bomb,'" March 4, 2003, http://news.bbc.co.uk/2/hi/business/2817995.stm (accessed January 9, 2009); Peter Goodman, "Taking a Hard Look at a Greenspan Legacy," *New York Times*, October 8, 2008, http://www.nytimes.com/2008/10/09/business/economy/09greenspan.html?em (accessed October 8, 2008).

38. Goodman, "Taking a Hard Look at a Greenspan Legacy"; Ellen Brown, "It's the Derivatives, Stupid! Why Fannie, Freddie, and AIG Had to Be Bailed Out," *Web of Debt Blog*, September 18, 2008, http://webofdebt.wordpress.com/2008/09/19/its-the-derivatives-stupid-why-fannie-freddie-and-aig-all-had-to-be-bailed-out (accessed February 2, 2009); "Following the A.I.G. Money," *New York Times*, March 14, 2009, http://www.nytimes.com/2009/03/15/opinion/15sun1.html (accessed March 31, 2009). "First Bank Failures of '09," *CNNMoney.com*, January 16, 2009, http://money.cnn.com/2009/01/16/news/economy/bank_failure/index.htm?postversion=2009011622 (accessed February 2, 2009); "Failed Banks for June 5, 2009," June 5, 2009, http://problembanklist.com/blog/failed-banks-for-june-5-2009 (accessed June 17, 2009).

39. Goodman, "Taking a Hard Look at a Greenspan Legacy"; John F. Burns and Landon Thomas Jr., "English-Speaking Capitalism on Trial," *New York Times*, March 29, 2009, WK-1.

40. "General Election: McCain vs. Obama," *Real Clear Politics*, http://www.realclearpolitics.com/epolls/2008/president/us/general_election_mccain_vs_

obama-225.html (accessed February 12, 2009); "Real Clear Politics Electoral College," *Real Clear Politics,* http://www.realclearpolitics.com/epolls/maps/obama_vs_mccain (accessed February 12, 2009).

41. Barack Obama, "Text of President-Elect Barack Obama's Speech on the Economy, *Los Angeles Times,* January 9, 2009, http://www.latimes.com/news/nationworld/nation/la-na-obama-economy-text9-2009jan09,0,4826774.story?page=2 (accessed January 9, 2009); Peter Nicholas, "Obama Puts His Trust in Government," *Los Angeles Times,* January 9, 2009, http://articles.latimes.com/2009/jan/09/nation/na-obama-economy9 (accessed April 21, 2009); Eric Dash, "U.S. Agrees to Raise Its Stake in Citigroup," *New York Times,* February 27, 2009, http://www.nytimes.com/2009/02/28/business/28deal.html (accessed March 14, 2009); Chris Isidore, "Bush Announces Auto Rescue," *CNNMoney.Com,* December 19, 2008, http://money.cnn.com/2008/12/19/news/companies/auto_crisis/?postversion=2008121911 (accessed December 22, 2008).

Notes for Chapter 2

1. Peter Beinart, "The *New* New Deal: What Barack Obama Can Learn from F.D.R.—and What the Democrats Need to Do," *Time,* November 24, 2008; Dave Demerjian, "Note to Next President: Modern-Day WPA Will Save the Economy," *Wired,* October 19, 2008, http://blog.wired.com/cars/2008/10/wall-street-bai.html (accessed November 5, 2008).

2. Scott Myers-Lipton, *Social Solutions to Poverty: America's Struggle to Build a Better Society* (Boulder, CO: Paradigm Publishers, 2006); Lucy G. Barber, *Marching on Washington: The Forging of an American Political Tradition* (Berkeley and Los Angeles: University of California Press, 2002); Carlos A. Schwantes, *Coxey's Army: An American Odyssey* (Lincoln: University of Nebraska Press, 1985).

3. Henry Vincent, *The Story of the Commonweal: Complete and Graphic Narrative of the Origin and Growth of the Movement* (Chicago: W. K. Conkey, 1894).

4. Public Works Administration, Division of Information, *America Builds: The Record of PWA* (Washington, DC: GPO, 1939), 35.

5. Jason S. Smith, *Building New Deal Liberalism: The Political Economy of Public Works, 1933–1956* (New York: Cambridge University Press, 2005); W. E. Upjohn Institute for Employment Research [by] Eugene C. McKean [and] Harold C. Taylor, *Public Works and Employment: From the Local Government Point of View* (Chicago: Public Administration Service, 1955); inflation calculator from the U.S. Department of Labor, Bureau of Labor Statistics, was used to determine 2008 figure, http://data.bls.gov/cgi-bin/cpicalc.pl (accessed February 12, 2009).

6. Harold L. Ickes, *Back to Work: The Story of PWA* (New York: Da Capo Press, 1973 [1935]); PWA, *America Builds.*

7. Smith, *Building New Deal Liberalism,* 107; Gwendolyn Mink and Alice O'Connor, eds., *Poverty in the United States: An Encyclopedia of History, Politics, and Policy* (Santa Barbara, CA: ABC-CLIO, 2004).

8. Bonnie F. Schwartz, *The Civil Works Administration, 1933–34: The Business of Emergency Employment in the New Deal* (Princeton, NJ: Princeton University Press, 1984); U.S. Federal Works Agency, *Final Report on the WPA Program: 1935–1943* (Washington, DC: GPO, 1939).

9. Smith, *Building New Deal Liberalism*; Harry L. Hopkins, *Spending to Save: The Complete Story of Relief* (New York: Norton, 1936).

10. Jeffrey B. Morris and Richard B. Morris, eds., *Encyclopedia of American History*, 7th ed. (New York: HarperCollins, 1996); Thomas H. Johnson, in consultation with Harvey Wish, *The Oxford Companion to American History* (New York: Oxford University Press, 1966); U.S. Federal Works Agency, *Final Report on the WPA Program*; Cass R. Sunstein, *The Second Bill of Rights: FDR's Unfinished Revolution and Why We Need It More Than Ever* (New York: Basic Books, 2004); inflation calculator from U.S. Department of Labor used to determine 2008 figure.

11. South Dakota Sports History, "Bureaucratic Structures of the New Deal Era," http://www.sdsportshistory.com/wpa/narr5.php (accessed October 28, 2008).

12. Smith, *Building New Deal Liberalism*; Jeannette Gabriel, "A Twenty-First-Century WPA: Labor Policies for a Federal Government Jobs Program," *Social Policy* 38, no. 2 (2007): 38–43.

13. PWA, *America Builds*, 35.

14. Leef Smith, "From Boys to Men: Depression-Era CCC Program Gave Workers Self-Respect," *Washington Post*, October 9, 2000, http://www.sfgate.com/cgibin/article/article?f=/c/a/2000/10/09/MN95572.DTL (accessed November 1, 2008); Civilian Conservation Corps Legacy, "CCC Facts," http://www.ccclegacy.org/ccc_facts.htm (accessed February 12, 2009); inflation calculator from U.S. Department of Labor used to determine 2008 figure.

15. Smith, *Building New Deal Liberalism*.

16. Myers-Lipton, *Social Solutions to Poverty*.

17. PWA, *America Builds*, 40.

18. U.S. Federal Works Agency, *Final Report on the WPA Program*, 81; Arthur M. Schlesinger, *The Politics of Upheaval, 1935–1936* (New York: Houghton Mifflin Harcourt, 2003).

19. PWA, *America Builds*, 84; William E. Leuchtenburg, *In the Shadow of FDR: From Harry Truman to Bill Clinton* (Ithaca, NY: Cornell University Press, 2001), 214.

20. Ken Dilanian, "$8B in Pork Clogs U.S. Infrastructure Plans," *USA Today*, September 13, 2007, http://www.usatoday.com/news/washington/2007-09-12-earmarks_N.htm (accessed February 12, 2009); Greg Thomas, "GO Zone Program: Too Many Projects, Too Little Money," *Times-Picayune*, October 27, 2007, http://blog.nola.com/times-picayune/2007/10/go_zone_program_too_many_proje.html (accessed February 12, 2009).

21. "America's Crumbling Infrastructure Requires a Bold Look Ahead," *The Economist*, July 3, 2008, http://seattlepi.nwsource.com/opinion/369517_fallingapart06.html (accessed February 12, 2009); "Roads to Nowhere," *Economist*, December 11, 2008, http://www.economist.com/world/unitedstates/displaystory.cfm?story_id=12775494 (accessed February 12, 2009); Richard Puentes, "Don't Raise That Gas Tax ... Yet!" *Brookings Institution*, August 22, 2007, http://www.brookings.edu/opinions/2007/0822transportation_puentes.aspx?rssid=puentesr (accessed February 12, 2009); U.S. House of Representatives, Committee on Government Reform, Minority Staff Special Investigations Division, "Waste, Fraud, and Abuse in Hurricane Katrina Contracts," August 2006, www.oversight.house.gov/documents/20060824110705-30132.pdf (accessed February 12, 2009).

22. PWA, *America Builds*; Smith, *Building New Deal Liberalism*, 105.

23. Jeffrey Buchanan, "Bush Heads to Gulf Coast, Still Misleading on How Little He Sent to Rebuild," *Huffington Post,* August 28, 2007, http://www.huffingtonpost.com/jeffrey-buchanan/bush-heads-to-gulf-coast_b_62248.html (accessed January 5, 2009).

24. Ibid.; Smith, *Building New Deal Liberalism,* 51.

25. Eric Rauchway, "Learning from the New Deal's Mistakes," *American Prospect,* December 22, 2008, http://www.prospect.org/cs/articles?article=learning_from_the_new_deals_mistakes (accessed February 6, 2009); David Sirota, "The Forgotten Math: Pre-WWII New Deal Saw Biggest Drop in Unemployment Rate in American History," *Campaign for America's Future,* January 6, 2009, http://www.ourfuture.org/blog-entry/2009010206/forgotten-math-pre-wwii-new-deal-saw-fastest-drop-unemployment-rate-american-h (accessed February 6, 2009); Mitch McConnell, "Leader McConnell Says Package Won't Work," *Real Clear Politics,* February 6, 2009, http://www.realclearpolitics.com/articles/2009/02/leader_mcconnell_wont_work.html (accessed February 11, 2009); Eric Rauchway, "(Very) Short Reading List: Unemployment in the 1930s," *Edge of the American West,* October 10, 2008, http://edgeofthewest.wordpress.com/2008/10/10/very-short-reading-list-unemployment-in-the-1930s (accessed February 11, 2009); inflation calculator from U.S. Department of Labor used to determine 2008 figure.

26. Smith, *Building New Deal Liberalism.*

27. Robert D. Leighninger Jr., *Long-Range Public Investment: The Forgotten Legacy of the New Deal* (Columbia: University of South Carolina Press, 2007); Gabriel, "A Twenty-First-Century WPA"; Rauchway, "Learning from the New Deal's Mistakes."

28. Roger Biles, *The South and the New Deal* (Lexington: University Press of Kentucky, 1994), 77.

29. James T. Patterson, *America's Struggle Against Poverty in the Twentieth Century* (Cambridge, MA: Harvard University Press, 2000), 62.

30. Michael E. Dyson, *Come Hell or High Water: Hurricane Katrina and the Color of Disaster* (New York: Basic Civitas Books, 2006).

31. Bill Quigley, "Trying to Make It Home: New Orleans a Year After Katrina," *Counterpunch,* August 22, 2006, http://www.counterpunch.org/quigley08222006.html (accessed February 11, 2009); Eamon Javers, "Anatomy of a Katrina Cleanup Contract," *Business Week,* October, 27, 2005, http://www.businessweek.com/bwdaily/dnflash/oct2005/nf20051027_8761_db038.htm (accessed February 12, 2009).

32. Justin Park, "Katrina Recovery Funds Wasted by Contractors, Govt.," *New Standard,* August 21, 2006, http://newstandardnews.net/content/index.cfm/items/3562 (accessed November 9, 2008); Lisa Myers and the NBC Investigative Unit, "Is Katrina Cleanup a Fleecing of America?" *MSNBC.com,* June 5, 2008, http://www.msnbc.msn.com/id/13153520 (accessed November 10, 2008); "Key Corporations Cited by House Oversight Committee," *Katrina Information Network,* http://katrinaaction.org/Katrina_contractors (accessed February 11, 2009).

33. "Fact Sheet: Casualties of Katrina," *CorpWatch,* September 15, 2007, http://www.corpwatch.org/article.php?id=14694 (accessed October 27, 2008).

34. "Fact Sheet"; Joseph Rhee, "Revolt in Mississippi: Indian Workers Claim 'Slave Treatment,'" *ABC News,* March 7, 2008, http://abcnews.go.com/Blotter/Story?id=4409785&page=1 (accessed February 10, 2009).

Notes for Chapter 3

1. David Bowman, director of research and special projects at the Louisiana Recovery Authority, information provided in an e-mail exchange, January 24, 2009; Anoop Prakash and Deborah Hernandez, "Post-Katrina New Orleans: The State of Affordable Rental Housing" (Washington, DC: U.S. Department of Housing and Urban Development, 2008); Amy Liu and Allison Plyer, "The New Orleans Index: Tracking the Recovery of New Orleans & the Metro Area," *Brookings Institution,* January 2009, http://www.gnocdc.org (accessed February 9, 2009).

2. John Mutter, "Hurricane Katrina Deceased-Victims List," *Earth Island Institute,* http://www.katrinalist.columbia.edu (accessed February 9, 2009); Amy Liu, "Building a Better New Orleans: A Review of and Plan for Progress One Year After Hurricane Katrina," *Brookings Institution,* August 2006, http://www.brookings.edu/reports/2006/08metropolitanpolicy_liu02.aspx (accessed February 9, 2009); Jack Reed, "Potential Economic Impacts of Hurricane Katrina," *Joint Economic Committee Democrats,* September 2005, http://www.jec.senate.gov/archive/Documents/Reports/katrinareportsep05.pdf (accessed February 9, 2009); Liu and Plyer, "The New Orleans Index."

3. Kevin F. McCarthy and Mark Hanson, *Post-Katrina Recovery of the Housing Market Along the Mississippi Gulf Coast* (Santa Monica, CA: RAND Corporation, 2008), http://www.rand.org/pubs/technical_reports/TR511 (accessed February 9, 2009); Garry Mitchell, "Rural Alabama Homeowners Still Waiting for Katrina Housing Aid," *Insurance Journal,* August 20, 2007, http://www.insurancejournal.com/news/southeast/2007/08/20/82854.htm (accessed March 31, 2009); Craig H. Baab, "Emergency Community Block Grant Funds in the Gulf Coast: Uses, Challenges, and Lessons for the Future," House Committee on Financial Services, http://financialservices.house.gov/hearing110/baab.pdf (accessed March 31, 2009).

4. Jeffrey Buchanan and Chris Kromm, "Where Did the Money Go?" *Blueprint for Gulf Renewal: The Katrina Crisis and a Community Agenda for Action* (August–September 2007), www.southernstudies.org/southern_exposure/2008/11/two-years-after-katrina.html (accessed September 15, 2007); Brad Heath, "$3.9B in Hurricane Aid Still Unspent," *USA Today,* February 8, 2009, http://www.usatoday.com/news/nation/2009-02-08-hurricane-aid_N.htm (accessed February 15, 2009).

5. Michael E. Dyson, *Come Hell or High Water: Hurricane Katrina and the Color of Disaster* (New York: Basic Civitas Books, 2006).

6. Ibid.; Bill Quigley, "How to Destroy an African-American City in Thirty-Three Steps: Lessons from Katrina," *Truthout,* June 29, 2007, http://www.truthout.org/article/bill-quigley-how-destroy-african-american-city-thirty-three-steps-lessons-from-katrina (accessed February 9, 2009); U.S. Census Bureau, "National per Student Public School Spending Nears $9,000," http://www.census.gov/Press-Release/www/releases/archives/education/010125.html (accessed April 24, 2009); Associated Press, "Hurricane Recovery Confronts Low Literacy Rate," August 26, 2008, http://www.msnbc.msn.com/id/26413788 (accessed April 24, 2009).

7. George W. Bush, "Rebuilding After Hurricane Katrina" September 15, 2005, http://www.presidentialrhetoric.com/speeches/09.15.05.html (accessed February 9, 2009).

8. Scott Myers-Lipton, "Effect of a Comprehensive Service-Learning Program on

College Students' Level of Civic Responsibility," *Teaching Sociology* 26, no. 4 (1998): 243–258; Scott Myers-Lipton, "Effect of a Comprehensive Service-Learning Program on College Students' Level of Modern Racism," *Michigan Journal of Community Service Learning*, no. 3 (1996): 44–54; Scott Myers-Lipton, "Effect of Service-Learning on College Students' Attitudes Toward International Understanding," *Journal of College Student Development* 37, no. 6 (1996): 659–668.

9. Republican Party of Louisiana, "Resolution 2008-E," June 7, 2008, www .rfkcenter.org/files/Louisiana%20Republican%20Party%20Resolution.pdf (accessed February 10, 2009).

Notes for Chapter 4

1. Will Straw and Michael Ettlinger, "How to Spend $350 Billion in a First Year of Stimulus and Recovery," *Center for American Progress,* December 5, 2008, http:// www.americanprogress.org/issues/2008/12/second_stimulus.html (accessed February 10, 2009).

2. Bruce Alpert, "Louisiana Delegation Urges Obama to Make Gulf Coast Recovery Office Part of White House Complex," *Times-Picayune,* March 3, 2009, http:// www.nola.com/news/index.ssf/2009/03/louisiana_delegation_urges_oba.html (accessed March 19, 2009).

3. "New Commitment to the Gulf Coast," *White House Blog,* http://www .whitehouse.gov/blog/09/02/20/New-commitment-to-the-Gulf-Coast (accessed March 19, 2009); "Our Views: A New Look at Recovery," *Advocate,* March 2, 2009, http://www.2theadvocate.com/opinion/40518507.html (accessed March 19, 2009).

4. Angelle Bergeron, "New Orleans Unions Plant Seeds for Growth with First Pre-apprentice Training Program," July 25, 2007, http://construction.com/CareerCenter/workforce/070725NewOrleansUnions.asp (accessed February 10, 2009).

5. Ross Eisenbrey, "Federal Support for Employment and Training Services Dwindles," December 6, 2006, http://www.epi.org/economic_snapshots/entry/webfeatures_snapshots_20061206 (accessed February 10, 2009).

6. Van Jones with Ariane Conrad, *The Green Collar Economy: How One Solution Can Fix Our Two Biggest Problems* (New York: HarperCollins, 2008), 10; Dave Burdick and Nicholas Sabloff, "Van Jones Q&A About His New Book 'The Green Collar Economy,'" *Huffington Post,* October 20, 2008, http://www.huffingtonpost .com/2008/10/20/van-jones-qa-about-his-ne_n_135928.html (accessed January 25, 2009).

7. Chuck Collins and Felice Yeskel with United for a Fair Economy and Class Action, *Economic Apartheid in America: A Primer on Economic Inequality and Insecurity* (New York: New Press, 2005), 70.

8. David Obey, "Summary: American Recovery and Reinvestment Act," U.S. House of Representatives, Committee on Appropriations, January 21, 2009, http:// www.appropriations.house.gov/pdf/PressSummary01-21-09.pdf (accessed January 21, 2009); Phillip Elliot, "Obama Seeks Major Change in Federal Contracting," *Associated Press,* March 4, 2009, http://news.yahoo.com/s/ap/20090304/ap_on_go_pr_wh/obama_waste_19 (accessed March 31, 2009).

9. Philip Rucker, "Beefy Résumé for a Giant Job: Policing Stimulus Spending,"

Washington Post, March 20, 2009, http://www.washingtonpost.com/wp-dyn/content/article/2009/03/19/AR2009031903360.html?hpid=topnews (accessed March 21, 2009).

10. David Leonhardt, "A Stimulus with Merit, and Misses Too," *New York Times,* January 27, 2009, http://www.nytimes.com/2009/01/28/business/economy/28leonhardt.html?hp (accessed January 27, 2009).

11. Sam Dillon, "Some Rich Districts Get Richer As Aid Is Rushed to Schools," *New York Times,* March 21, 2009, http://www.nytimes.com/2009/03/22/education/22schools.html?partner=rss&emc=rss (accessed March 21, 2009).

12. Foon Rhee, "Poll: Tax Cuts Will Help Economy More Than Spending," *Boston.com,* January 21, 2009, http://www.boston.com/news/politics/political intelligence/2009/01/poll_tax_cuts_w.html (accessed January 21, 2009).

13. Obey, "Summary."

14. "Obama Details $825B Stimulus," *HonoluluAdvertiser.com,* January 25, 2009, http://www.honoluluadvertiser.com/article/20090125/NEWS21/901250394/-1/RSS02?source=rss_localnews (accessed January 26, 2009); David Sanger, "Nationalization Gets a New, Serious Look," *New York Times,* January 25, 2009, http://www.nytimes.com/2009/01/26/business/economy/26banks.html (accessed January 25, 2009).

15. Obey, "Summary"; Paul Krugman, "The Obama Gap," *New York Times,* January 9, 2009, A23; Tim King, "Obama Economic Advisor Addresses the American Recovery and Reinvestment Plan's Job Impact," *Salem-News.com,* January 12, 2009, http://www.salem-news.com/articles/january122009/obama_recovery_plans_1-12-09.php (accessed January 25, 2009).

16. Associated Press, "Highlights of House-Senate Economic Stimulus Plan," *Yahoo News Singapore,* February 13, 2009, http://sg.news.yahoo.com/ap/20090213/twl-congress-stimulus-highlights-1be00ca.html (accessed February 14, 2009); Michael Cooper, "House Plan for Infrastructure Disappoints Advocates for Major Projects," *New York Times,* January 19, 2000, http://www.nytimes.com/2009/01/20/us/politics/20publicworks.html?em (accessed January 19, 2009); Andrew Taylor, "Much in Obama Stimulus Bill Won't Hit Economy Soon" *Associated Press,* January 20, 2009, http://abcnews.go.com/Politics/wireStory?id=6686139 (accessed January 26, 2009); Richard Cowan and Susan Cornwell, "Congress Sends $787 Billion Stimulus to Obama," *Reuters,* February 13, 2009, http://ca.news.yahoo.com/s/reuters/090214/us/politics_us_usa_stimulus_98 (accessed February 14, 2009).

17. Cooper, "House Plan for Infrastructure Disappoints Advocates for Major Projects"; Taylor, "Much in Obama Stimulus Bill Won't Hit Economy Soon"; William Brantley, "ASCE Report Card for Pennsylvania Infrastructure: Bridges," *American Society of Civil Engineers,* http://www.pareportcard.org/graphics/PABridges2006.pdf (accessed March 21, 2009); Gary Richard, "$6 Million to Speed Up Silicon Valley Commutes," *San Jose Mercury News,* March 26, 2009, 1A.

18. Jeff Zeleny and David Herszenhorn, "Obama Seeks Wide Support in Congress for Stimulus," *New York Times,* January 6, 2009, A15.

19. *PolicyLink,* "The PolicyLink Center for Infrastructure Equity," http://www.policylink.org/InfrastructureEquity/default.html (accessed February 10, 2009).

20. Robert Reich, "The Stimulus: How to Create Jobs Without Them All Going to Skilled Professionals and White Male Construction."

21. Louis Uchitelle, "Economic Dive Deepens, Giving Stimulus Urgency," *New York Times,* January 31, 2009, A1; Bureau of Economic Analysis, "Gross Domestic Product: Fourth Quarter, 2008," March 26, 2009, http://www.bea.gov/newsreleases/national/gdp/gdpnewsrelease.htm (accessed April 25, 2009).

22. Reich, "The Stimulus"; Eileen Boris, Linda Gordon, Jennifer Klein, and Alice O'Connor, "More Than 1,000 American Historians Call for Equity in the Stimulus Package in an Open Letter to Obama," *Center for Research on Women and Social Justice,* http://www.femst.ucsb.edu/projects/crwsj/feminist_historians.php (accessed January 31, 2009).

Notes for Chapter 5

1. Jason Scott Smith, *Building New Deal Liberalism: The Political Economy of Public Works, 1933–1956* (New York: Cambridge University Press, 2005).

2. Amity Shlaes, *The Forgotten Man: A New History of the Great Depression* (New York: HarperPerennial, 2008).

3. "Nationalized Banks Are 'Only Answer,' Economist Stiglitz Says," *Deutsche Welle,* February 6, 2009, http://www.dw-world.de/dw/article/0,4005355,00.html (accessed February 10, 2009); Edmund L. Andrews, "Rescue of Banks Hints at Nationalization," *New York Times,* January 15, 2009, http://www.nytimes.com/2009/01/16/business/16banking.html (accessed February 10, 2009); Dan LaBotz, "The Financial Crisis: Will the U.S. Nationalize the Banks?" *ZNet,* September 29, 2008, http://www.zmag.org/znet/viewArticle/18956 (accessed February 10, 2009).

4. Heidi Shierholz, "Job Losses Ballooned in Final Quarter of 2008," *Economic Policy Institute,* January 9, 2009, http://www.epi.org/publications/entry/4236 (accessed January 13, 2009); Steven C. Pitts, "Unionization and Black Workers," *American Prospect,* September 22, 2008, http://www.prospect.org/cs/articles?article=unionization_and_black_workers (accessed February 1, 2009).

5. Alexander Cockburn and Jeffrey St. Clair, *Whiteout: The CIA, Drugs, and the Press* (New York: Verso, 1998); Gary Webb, *Dark Alliance: The CIA, the Contras, and the Crack Cocaine Explosion* (New York: Seven Stories Press, 2003); statistics from the U.S. Bureau of the Census from August 2008 indicate that poverty rates for Hispanics were 21.5 percent in 2007 and for blacks were 24.5 percent as compared to an 8.2 percent poverty rate for whites. In addition, the poverty rate for the foreign-born was 16.5 percent and for U.S. noncitizens was 21.3 percent in 2007.

6. World Bank, *World Development Report 1990: Poverty* (Oxford: Oxford University Press, 1991); Rockefeller Foundation, "Time Campaign for American Workers Survey 2008," July 17, 2008, http://www.rockfound.org/library/caw_poll_exec_summary.pdf (accessed February 10, 2009); Farrukh Iqbal, *Sustaining Gains in Poverty Reduction and Human Development in the Middle East and North Africa* (Washington, DC: World Bank, 2006).

7. Economic and Statistics Analysis Unit, "Public Works as a Solution to Unemployment in South Africa? Two Different Models of Public Works Programme

Compared," *Overseas Development Institute,* November 2004, http://ideas.repec.org/p/odi/bpaper/2.html (accessed February 10, 2009).

8. Martin Ravallion, "Reaching the Rural Poor Through Public Employment: Arguments, Evidence, and Lessons from South Asia," *World Bank Research Observer* 6, no. 2 (1991): 153–175; Philippe Garnier and Jean Majeres, "Fighting Poverty by Promoting Employment and Socio-economic Rights at the Grassroots Level," *International Labour Review* 131, no. 1 (1992): 63–75; Ephraim W. Chirwa, Evious K. Zgovu, and Peter M. Mvula, "Participation and Impact of Poverty-Oriented Public Works Projects in Rural Malawi," *Development Policy Review* 20, no. 2 (2002): 159–176.

9. Michael Lipton, *Successes in Anti-poverty* (Geneva: International Labour Office, 1998); Anna McCord, "Win-Win or Lose? An Examination of the Use of Public Works as a Social Protection Instrument in Situations of Chronic Poverty," paper presented at the Conference on Social Protection for Chronic Poverty, Institute for Development Policy and Management, University of Manchester, United Kingdom, February 23–24, 2005.

10. Thomas Jefferson, "Public Works and Public Assistance," *Thomas Jefferson Digital Archive,* http://etext.virginia.edu/jefferson/quotations/jeff1310.htm (accessed March 31, 2009).

11. Diana Pearce and Jennifer Brooks, "The Self-Sufficiency Standard for the Washington, DC, Metropolitan Area," *Wider Opportunities for Woman* (Fall 1999), http://www.sixstrategies.org/files/Resource-StandardReport-DC.pdf (accessed February 10, 2009); "Female Statistics: Social and Economic Autonomy," *Institute for Women's Policy Research,* 2006, http://www.iwpr.org/femstats/Excel/econ_aut.xls (accessed February 10, 2009).

12. Christopher Cooper, "Old-Line Families Plot the Future in New Orleans," *Wall Street Journal,* September 8, 2005, http://www.commondreams.org/headlines05/0908-09.htm (accessed February 12, 2009).

13. John Harwood, "Louisiana Lawmakers Aim to Cope with Political Fallout," *Wall Street Journal,* September 9, 2005, http://online.wsj.com/article/0,SB11262292 3108136137,00.html?mod=todays_us_page_one (accessed February 12, 2009).

14. Joel Havemann, "HUD Boss Says New Orleans 'Not Going to Be as Black,'" *Seattle Times,* October 1, 2005, http://seattletimes.nwsource.com/html/nationworld/2002532703_canenawlins01.html (accessed February 12, 2009).

15. Charles M. Payne, *I've Got the Light of Freedom: The Organizing Tradition and the Mississippi Freedom Struggle* (Berkeley and Los Angeles: University of California Press, 1995).

16. Belden Russonello, "Public Opinion Research on Human Rights in the U.S.," *Opportunity Agenda* (August 2007): 2–4, http://209.85.173.132/search?q cache:7vhlRPXuJgJ:environmentandhumanrights.org/resources/public%2520opinion%2520research%2520on%2520HR%25208-07%2520exec%2520summ.pdf+Opportunity+Agenda,+%E2%80%9CPublic+Opinion+Research+on+Human Rights+in+the+U.S.%E2%80%9D&hl=en&ct=clnk&cd=1&gl=us&client=firefox-a (accessed February 15, 2009).

17. John Zogby, "Katrina Will Prove to Be a More Defining Moment in American History Than Terrorist Attacks of 9-11," *Dissident Voice,* June 15, 2007, http://www.dissidentvoice.org/2007/06/katrina-will-prove-to-be-a-more-defining-

moment-in-american-history-than-terrorist-attacks-of-9-11 (accessed February 15, 2009).

18. Chris Kromm and Sue Sturgis, "Hurricane Katrina and the Guiding Principles on Internal Displacement," *Institute for Southern Studies* (January 2008), www .southernstudies.org/ISSKatrinaHumanRightsJan08.pdf (accessed February 15, 2009); "Jobs and Business: The State of Opportunity for Workers Restoring the Gulf," *Opportunity Agenda* (2006), https://opportunityagenda.org/files/field_file/Katrina% 20Jobs.pdf (accessed February 15, 2009); Barbara Gault, Heidi Hartmann, Avis Jones-DeWeever, Misha Werschkul, and Erica Williams, "The Women of New Orleans and the Gulf Coast: Multiple Disadvantages and Key Assets for Recovery," *Institute for Women's Policy Research,* October 2005, www.iwpr.org/pdf/NewOrleans_Part1.pdf (accessed February 15, 2009); Laurel E. Fletcher, Phuong Pham, Eric Stover, and Patrick Vinck, "Rebuilding After Katrina: A Population-Based Study of Labor and Human Rights in New Orleans," University of California Boalt Hall School of Law, June 2006, hrc .berkeley.edu/pdfs/report_katrina.pdf (accessed February 15, 2009); Dana Alfred, "Where Did They Go and Are They Coming Back?" *Louisiana Family Recovery Corps,* August 7, 2007, www.recoverycorps.org/media/files/WhereDidTheyGo.pdf (accessed February 15, 2009); Amy Liu and Allison Plyer, "The New Orleans Index Anniversary Edition: Three Years After Katrina," *Brookings Institution,* August 2008, www.brookings .edu/reports/2007/08neworleansindex.aspx (accessed February 15, 2009).

19. Jeffrey Buchanan, "Katrina 3-Year Coverage: Building on Community-Driven Successes with the Gulf Coast Civic Works Act," *Institute for Southern Studies,* August 28, 2008, http://www.southernstudies.org/2008/08/katrina-3-year-coverage-building-on .html (accessed February 16, 2009).

20. Kromm and Sturgis, "Hurricane Katrina and the Guiding Principles on Internal Displacement."

Notes for Chapter 6

1. Cullen Murphy and Todd S. Purdum, "Farewell to All That: An Oral History of the Bush White House," *Vanity Fair,* http://www.vanityfair.com/politics/ features/2009/02/bush-oral-history200902?printable=true&currentPage=all (accessed February 9, 2009); Melissa Harris-Lacewell and James Perry, "Obama's Debt to New Orleans," *The Nation,* March 12, 2009, http://www.thenation.com/doc/20090330/ harris-lacewell_perry?rel=hp_currently (accessed March 29, 2009).

2. Franklin D. Roosevelt, State of the Union Address, in Samuel Rosenman, ed., *The Public Papers and Addresses of Franklin D. Roosevelt* (New York: Harper, 1950), vol. 13, 40–42.

3. G. J. Santoni, "The Employment Act of 1946: Some Historical Notes," *Review* (St. Louis, MO: Federal Reserve Bank of St. Louis, 1986), 12; Harry Truman, "Text of Truman Plea for Public Health Program," in Cynthia Rose, ed., *American Decades Primary Sources, 1940–1949* (Detroit, MI: Thompson/Gale, 2004).

4. David J. Garrow, *Bearing the Cross: Martin Luther King, Jr., and the Southern Christian Leadership Conference* (New York: Vintage, 1986).

5. Garrow, *Bearing the Cross*; Martin Luther King, Jr., "Interview by Alex Haley," *Playboy* (January 1965): 76.

6. Martin Luther King, Jr., "Showdown for Nonviolence," in James M. Washington, ed., *A Testament of Hope: The Essential Writings of Martin Luther King, Jr.* (San Francisco: Harper and Row, 1986), 64–72; Martin Luther King, Jr., "Where Do We Go from Here: Chaos or Community?" in James M. Washington, ed., *A Testament of Hope: The Essential Writings of Martin Luther King, Jr.* (San Francisco: Harper and Row, 1986), 248; Martin Luther King, Jr., transcription of a speech from video "The Promised Land, 1967–1968," in *Eyes on the Prize II* (Boston: Blackside, 1990), pt. 4.

7. Michael E. Dyson, *Come Hell or High Water: Hurricane Katrina and the Color of Disaster* (New York: Basic Civitas Books, 2006).

8. Jesse McKinley, "Tent Cities Arise and Spread in Recession's Grip," *New York Times*, March 26, 2009, A1.

9. Timothy Wirth, "Open Letter to Senator Reid," *Energy Futures Coalition*, http://www.energyfuturecoalition.org/files/webfmuploads/Efficiency%20Docs/TEW_SenReid_letter_1-28-09.pdf (accessed March 23, 2009).

10. Christopher Conkley, "Business, Labor Join to Push for Public-Works Projects," *Wall Street Journal*, January 26, 2009, http://online.wsj.com/article/SB123325881549029813.html (accessed March 23, 2009); U.S. Chamber of Commerce, "H.R. 1, the 'American Recovery and Reinvestment Act of 2009' and Beyond," http://www.uschamber.com/lra/default (accessed March 23, 2009).

11. "Clean Energy Solutions: Repower and Rebuild America," *Sierra Club*, http://www.sierraclub.org/energy (accessed March 23, 2009); Jonathan Rose, "Rebuild America for Climate Prosperity," *Huffington Post*, December 8, 2008, http://www.huffingtonpost.com/jonathan-fp-rose/rebuild-america-for-clima_b_149254.html (accessed March 23, 2009).

12. U.S. Chamber of Commerce, "The Road to U.S. Economic Growth," http://www.uschamber.com/lra/default (accessed March 23, 2009).

13. King, "Where Do We Go from Here?", 615; Daniel H. Weinberg, "Press Briefing on 1999 Income and Poverty Estimates," *U.S. Census Bureau*, http://www.census.gov/hhes/www/income/income99/prs00asc.html (accessed February 9, 2009).

INDEX

About the Author

Scott Myers-Lipton, associate professor at San José State University, is the author of *Social Solutions to Poverty: America's Struggle to Build a Just Society* as well as numerous scholarly articles on civic engagement, education, and racism.

For the past twenty years, Scott has helped students examine solutions to poverty by taking them to live at homeless shelters, the Navajo and Lakota nations, Kingston, Jamaica, and the Gulf Coast. He is also the cofounder of the Gulf Coast Civic Works campaign.

Scott is the recipient of San Jose/Silicon Valley NAACP Freedom and Friendship Award, the Mover of Mountains Award from the Martin Luther King Jr. Association of Santa Clara County, and the Manuel Vega Latino Empowerment Award. He lives with his wife, Diane, and his two children, Gabriela and Josiah, in the Bay Area, where they are the proprietors of the Sequoia Retreat Center, a meeting space dedicated to individual and social transformation.